History of the English Language

Thomas Raynesford Lounsbury

HANDBOOKS for Students and General Readers.

HISTORY

OF THE

ENGLISH LANGUAGE

BY

T. R. LOUNSBURY

PROFESSOR OF ENGLISH IN THE SHEFFIELD SCIENTIFIC
SCHOOL OF YALE COLLEGE.

NEW YORK
HENRY HOLT AND COMPANY
1891.

PREFACE.

The general plan of this volume is so fully stated in the conclusion of the introductory chapter, that little needs to be said in addition. One or two explanatory statements it may be advisable to make.

The history is a history of the language, and not at all of the literature. To any real comprehension of the former, however, some knowledge of the latter is essential; and inasmuch as, in the case of Anglo-Saxon and Early English, sources of information on this subject are not easily accessible to most readers, a slight sketch of the literature of those periods has been given.

The division of the history into two parts, each to a certain extent complete in itself, has involved in a few instances the necessity of going over the same ground. In no case, however, will this be found to be mere repetition. And, while the second part has been more particularly prepared for the special student, it is hoped that there is nothing in it which will present any difficulty to any reader of ordinary intelligence who cares to investigate the subject.

EXPLANATORY.

THIS Series is intended to meet the requirement of brief text-books both for schools and for adult readers who wish to review or expand their knowledge.

The grade of the books is intermediate between the so-called "primers" and the larger works professing to present quite detailed views of the respective subjects.

Such a notion as a person beyond childhood requires of some subjects, it is difficult and perhaps impossible to convey in one such volume. Therefore, occasionally a volume is given to each of the main departments into which a subject naturally falls—for instance, a volume to the Zoölogy of the vertebrates, and one to that of the invertebrates. While this arrangement supplies a compendious treatment for those who wish, it will also sometimes enable the reader interested in only a portion of the field covered by a science, to study the part he is interested in, without getting a book covering the whole.

Care is taken to bring out whatever educational value may be extracted from each subject without impeding the exposition of it. In the books on the sciences, not only are acquired results stated, but as full explanation as possible is given of the methods of inquiry and reasoning by which these results have been obtained. Consequently, although the treatment of each subject is strictly elementary, the fundamental facts are stated and discussed with the fulness needed to place their scientific significance in a clear light, and to show the relation in which they stand to the general conclusions of science.

Care is also taken that each book admitted to the series shall either be the work of a recognized authority, or bear the unqualified approval of such. As far as practicable, authors are selected who combine knowledge of their subjects with experience in teaching them.

CONTENTS.

INTRODUCTORY CHAPTER.

LANGUAGES ALLIED TO THE ENGLISH.

PART I.

GENERAL HISTORY.

CHAPTER I.

THE ROMAN AND THE TEUTONIC CONQUESTS OF BRITAIN.

CHAPTER II.

THE ANGLO-SAXON LANGUAGE AND LITERATURE.

CHAPTER III.

INFLUENCE OF FOREIGN TONGUES UPON THE ENGLISH OF THE ANGLO-SAXON PERIOD.

CHAPTER IV.

THE NORMAN CONQUEST AND THE FRENCH LANGUAGE IN ENGLAND.

CHAPTER V.

PERIODS IN HISTORY OF THE ENGLISH LANGUAGE, AND THE CHANGES WROUGHT IN IT BY THE NORMAN CONQUEST.

CHAPTER VI.

THE THREE DIALECTS OF EARLY ENGLISH, AND THE RISE OF THE MIDLAND.

CHAPTER VII.

CHANGES IN THE MIDDLE ENGLISH PERIOD (1350–1550).

CHAPTER VIII.

MODERN ENGLISH.

PART II.

HISTORY OF INFLECTIONS.

CHAPTER I.

SOME FEATURES COMMON TO ALL THE TEUTONIC TONGUES.

CHAPTER II.

THE NOUN.

CHAPTER III.

THE ADJECTIVE.

CHAPTER IV.

THE PRONOUN.

CHAPTER V

THE VERB.

ENGLISH LANGUAGE.

INTRODUCTORY CHAPTER.

LANGUAGES ALLIED TO THE ENGLISH.

THE most superficial student of speech is well acquainted with the fact that English is no isolated, independent tongue, but one of the members of a vast family, embracing tongues far removed from one another, both in time and in space. This family occupied, at an early period, large districts of Asia, and nearly the whole of Europe; and during the last four hundred years its domain has been extended still farther, over a great portion of the habitable globe. Various names have been employed to designate it as a whole; of which those most in use are Indo-Germanic, Indo-European, and Aryan, especially the last two. Every one of the Indo-European languages is more or less closely related to every other by the fact of descent from a common mother tongue. Yet of this common mother-tongue not only have no monuments been handed down, but also the time when and the place where it was spoken are unknown, and are likely to remain forever unknown. This only we can say, that, at some remote periods of the past, members of the race that spoke the primitive Indo-European speech or later descendants of it, parted company from one another, wandered in various directions, and finally formed permanent settlements far apart. Lapse of time, and separation in space, caused differences to spring up between these dispersed communities, — differences in customs, in beliefs, and, what most concerns us here, in language. The divergences that arose became, in the course of events, so much more important and conspicuous than the resemblances which had been preserved, that, when the scattered races and peoples that had sprung from this one primitive Indo-European tribe appear to us in recorded history, they are totally unaware of the tie of blood or of speech that subsists between them; in fact, it was not discovered until within a hundred years. The scientific study which has been carried on in the present century of the languages of the Indo-European family shows that in all branches of it there is a certain number of the same grammatical forms and of the same words. These are not merely proofs of a common descent: their common existence makes it clear that these forms and words must have belonged to the speech of the primitive Indo-European community before its dispersion into separate ones; and from it they must have been transmitted to all its descendants. By a comparison of the forms and words thus preserved in the derived languages, it has been possible to construct a theoretical primitive language, which is the remote parent of every tongue included in this family.

Bound to each other, therefore, by the fact of common descent, all Indo-European tongues necessarily are; but it likewise follows that some are much more closely related to one another than they are to others. According to the nearness of this relationship among themselves, the languages of the Indo-European stock have been divided into the following distinct branches: —

I. The Indian. — This embraces the languages of Northern Hindostan. Its great representative is the Sanskrit, which, as a spoken tongue, died out three centuries before Christ. It is the oldest of all the languages of the Indo-European family, and as a whole comes nearest to the primitive speech.

II. The Iranian. — This includes the languages of both Ancient and Modern Persia and of provinces and tribes adjoining or belonging to that country.

III. The Hellenic. — This includes the Ancient Greek, with its various dialects, and its existing representative, the Romaic or Modern Greek.

IV. The Slavonic, or Slavo-Lettic. — This includes the languages spoken over a large portion of Eastern Europe. Of this branch the Russian is much the most important.

With none of these has the English any intimate

relationship, though from the Ancient Greek. it has borrowed a moderately large number of words. With the three remaining branches its connections are nearer, though varying in their nature. With the first it has come into close geographical contact; from the second it has taken full half of its literary vocabulary; of the third it is itself a member.

V. The Celtic. — This branch was once widely spread over Western Europe; but it is now confined to portions of the British Isles, and, in North-western France, to the Peninsula of Britanny, a part of the ancient Armorica. It is divided into the two following clearly-defined groups: 1st, The Cymric. To this belong the languages or dialects once used throughout the whole of England and Southern Scotland, but now limited to the principality of Wales, and represented in it by the tongue we call the Welsh. The Cornish, the language of the extreme south-west of Britain, which died out entirely in the last century, was also a member of this group, which includes one other living tongue besides the Welsh, — the Breton or Armorican, spoken in the Peninsula of Britanny, as already mentioned. 2d, The Gadhelic or Gaelic. Of this group the most important members are the Irish, the native language of Ireland, and the Erse, the language of the Scottish Highlands. The Manx, spoken by a portion of the population of the Isle of Man, is also included in it. The Celtic tongues are all gradually dying out; giving way in the British Isles to the encroachment of the English, and in France to that of the French. Linguistically they are widely removed from our tongue, and, in spite of their geographical nearness, have had no influence worth speaking of on its vocabulary, and none at all on its grammar.

VI. The Italic. — Of the ancient languages included in this branch, the Latin is the great representative; and from that tongue have descended all the modern ones belonging to it. These are collectively called Romanic or Romance. The most important of the descendants of the Latin are the Italian, the Spanish, the Portuguese, the French, and the Provençal. French was at first the language of Northern France only; while Provençal, or the Languedoc, was the language of the south of that country. The latter, during the twelfth and thirteenth centuries especially, flourished as a language of literature, and in it was then composed the poetry of the troubadours. But the political preponderance of Northern France carried with it the supremacy of the tongue spoken in it; and the Provençal sunk from the position of a cultivated language to that of a dialect. The influence of this branch upon the English has been very great so far as regards its vocabulary. The Latin and Romance elements in our tongue, owing to circumstances connected with its history, make up fully one-half of the number of words used in literature.

VII. The Teutonic. — Of this branch English is one of the most important members, and may, perhaps, be justly called the most important. As we have no remains of the primitive Indo-European, so we have none of the primitive Teutonic speech, from which all the tongues belonging to this stock have descended. This whole branch is subdivided into four groups: —

1. *The Gothic, or Mœso-Gothic.* — This was the tongue spoken by the Goths who dwelt in Mœsia, on the Lower Danube. It is the eldest of the Teutonic tongues that have been preserved, and naturally much the most ancient in its forms; standing, indeed, in the same relation to the other members of this branch that the Sanskrit does to all the members of the Indo-European family. Its principal literary monument is only partially preserved. This was a translation of the Bible made in the fourth century into the language of the Goths dwelling in the province of Mœsia on the Lower Danube, by Ulfilas, their bishop. The speech died out in the ninth century, and has left no descendants.

2. *The Norse, or Scandinavian.* — The oldest representative of this group is the Old Norse, or, as it is sometimes called, the Old Icelandic. To Iceland it was carried in the ninth century by settlers from Norway, and there gave birth to a brilliant literature. The modern Scandinavian tongues are the Icelandic, the Swedish, the Danish, and the Norwegian. The last is a popular dialect only.

3. *The High-Germanic.* — This is so called because originally spoken in Upper or Higher Germany. The history of the dialects belonging to it is divided into three periods. The first is that of the Old High Ger-

man, extending from the eighth to the twelfth century. The leading literary dialect of the Old High German was the Frankish, though others were employed. The second period was that of Middle High German, extending from the twelfth to the sixteenth century. This literature was very abundant in quantity, and rich in quality: the dialect in which it was written was the Swabian. The New High German begins with the writings of the reformer Luther, in the first half of the sixteenth century, especially with his translation of the Bible. It is the language of all modern German literature, and is by us usually termed simply the German.

4. *The Low Germanic.*—This was so called because originally spoken in Northern or Low Germany. This group consists of several tongues, of which some are now only popular dialects, having been reduced to this condition by the predominance of High German as the language of literature. The four ancient tongues of this group are the Friesic, the Netherlandish, the Old Saxon, and the Saxon or English. The Friesic was once spoken on the coasts of the North Sea and on the adjoining islands. Its oldest records consist of legal documents of about the thirteenth century, and it is now only an idiom of the common people. The Netherlandish and the Old Saxon were closely related. From them have descended the Dutch of Holland, the Flemish of portions of Belgium, and the Platt Deutsch, or Low German proper. This last is still a wide-spread popular idiom in Northern Germany, and

is occasionally employed in literature. Last and most important of this group is the Saxon, or English, carried in the fifth and sixth centuries to Great Britain by the Saxons and Angles, and there having a history, and developing a literature peculiarly its own. The earliest form of it is commonly designated by modern writers as Anglo-Saxon.

While English is, therefore, spoken of with sufficient accuracy as a member of the Indo-European family of languages, it is more specifically to be described as a member of the Low Germanic group of the Teutonic branch of that family. Its history, like that of all other tongues, naturally divides itself into two parts. The first embraces what, for lack of a better term, may be called its general history; that is, the account of the circumstances and conditions under which it developed its present form, of the external agencies that operated upon it, especially the social and political influences that affected it, that modified it, and, in particular, that changed the character of its vocabulary, and transformed it from an inflectional speech into one nearly non-inflectional. The second is the history of the internal changes which took place within the l[illegible]guage itself. It is obvious at a glance that the latte[illegible] a far more intricate and extensive subject than the former. It embraces, indeed, a vast variety of subjects, the full consideration of any one of which would require a separate volume. This work will treat of so much only of this internal history as is concerned with the variations of form that have taken place in the noun, the adjective, the pronoun, and the verb, caused by change or loss of inflection. Some notice will necessarily be taken, in addition, of the steps which the language has resorted to in order to increase its resources, and to repair the losses it has sustained, either by the development of forms entirely new, or the application of old forms to new uses. This is but a small portion of the immense field which must be covered in any full account of the interior growth and development of our speech; but beyond these limits there will, in this treatise, be no attempt to go.

CHAPTER I.

THE ROMAN AND THE TEUTONIC CONQUESTS OF BRITAIN.

The English tongue is at the present time the speech of communities scattered over all the globe; but its history as a language is almost wholly confined to the Island of Great Britain. There it was that the violent changes which took place in the social and political condition of the people were indirectly followed by as violent changes in the character and grammatical structure of the words they spoke. Without an adequate knowledge of the former, no one can gain a satisfactory conception of the latter. The Celts, the Romans, the Saxons, the Northmen, and the French have met or succeeded one another upon British soil; and the occupation of the country by each has left ineffaceable records of itself in the tongue we use to-day. But English was not the original speech of the island. In the modern form in which we know it, it can, indeed, hardly lay claim to a higher age than five hundred years. It is, therefore, quite as important to understand clearly what English is not, as well as what it is.

The Roman Conquest. — Great Britain can hardly be said to be known to history until a short time before the Christian era. Our first positive information in regard to it we owe to Julius Cæsar, who, after his conquest of Gaul, turned his attention to the island, and twice invaded it, — once in 55 B.C., and again in the following year. He found there a people allied in blood and speech to the one he had just brought under Roman sway, and both belonging to the race called Celtic, then widely spread over Western Europe. It was the Cymric branch of this family, now represented in Great Britain by the Welsh, that had possession of most of the island; and it was with this that Cæsar came into contact. His success was rather nominal than real; for though he marched a little way into the interior, and exacted the payment of a tribute, he seems, in the words of Tacitus, to have handed down to posterity the discovery of the country rather than its possession. For nearly a hundred years afterward it remained unmolested by the Romans. But in the reign of the Emperor Claudian a renewed attempt at conquest began, in A.D. 42, and was kept up without intermission till near the close of the first century. By that time the reduction of the island was accomplished as far north as the Forth. Beyond that the invaders never gained any thing but a temporary foothold.

With the conquest of the greater portion of the

island the Romans began that energetic administration, which, in the case of Gaul and Spain, ended in making the native inhabitants of those countries as Latin as the inhabitants of Italy itself. Colonies were established, towns were fortified, military roads were constructed. With their laws and customs, the invaders introduced also their language and literature. These last early became popular; and the attention paid to them must have steadily increased during the more than three hundred years in which the Romans occupied the island. Yet, however widely the Latin tongue was then used, it manifestly never made its way in Britain as it did in Gaul and Spain. It was without doubt chiefly confined to the educated classes and to the dwellers in cities; for, with the withdrawal of the Romans in the early part of the fifth century, their language disappeared almost as completely. Some of its words were retained in the speech of the native population, and have been handed down in the speech of their descendants; but perhaps not a single one of these has passed directly from this source over into the English tongue. Traces of the Roman occupation are, indeed, to be found in names of towns. The Latin *colonia*, 'colony,' is seen in the final syllable of Lincoln; the Latin *castra*, 'camp,' is preserved in the names of a large number of places ending in *-caster*, *-cester*, and *-chester*, as Lancaster, Worcester, and Winchester. Likewise the word 'street,' which is nothing more than the first word of *strata via*, 'paved way,' may have come to us in consequence of the Teutonic invaders hearing the term first applied by the Britons to the Roman military roads; but this is doubtful, for the same term appears very early in all the Teutonic dialects. It is possible that one or two other words may have been derived in this way from this source; but it is evident that the Latin of the Roman occupation exercised no appreciable influence upon the English speech properly so called. Still, as the Roman names of towns have been retained to this day, to the words denoting these is often given the title of "Latin of the First Period."

The Teutonic Conquest.—Up to this time, English was not known in the island. It was to the Teutonic invasion, that followed soon after the Roman occupation ceased, that we owe the introduction of our language into Great Britain, and the gradual displacement of the Celtic tongues.

The story of this Teutonic invasion and conquest is in many respects obscure and uncertain; but, while numerous details may be mythical rather than historical, the general statement cannot be far from the truth. The common account runs somewhat as follows: Of the western provinces of the Roman Empire, Great Britain was the last to be conquered, the first to be abandoned. Its inhabitants were left, in the first half of the fifth century, exposed to the attacks of the dwellers in the northern part of the island, the Picts and Scots, who had never been really subdued, and whose incursions had always been, from the time of the first conquest, a source of annoyance and alarm. In their extremity the wretched population called for aid upon certain Teutonic tribes dwelling upon the north coast of Germany. It was by these the English language was brought into Great Britain; for the new auxiliaries did not long remain contented with the limited territory which had been assigned them, but, soon turning their arms against their allies, ended at last in conquering the country they came to save. This invasion is said to have begun about the middle of the fifth century. It is more than probable, to be sure, that, previous to this time, Teutonic bands had made marauding descents upon the coast: it is not impossible that they had formed scattered settlements. About the end of the fourth century one of the Roman military officers stationed in Britain was styled "Count of the Saxon frontier" (*Comes Limitis Saxonici per Britanniam*); and his jurisdiction extended from the Wash to Southampton. This stretch of coast may have been called the Saxon frontier because Saxons inhabited it: there is little doubt it was so called because the Saxons molested it.

Names of the Teutonic Invading Tribes, and Kingdoms founded by them.—The Teutonic invaders were Low Germans, and belonged to three tribes,—the Jutes, the Saxons, and the Angles. According to the dates furnished by the Anglo-Saxon chronicle, Hengist and Horsa came over in 449 with a body of Jutes, and subsequently founded the kingdom of Kent. In 477 Ælla landed near the present city of Chichester, and founded the kingdom of the

South Saxons, or Sussex. In 495 Cerdic came over, and in 519 founded the kingdom of the West Saxons, or Wessex, which by successive conquests came finally to include nearly all South-west England, with a portion of the country north of the Thames. There was also one other Saxon kingdom, that of the East Saxons, or Essex, which seems to have been founded during the sixth century. Essex, Wessex, and Sussex were the three Saxon monarchies; and there were likewise three kingdoms founded by the Angles, whose collective territory embraced much the larger part of Great Britain, but whose origin is wrapped in even deeper obscurity than the other. The largest of these was the kingdom of Northumbria, which extended from the Humber to the Forth. We know nothing of its early history. The establishment of its monarchy is ascribed to the year 547, under which date the Anglo-Saxon chronicle states that "Ida came to the throne, from whom sprang the royal race of the Northumbrians." Besides this, there was the kingdom of East Anglia, which included the modern Norfolk and Suffolk, and parts of other counties. The last Anglian kingdom to be formed was that of Mercia, — the "March," or frontier, which in process of time came to embrace most of the central counties of England. These seven monarchies are often popularly but loosely spoken of as the Heptarchy.

From the above account it is evident that the Teutonic conquest of Great Britain was chiefly the work of two tribes, — the Saxons and the Angles, — and that the former settled mainly in the southern part of the island; while the latter occupied the centre and north of England and the southern half of Scotland. The Angles had a marked superiority, both in their numbers and in the extent of territory they occupied. When, therefore, any characteristic differences that may have originally existed between the tribes began to disappear, and the two peoples blended in one, it is no matter of wonder that the name of the larger body was given to the country the two possessed in common. *Englisc*, or English, was the title usually given, after the ninth century, to the race and language. *Englaland* (contracted, *England*), or "the land of the Angles," came later to be the name applied to the whole country from the Channel to the Frith of Forth. But, though the Angles were the most numerous, the Saxons must have been the first to come into contact with the native population, probably through marauding descents upon the coasts; for it was the title which the conquered race gave to all the invaders. Even to this day, to the Celtic inhabitant of the British Isles, whether Cymric or Gaelic, the Englishman is not an Englishman, but a Saxon. On the other hand, the invaders spoke of the native population sometimes as Britons, sometimes as Welsh (A. S. *Welisc*, *Welsc*, 'foreign,' from A. S. *Wealh*, a 'foreigner,' from Latin *Gallicus*, 'belonging to Gaul').

Rise of the Kingdom of Wessex. — The conquest of the country was no rapid or easy task. The native population resisted fiercely, and gave way slowly. Every accession of territory was gained at the cost of hard fighting. Still, under incessant attacks, the Britons were steadily, though slowly, pushed back towards the western shore of the island; and at the beginning of the ninth century the portion of country directly under their sway was limited to the present county of Cornwall (West Wales), to the present principality of Wales (North Wales), and to a strip along the northern coast of England and southern coast of Scotland, which was termed Strathclyde. But the invaders were not only constantly fighting the original Celtic inhabitants, they were as constantly engaged in hostilities among themselves. With the accession, however, in 802, of Egbert to the throne of Wessex, the kingdom of the West Saxons became the ruling one, — a supremacy which it never after lost. Before the death of that monarch, which took place in 838, his authority was acknowledged by all the invaders that had settled in Great Britain, and was submitted to by the people of West and of North Wales. In the following century, during the reigns of Edward the Elder (901–925) and Athelstan (925–940), the son and grandson of Alfred the Great, the power of the house of Wessex became permanently established over the whole island; and the kings of that line were recognized as immediate lords of all the English inhabitants, and as superior lords of all the Celtic. At this point the Teutonic conquest of Britain may be said to have been fully achieved.

CHAPTER II.

THE ANGLO-SAXON LANGUAGE AND LITERATURE.

Language of the Teutonic Invaders. — Up to the accession of Egbert, the speech of the Teutonic invaders of Britain, while everywhere the same essentially, was broken up into a number of dialects. It is not likely that any one of them had any authority outside of its own district: none of them, except, possibly, the Northumbrian, possessed a literature. The Latin charters of the early kings in several places make distinct mention of the dialect of Kent; but in that no literary work was then composed, or, if composed, it has not been handed down in its original form. With the accession, however, of the royal house of Wessex to the rule of Teutonic England, this state of affairs underwent a change. Linguistic supremacy, other things being equal, is sure to follow political: the dialect of Wessex, accordingly, became the cultivated language of the whole people, — the language in which books were written, and laws were published. During the reign of Alfred (871–901) it began to develop a literature, which, before the Norman conquest, attained no slight proportions; and it is in this West-Saxon dialect that nearly all the existing monuments of our earliest speech were composed. Still, besides these we have extant a few interlinear glosses written in the language of Northumbria, the parent-tongue of the present dialects of the north of England and of the Scottish Lowlands.

The language of the Teutonic invaders was originally called by them Saxon or English, according as they themselves were Saxons or Angles; and it continued, even down to the eleventh century, to be thus variously designated in their own Latin writings. Still the superiority of the Angles, arising from vastly greater numbers, from larger territory, and perhaps from an earlier cultivation of literature, survived the decay of their political power; and though the kings of the West Saxons attained to the supremacy, though the West-Saxon dialect became the language of all who wrote, the name applied both to the race and the tongue was usually *Englisc*, that is, "English." From the ninth century on, it is almost the only term used by those who spoke it. When, in the sixteenth and seventeenth centuries, a revival of the study of our early speech took place, it was sometimes called Saxon, sometimes English-Saxon, and sometimes Anglo-Saxon; and the last designation, as recognizing the names of the two principal invading tribes, has been the one generally adopted. In this work Anglo-Saxon will be used to mark a period in the history of the English language extending from 450 to 1150, or nearly a century after the Norman conquest; and, when employed without limitation, will designate that dialect called specifically the West Saxon. As an equivalent phrase, "English of the Anglo-Saxon period" will also be used.

Differences between Anglo-Saxon and modern English. — Both in grammar and in vocabulary Anglo-Saxon differed widely from modern English. It was what, in the technical language of grammarians, is called a synthetic language; that is, a language, like the Latin, which expresses by changes in the form of the words themselves, the modifications of meaning they undergo, and their relations to one another in the sentence. It had two principal declensions of the noun, with several subordinate declensions under one of them; it had two declensions of the adjective, according as its substantive was definite or indefinite; it had a distinct form for four cases in the substantive; it had two leading conjugations of the verb, with subordinate conjugations under each; and, as a necessary accompaniment of this fulness of inflection, it possessed a complicated syntax. On the other hand, modern English is what is called an analytic tongue. The relations of ideas which were once expressed by termination and inflection are now, with the disappearance of these, expressed, instead, by the use of prepositions and their cases, and by the arrangement of words in the sentence. Still the grammatical structure, what there is left of it, is purely Teutonic. Even more marked is the difference between the ancient and the modern tongue in the vocabulary. A vast number of words belonging to the Anglo-Saxon no longer exist for us, even in a changed form: their places have been supplied by borrowing from other languages, especially Latin and French, to an extent which, if vocabulary alone were considered, would make it doubtful whether our tongue is Teutonic or Romanic. These differences between the earliest and modern English are essential differences: they are not the characteristics of a development of language, but of an actual transformation. Hence has arisen the necessity of a special term applied to this period of our speech. A nomenclature which, in the history of our tongue, includes under one name the English of Cadmon and of Tennyson is unsatisfactory and misleading,—full as much so one which confounds the language of Cadmon and of Chaucer.

Anglo-Saxon Literature.—Poetry.—No written literature existed among the Teutonic invaders before their conversion to Christianity in the seventh century; and of the two dialects of Anglo-Saxon, the West-Saxon and the Northumbrian, the former is the only one that has handed down productions of any value. In this were composed no small number of works, both in prose and poetry. The latter, as in all early literatures, was much the most important, and presents a marked contrast, alike in character and construction, to the verse of later times. Its distinguishing peculiarity, as regards form, was, that it was alliterative; that is to say, it depended, not upon final rhyme, nor upon regularity of accent, nor upon the existence of a fixed number of syllables in the line, but upon the fact that a certain number of the most important words in the same line began with the same letter. According to the usual, though not invariable, arrangement, two important words in the first section of the line, and one in the second section, began with the same letter (if a consonant), or with vowels, which were not required to be the same. Unaccented prefixes were not regarded, as the *ge* in *ge-wât* of the following illustration of this method of versification: —

> Ge-*w*ât þâ ofer *w*ǣg-holm · *w*inde ge-fŷsed
> *F*lota *f*âmig-heals · *f*ugle gelîcost.
>
> *W*ent then over the sea-*w*ave, *w*ind-impelled,
> The *b*oat with *b*ow of foam, likest a *b*ird

As regards subject, Anglo-Saxon poetry was mainly of a religious character, consisting largely of versifications of the narratives contained in the Bible, and of legends of saints and martyrs. Still its most important work is the epic of Beowulf, which celebrates the deeds of a Danish hero of that name; and, though it exists in only a single imperfect manuscript of the tenth century, its original composition is generally thought to go back to the period before the conversion of the people to Christianity. The next most important work is a version of some of the Bible narratives, generally attributed to Cadmon, a Northumbrian monk who flourished in the middle of the seventh century. But the work as it now exists is in the West-Saxon dialect, and not in that in which it was originally composed. The whole of Anglo-Saxon poetry which is extant amounts to about thirty thousand lines, and a large proportion of this has been preserved in two volumes. One of them is the Codex Exoniensis; or, Exeter Book, — a collection which is supposed to be the one mentioned among the gifts made in the eleventh century to St. Peter's monastery in Exeter by Bishop Leofric. It is there spoken of as "a large English book of various matters composed in songwise" (*mycel Englisc bôc be gehwylcum þingum on leóðwísan geworht*). The other is the Codex Vercellensis, — a collection found in 1832 at Vercelli in Italy.

Prose. — The language of Anglo-Saxon poetry stands at the farthest possible remove from that of daily life. It constantly repeats the same ideas in slightly varying phrases; it uses numerous compound words peculiar to itself; the construction of its sentences is often involved and intricate, and the meaning in consequence obscure; and through it all, with a certain grandeur, there is joined a certain monotony from the little range of thought or expression found in it. On the other hand, Anglo-Saxon prose is exceedingly simple in its construction. It may be said to begin with King Alfred, who is, indeed, its most prominent author. Like the poetry, its subject-matter was mainly religious, and to a large extent it was made up of translations from the Latin. Still its most valuable monuments were purely original; one being a collection of the laws of various kings, and the other a series of annals called "The Anglo-Saxon Chronicle," in which the events of each year are recorded under that date. Of this work one manuscript extends down to the death of King Stephen in 1154. Anglo-Saxon prose is of great interest from a linguistic point of view: as literature, it is, in general, dull beyond description.

The following specimen of Anglo-Saxon prose is taken from the account given to King Alfred by Ohthere, one of his Norse subjects, and inserted by the former into his translation of the History of Paulus Orosius, a Spanish priest of the fifth century. In the interlinear gloss the modern forms of the Anglo-Saxon words are, when not used, placed between parentheses: and some of the words not found or implied in the Anglo-Saxon, but employed in the gloss, are placed between brackets. The characters ð þ represent the two sounds of *th*, heard in such words as *this*, *think*, *then*, *than*, *death*, *tithe*.

Ohþere sǣde his hlâforde, Ælfrede kynincge, þæt
Ohthere said to his lord, King Alfred, that
he ealra Norðmanna norðmest bûde. He cwæð þæt
he of all Northmen northmost dwelt. He said (quoth) that
he bûde on þæm lande norðweardum wið þâ West-sǣ.
he dwelt in the land northward along (with) the West-sea.
He sǣde, þeâh, þæt þæt land sŷ swîðe lang norð þanon;
He said, though, that that land is very long north thence;

ac hit is eal wêste, bûtan on feâwum stôwum, sticcemælum wîciað Finnas on huntôðe on wintra, and on sumera on fiscôðe be þære sæ. He sæde þæt he, æt sumum cyrre, wolde fandian hû lange þæt land norðrihte læge; oððe hwæþer ænig man be-norðan þæm wêstene bûde. Þâ fôr he norðrihte be þæm lande: let him ealne weg þæt wêste land on þæt steôrbord, and þâ wîd-sæ on bæcbord, þrŷ dagas. Þâ wæs he swâ feor norð swâ þâ hwæl-huntan fyrrest farað. Þâ fôr he þâ-gyt norðrihte, swâ feor swâ he mihte on þæm ôðrum þrîm dagum geseglian.

but it is all waste, except (but) in a few places, [where] here and there dwell Finns, for (in) hunting in winter, and in summer for (in) fishing along (by) that sea. He said that he, at a certain [some] time, wished [would] to find out by trial how long the land due north lay; or whether any man north of the waste dwelt. Then went (fared) he due north along (by) the land: [he] left all [the] way the waste land on the starboard, and the wide-sea on [the] larboard three days. Then was he so far north as the whale-hunters farthest go (fare). Then went (fared) he still (then-yet) due north, so far as he might in the second [other] three days sail.

CHAPTER III.

INFLUENCE OF FOREIGN TONGUES UPON THE ENGLISH OF THE ANGLO-SAXON PERIOD.

DOWN to the time of the Norman conquest the Anglo-Saxon form of the English language remained essentially the same. The grammatical modifications, in particular, that it underwent, were comparatively few in number, and slight in importance. Some inflections were lost; cases originally possessing different endings came to have the same; and the tendency of verbs of the strong conjugation to pass over to the weak began even thus early to show itself. Still none of these changes were violent or extensive: all of them took place in accordance with the natural law of development. But during this period the language came into contact with three other tongues, which to some extent affected the vocabulary, and perhaps, also, the form of expression. These were, first, the speech of the native Celtic inhabitants; secondly, the Latin; and, thirdly, the Norse. Of these, Latin was the only one which at that time added any appreciable number of words to the language of literature. Terms from the Celtic or the Norse may have been adopted into the colloquial speech; but it was not until the break-up of the classic Anglo-Saxon, which followed the Norman conquest, that they occur to any extent in writing.

Celtic.—The native inhabitants found by the Teutonic invaders in the part of Britain they overran belonged to the Cymric branch of the Celtic stock. As the conquest was the work of several hundred years, it might be supposed that the vocabulary of each people would have received large accessions from that of the other; but such was not the case. Very few Celtic terms are found in Anglo-Saxon literature; and not many, indeed, appear to have made their way into written English in the centuries immediately following the coming of the Norman-French. This was, without doubt, due mainly to the little intercourse that prevailed between the two races and the feelings of hatred developed by long years of war. The fact that the native inhabitants were Christians, and the invaders heathen, tended also to widen the breach between them; but, even after the conversion of the Anglo-Saxons, religious differences came in to impart additional bitterness to the hostility that sprang from political and military conflicts. Bede, writing in the earlier half of the eighth century, says, that in his day it was not the custom of the Britons to pay any respect to the faith and religion of the English, nor to correspond with them any more than with pagans. In consequence, very few of the Celtic words in our speech go back to a very early date. Most of them, indeed, that came into the language before a comparatively late period, were usually not borrowed directly, but apparently went first into Latin or French, and from them found their way into English. Thus *glen*, which occurs in our earliest speech, may have been borrowed directly from the speech of the Britons; but other early, though not Anglo-Saxon words, such as *basket*, *bran*, *brisket*, *cabin*, *piece*, *quay*, if in all cases of Celtic origin, have in every case gone first into the French, and from that tongue have been borrowed by us. It is rarely safe, indeed, to assert positively that any particular word found in our primitive language has been taken from the Celtic; for the derivation is sure to be disputed. Certainly the modern importations from that quarter far exceed in number the earlier ones. Moreover, they have generally come to us from the Gaelic branch, and not from the Cymric: and in most cases they denote objects peculiar, or originally peculiar, to the race by which they were first employed. The words *bard*, *brogue*, *clan*, *druid*, *plaid*, *shamrock*, *whiskey*, for illustration, are all of Celtic origin; but none of them go back to the Anglo-Saxon period, and most of them are of comparatively recent introduction. In proper names, whether of persons or places, Celtic terms are naturally much more common. There is an old English saying which runs as follows: —

By Tre,[1] Ros,[2] Pol,[3] Lan,[4] Caer,[5] and Pen[6]
You know the most of Cornish men.

And these prefixes and several others are still numerous in names of persons and places.

It is to be added, that the influence of Celtic upon English has never been made the subject of thorough scientific investigation. Extravagant claims have been and are still put forth as to the extent of this element in our tongue. In particular, long lists of English words have been often given as derived from Celtic ones more or less resembling them. These lists are as a general rule, utterly untrustworthy. In many instances there is no relationship whatever between the words compared; in other instances the relationship is due to the fact that the same word has come down from the primitive Indo-European to both the Celtic and Teutonic branches; and in other instances still, where there has been actual borrowing, it is the Celtic tongues that have borrowed from the English, and not the English from the Celtic. At best, the influence of the languages of this stock upon our speech has been slight.

Latin. — Far greater, even as regards Anglo-Saxon, was the influence of the Latin. This first manifested itself in the seventh century, and was due, like most other changes in the vocabulary, to the operation of causes not in themselves of a linguistic nature. In the

[1] A place or dwelling.
[2] Cymric *rhos*, a moor; Gaelic *ros*, a headland. [3] A marsh, pool.
[4] An enclosure, church. [5] A cairn; or, from Lat. *castra*, a camp.
[6] A mountain; in Gaelic, *ben*.

year 597 a band of Roman missionaries, sent by Pope Gregory I., came, under the leadership of Augustine, to the kingdom of Kent, with the object of converting the people. Their efforts were successful; and by the end of the following century all of the Teutonic inhabitants of Britain had gone over from heathenism to the Christian faith. One immediate consequence was to bring into prominence and power in the country a body of ecclesiastics who not only carried on the church-service in Latin, but were in the habit of using that language largely in conversation and in writing. For the first time in its history, Teutonic Britain was brought into contact with the superior literature and civilization of the Continent. The inevitable result was to introduce into the Anglo-Saxon a number of words taken from the Latin. At first these were naturally connected with the church-service, or with ecclesiastical proceedings; but, as time went on, a variety of terms came in, denoting objects in no way connected with religion.

As the influence of Celtic in this early period has been overrated by many, that of Latin has been underrated by most. The words borrowed from it were not only considerable in number, they were, to a great extent, thoroughly assimilated. From the Latin nouns introduced, new adjectives and verbs and adverbs were formed by the addition of Teutonic endings; as from *cuc*, 'cook' (from Lat. *coquus*), was formed the verb *cucean*, 'to cook;' from *regol*, 'rule' (from Lat. *regula*), were formed the adjective *regollic*, 'rule-like,' 'regular,' and the adverb *regollīce*, 're[illegible]gularly.' The new words also were used with perfect f[illegible]reedom to form compounds with the native ones; as, [illegible]erous for instance, *biscop*, 'bishop' (from Lat. *episcopus*), [illegible]s enter into composition with more than a dozen Anglo-Saxon ones, of which list *biscop-rīce*, 'bishopric,' will serve as an illustration. In fact, all the results that take place now when words from one tongue are brought in large numbers into another can be found exemplified in the influence of Latin upon the English of this early period. Some of the native words began to disappear entirely; thus, *fefor*, 'fever' (from Lat. *febris*), drove out *hriðe*, the original word denoting that disease. Again: the borrowed and the native words would frequently stand side by side; thus, in King Alfred's writings, as well as later ones, *munt*, 'mount' (from Lat. *mons*, *mont-is*), is used interchangeably with *dûn*, the present 'down,' and *beorg*, seen in our 'iceberg.' Before the Norman conquest six hundred words at least had been introduced from Latin into the Anglo-Saxon; some of them occurring but once or twice in the literature handed down, others met with frequently. Were we to include in this list of borrowed terms the compounds into which the borrowed terms enter, the whole number would be swelled to three or four times that above given. It is also to be marked, that not [illegible]ly were nou[illegible]directly borrowed, but also adjectives and verbs, though to a far less extent. The words that came int[illegible] Anglo-Saxon from the seventh century on constitute [illegible] the first real introduction of the Latin element into our tongue; but, in accordance with the terminology generally adopted, it is styled "Latin of the Second Period."

Scandinavian. — The extent of this Latin influence upon Anglo-Saxon is something that is capable of pretty definite determination; but such is not the case with the Scandinavian element that comes now to be considered. The descendants of the Teutonic invaders, not much more than a century after their conversion to Christianity, were to suffer the same evils that had been inflicted by their own heathen freebooting forefathers upon the original Celtic population. Under the year 787 the Anglo-Saxon Chronicle states, that in the days of Bertric, King of Wessex, three shiploads of Northmen landed upon the coast of Britain, and slew the officers who went out to meet them with the intent of taking them prisoners. "These," it continues, "were the first ships of Danish men who sought the land of the English race." This event marks the beginning of a steadily increasing series of marauding descents upon the seaboard, and inroads into the interior, which, in the latter part of the ninth century, culminated in the devastation or subjection of nearly all the Anglo-Saxon territory, and the permanent settlement of a large part of it. East Anglia was conquered in 870, and became and thenceforward remained a Danish kingdom. The invaders also overran or subdued the greater portion of what is now Northern and Eastern England. Their attempts upon Wessex were finally, however, effectually checked by the defeat they received from King Alfred at Edington, in Wiltshire, in 878. This was followed by the Peace of Wedmore, in accordance with which the whole country was divided between the two nations, the Danes on their part agreeing to adopt tne Christian faith. Even after this, incursions continued to be made; and toward the close of the tenth century the invasion was renewed on a grander scale. It ended in establishing upon the English throne, from 1013 to 1042, a Danish dynasty, to which belonged Sweyn, Canute, Harold Harefoot, and Hardicanute. But in every case the new-comers seem to have made no effort to keep up their own tongue, but adopted the speech of the people among whom they had fixed their homes. The Scandinavian settlements are, for the most part, limited to East Anglia (Norfolk and Suffolk), to Lincolnshire and the neighboring counties on the west, to Yorkshire, Lancashire, Westmoreland, and Cumberland. Their existence is generally conceded to be indicated by various names of towns, of which those ending in *-by* (Old Norse *býr*, a 'dwelling,' 'village'), in *-thorp* or *-torp* (O. N. *þorp*, a 'hamlet,' 'village'), in *-toft* (O. N. *tóft*, a 'homestead,' 'enclosure'), and in *-thwaite* (O. N. *þveiti*, a 'clearing'), are among the most common. Examples of these can be seen in Whitby, Althorp, Lowestoft, and Braithwaite.

There was, accordingly, no slight infusion of the Scandinavian element in the population that inhabited Britain. But the extent of Scandinavian influence upon the language is difficult to ascertain for the following reasons: the Old Norse and the Anglo-Saxon are both Teutonic tongues; they both descended from a common ancestor. A large number of words were the same, or nearly the same, in both. It is not conceivable that all the vocabulary possessed by either has been handed down in the literature of each that has been saved. When, therefore, a word occurs in modern English which is not found in Anglo-Saxon, or any other Low German tongue, but is found in Old Norse, we can say that there is every probability that it came from the latter; but we cannot say this with certainty, for it may have existed in the former, and not have been preserved. There is, moreover, a special difficulty in this question, from the fact that it was in the Anglian kingdoms that these foreign settlements were made. Now, the existing remains of Northumbrian speech, which is an Anglian dialect of the Anglo-Saxon, show plainly that this dialect was much closer allied to the Old Norse than is the West-Saxon, which is a Saxon dialect of Anglo-Saxon. In the last-named the infinitive of the verb, for illustration, regularly ends in *-an;* while in the other two the *n* is entirely or occasionally dropped. In West-Saxon 'to tell' is *tellan;* in Northumbrian it is *tellan* or *tella;* in Norse it is *telia.* It is, therefore, quite conceivable, though it may not be very probable, that words and forms which we ascribe to the Scandinavian element may, in fact, have not come from it, but from the speech of the Anglian population; for we have no such extensive vocabulary of the Northumbrian dialect as we have of the West-Saxon.

Still there is no doubt that a large number of Norse words were introduced at this time into the spoken tongue; and many of these have spread beyond their original limits, and linger to this day in all the local dialects of Northern England and Southern Scotland. In these, indeed, this foreign element is far more conspicuous than in the language of literature. Still, in regard to the latter also, it is reasonable to suppose that the Norse words, and meanings of words, in many cases, have supplanted those, which, up to the time of its introduction, had been the prevailing or exclusive ones in Anglo-Saxon. For illustration, *sindon* was the ordinary form for the plural of the present tense of the verb *be:* its place is now supplied by *are*, the original of which is rare in Anglo-Saxon, but the regular form in the Norse. So from the Norse *kalla* we seem to get our verb *call;* for in Anglo-Saxon the corresponding word is *clipian*, 'to clepe.' Again: the word *dream* is common to both tongues; but in Anglo-Saxon it means 'joy,' 'music;' and it is from the Norse that we have taken the modern signification. Still it was not till the break-up of the native speech, that followed upon the Norman conquest, that Norse words came to be used to any extent in the language of literature.

CHAPTER IV.

THE NORMAN CONQUEST AND THE FRENCH LANGUAGE IN ENGLAND.

UP to the middle of the eleventh century the influences that had been at work upon the language had not been productive of great changes; still less were they revolutionary in their nature. The Norsemen for a time brought ruin everywhere; but whether they desolated temporarily, or settled permanently, they did not anywhere materially disturb the native speech as an instrument of communication, or affect in the slightest its literary supremacy. Even during the time they ruled the country, they seem not to have made any effort to introduce into it the use of their own tongue. But a series of events was now to take place which completely changed the future political history of the English people; and it was attended by as profound and wide-reaching a change in the character of English speech. In the latter half of the eleventh century came the Norman conquest and the introduction into the island of the French as the language of the higher classes. The most powerful effects produced by these upon the native tongue did not fully show themselves until three centuries had passed; but a very early and almost immediate effect wrought upon it was to throw it into a state of confusion. The English of the Anglo-Saxon period sank at once from its position as the language of culture, whatever that culture was; and when, in the fourteenth century, it once more re-appears as the language of classic literature, it is a language and literature widely different from that which had been supplanted or degraded by the coming of a stranger race. From the Norman conquest on, the native speech no longer followed the natural law of development which it would have followed as a pure Teutonic tongue.

To explain the nature of the changes that were wrought in it, it will be necessary to give some account of the men whose coming caused them, and of the relations which for a long time existed on English soil between the French and English languages.

The Norman-French.—Toward the close of the ninth century a band of Northmen, under a renowned leader named Rolf, or Rollo, sailed up the Seine, captured Rouen, and, from that point as a centre, carried on a continuous and destructive war with the native inhabitants. At last, in 912, peace was made. To the invaders, Charles the Simple, the King of the French, ceded a large territory bordering upon the British Channel, which was called from them Normandy. On the other hand, Rollo agreed to become the feudal vassal of the French monarch, and to embrace the Christian religion. These conditions were fully carried into effect; and the Northmen became the undisturbed owners of the district given up to them, and, along with the religion of their subjects, they also adopted their language.

The Norman Conquest.—The relations between the English and the Norman-French began to assume about the beginning of the eleventh century a somewhat close character by the marriage, in 1002, of the Anglo-Saxon king, Ethelred II., to Emma, sister of Richard III., the fifth duke of Normandy. One fruit of this union was a son, Edward, usually styled the Confessor, who reigned over England from 1043 to 1066. But the early years of this prince were spent at the court of his uncles Richard and Robert, dukes of Normandy; and when, after the termination of the Danish dynasty in 1042, he was recalled to his native country, and placed upon the throne, he continued to retain a preference for the friends and the tastes of his youth. Norman-French noblemen were assigned positions of responsibility and power; Norman-French priests were made English bishops; and, though a revolution in 1052 drove out most of the foreign favorites, the foreign influence could not have passed away utterly. Early in 1066 Edward the Confessor died; and Harold, the most powerful nobleman in the kingdom, was chosen king in his stead. But a claim to the throne was immediately made by William, Duke of Normandy, a cousin of the deceased monarch. To support it, he invaded England in the autumn of the same year; and the battle of Hastings, fought on the 14th of October, 1066, resulted in tne defeat and death of Harold and the subjection of the whole country.

Effect of the Conquest upon the Native Language. — Two general facts in regard to language are at once apparent as the effect of the conquest. One is, that, though the native tongue continued to be spoken by the great majority of the population, it went out of use as the language of high culture. It was no longer taught in the schools; it was no longer employed at the court of the king, or the castles of the nobles, or in the services of the church. This displacement was probably slow at first; but it was done effectually at last. The second fact is, that, from the first, the higher classes, both lay and ecclesiastical, that came in with the conquest, used either Latin or French; the latter, in process of time, growing more and more to be the language, not alone of polite society, but of literature. We have, in consequence, the singular spectacle of two tongues flourishing side by side in the same country, and yet for centuries so utterly distinct and independent, that neither can be said to have exerted much direct appreciable influence upon the other, though in each case the indirect influence was great. To understand the relations between these two tongues involves an acquaintance with the relations existing between the two races that spoke them; and in both cases the knowledge we have, especially of the earlier period, is obscure. Our information, indeed, in regard to our speech, is based almost exclusively upon incidental notices contained in the Latin chronicles written in the twelfth century and in the beginning of the thirteenth; and as in these the subject of language is rarely treated of specifically, and never at any length, the inferences that are drawn can only be looked upon as probable, and not as certain. From the latter part of the thirteenth century on, the native tongue is more an object of consideration in itself, and our knowledge of the relations between French and English becomes far more positive and precise. A few of the more important statements will be quoted; but in every case it is necessary to bear in mind, not only what was said, but when it was said.

Up to a comparatively late period, the History which purported to be written by Ingulph, appointed Abbot of Croyland in 1076, was regarded as authentic, and its statements were implicitly credited. In this work it was asserted, that, after the accession of William, the English race was held in contempt and detestation; that the Normans so abhorred the language, that the laws of the land and the decrees of the king were put into Latin; and that in the schools the elements of grammar were imparted in French. Though this History was professedly the production of a contemporary of the Conqueror, there is no doubt that much, if not all, of it, was a forgery of several centuries later. Its statements can therefore have no further weight than would belong to writings of that later period; that is, really none at all. Nevertheless, there is satisfactory evidence that contempt was both felt and expressed by the foreigners for the native population, — a contempt which was naturally extended to the language. Henry of Huntingdon, who flourished in the former half of the twelfth century, in speaking of the state of the country at the death of William the Conqueror, asserted that it was a disgrace to be even called an Englishman. About the beginning of the thirteenth century Gervase, who was born at Tilbury in Essex, but entered the service of the Emperor of Germany, wrote, among other things, an account of his native land. In this, while speaking of Harold, the last of the Anglo-Saxon kings, he stated that it was then the custom of the noblest of the English to have their sons educated among the French for the sake of gaining proficiency in arms and for the purpose of removing the barbarism of the native language. While this assertion is of not the slightest value as evidence of the state of affairs in the time of Edward the Confessor, it is of value as to the state of opinion in the time of King John. The tongue of the common people was, in truth, in the eyes of the Norman a barbarous one. He made not the slightest attempt to destroy it: he contented himself with simply despising it. To him it was the rude speech of a rude people which had been subjected to the sway of a superior race

French and English Languages on English soil. — English, indeed, after the conquest, did not cease to be a written language: it did cease to be a cultivated one. None of those conservative influences were cast about it which are sure to prevent rapid and radical changes in any tongue that is regularly employed by the educated. But the great body of the people clung to it. They were ignorant, and they corrupted it; but, as they could not or would not learn the language of the higher classes, they preserved it. While French, therefore, continued to remain for centuries the tongue employed in polite conversation, while it and Latin were the ones mainly employed in literature, the native speech could not fail, as time went on, to make its influence more and more felt by the mere weight of numbers on the part of those using it. There is a general impression that the nobility did not learn to speak English till the fourteenth century; and this may be true to this extent, that the subjects of the English king who were born on the Continent, and spent there most of their lives, never learned to speak it at all. But it is against all probability that those members of the higher classes who were brought up in the island, whose interests mainly lay there, whose lives were largely passed there, should not have been able to understand and make use of the speech of the great body of the common people with whom they came into daily contact. From the very first, necessity would have forced them at times to employ English, though French were the language of their choice. This view is borne out by numerous incidental references to the subject which have been handed down. In particular, ignorance of English on the part of the clergy came to be regarded as a serious objection. The historian Matthew of Paris, who flourished during the reign of Henry III. (1216–1272), relates that Sewal, Archbishop of York, who died in 1258, wrote a letter of remonstrance to the Pope, complaining of the way in which he had been harassed by suspensions, examinations, and in other ways, because he refused to accept of inexperienced persons recommended by the pontiff to benefices, on the ground that they were ignorant of the English language. One of the chief reasons of the unpopularity of Henry III. was his preference for favorites who came from his dominions on the Continent; and the writer of the chronicle which goes under the name of Matthew of Westminster's, in giving an account of the events which took place in 1263, during the civil war between the barons and that monarch, states that whoever was unable to speak the English language was regarded by the common people as a vile and contemptible person. If this assertion be true, there is no escape from the legitimate inference that the nobility whose homes were in the island must have been familiar with the native speech.

Rise in Importance of the English. — But as it was political events that had brought about the degradation of the English language, so it was to political events that its gradual rise in importance and estimation was mainly due. The continued, and within certain limits probably increasing, use of the

French speech on the soil of Great Britain, lay largely in the fact that it was likewise the speech of a vast population on the Continent who were subject to the same ruler as the islanders. The possessions of Henry II., for instance, embraced full half of what is now France, and far exceeded in extent the territory under the direct control of the French monarch himself. So long as this state of things lasted, an uncultivated tongue like the English was at an immense disadvantage as compared with a cultivated one existing alongside of it. Even the island itself was, to a great degree, simply looked upon as a storehouse of men and materials, from which its kings could draw supplies to prosecute their designs of conquest upon the Continent; and the language itself could not hope to be rated at as high a value as the country in which it was the speech of the lower classes only. But during the thirteenth century events occurred that changed the condition of affairs. Chief among these was the gradual loss of the possessions held by the English kings in France, and, in particular, the loss of Normandy in 1204, during the reign of John. This had the inevitable effect of largely transferring the interests of the nobility from the Continent to the Island. Henceforth their lot was to be cast amid the English-speaking race that dwelt upon the estates held by them in England. The breach which naturally arose, in consequence, between the people of the Island and of the Continent, was still further widened by the action taken in 1244 by the French king, Louis IX.

In that year he summoned to Paris all the nobility of England who had possessions in France, and gave them their choice of relinquishing their property in the one country or the other, because it was impossible for the same man to be the subject of two rulers, always in rivalry, and often in hostility. They were, accordingly, obliged to give up one or the other. As soon as the knowledge of this transaction came to the ears of the English king, he at once ordered that all Frenchmen, especially Normans, who had possessions in England, should be deprived of their property.

The necessary effect of these political changes was first to cause the English and the French to look upon each other more and more as different peoples; secondly, to hasten the union between the English of native and of foreign descent, and to wipe out distinctions of any kind heretofore existing between them. Yet it is clear that there could never be a complete union without the adoption of a common language; and, in spite of these events, this had not yet taken place at the end of the thirteenth century. On this point we have the direct and unimpeachable testimony of a contemporary writer, which, though often quoted, is too important to be passed over here. Robert of Gloucester, a monk who flourished in the latter half of the thirteenth century, wrote a rhymed chronicle of Britain and England, down to the year 1272. In giving an account of the conquest by William, he is led to speak of the two languages still existing in the country side by side, and this he does in the following words: —

Thus com, lo! Engelond into Normandies hond.
And the Normans ne couthe speke tho bote hor owe speche,
And speke French as hii dude atom and hor childen dude also teche.
So that heiemen of this lond, that of hor blod come,
Holdeth alle thulke speche that hii of hom nome.
Vor bote a man conne Frenss, me telth of him lute;
Ac lowe men holdeth to Engliss and to hor owe speche yute.
Ich wene ther ne beth in al the world contreyes none
That ne holdeth to hor owe speche bote Engelond one.[1]

From this it is evident that French was still the language of the higher classes, and that to be ignorant of it was in a measure a social stigma. Nor did this feeling speedily die out. In the earlier half of the following century Ralph Higden, a monk of St. Werburgh's, in Chester, wrote in Latin a chronicle of the world, under the title of "Polychronicon;" and in it he gave an account of the languages spoken in England, and of the corruption that had crept into the native speech. A translation of this work was completed in 1387, by John of Trevisa, vicar of Berkeley;

[1] Lo! thus came England into the possession of Normandy.
And the Normans could then speak only their own speech,
And spoke French as they did at home, and caused their children also to be taught it.
So that noblemen of this land, that come of their blood,
Hold all the same speech that they from them received.
For unless a man knows French, he is little thought of;
But low men keep to English, and to their own speech yet.
I think there be not in all the world any countries
That do not hold to their own speech but England alone.

and the passage explanatory of the co uption that had overtaken the tongue he rendered in the following words: —

This apeyryng of the burth-tonge ys bycause of twey thinges: — on ys, for chyldern in scole, agenes the vsage and manere of al other nacions, buth compelled for to leue here oune longage, and for to construe here lessons and here thinges a Freynsch, and habbeth, suththe the Normans come furst into Engelond. Also gentil men children buth ytaught for to speke Freynsch fram tyme that a buth yrokked in here cradel, and conneth speke, and playe with a child hys brouch; and oplondysch men wol lykne ham-sylf to gentil men, and fondeth with gret bysynes for to speke Freynsch, for to be more ytold of.[1]

Such was the state of things in the former part of the fourteenth century. But by the middle of that century the movement toward the general adoption of the native speech had acquired a momentum which could no longer be resisted. From this period, signs of the employment of English by all classes in the community begin to multiply. Traditions connected with education are among the last to lose their hold upon the mind: practices connected with it are among the last to be abandoned. But, in the latter half of the fourteenth century, instruction through the

[1] This impairing of the birth-tongue is because of two things: one is, because children in school, against the usage and manner of all other nations, are compelled to leave their own language, and to construe their lessons and their matters in French, and have, since the Normans came first into England Also, gentlemen's children are taught to speak French from (the) time that they are rocked in their cradle, and can speak, and play with a child's brooch: and back-country men (or rustics) wish to make themselves like gentlemen, and strive with great earnestness to speak French, in order to be thought the more of.

medium of the French had to a great extent been supplanted by instruction through the medium of the English. Here, again, we have positive testimony. John of Trevisa, to his version, which has just been given, of Higden's account, added a correction of his statements, which was rendered necessary by the changes that had taken place between the time the book was written and the time it was translated. He asserted, that, since the great pestilence of 1349, the system of instruction had been revolutionized. Upon the remark of his author that the children of the higher classes were taught French from their cradles, he makes the following comment: —

Thys manere was moche yvsed tofore the furste moreyn, and ys seththe somdel ychaunged. For Iohan Cornwal, a mayster of gramere, chayngede the lore in gramer-scole, and construccion of Freynsch into Englysch; and Richard Pencrych lurnede that manere techyng of hym, and other men of Pencrych; so that now, the yer of oure Lord a thousond thre hondred foure score and fyue, of the secunde Kyng Richard after the conquest nyne, in al the gramer-scoles of Engelond childern leueth Frensch and construeth and lurneth an Englysch, and habbeth therby avauntage in on syde and desavauntage yn another: here avauntage ys, that a lurneth here gramer yn lasse tyme than childern wer ywoned to do; disavauntage ys, that now childern of gramer-scole conneth no more Frensch than can here lift heele, and that ys harm for ham, and a scholle passe the se and trauayle in strange londes, and in meny caas also. Also gentil men habbeth now moche yleft for to teche here childern Frensch.[1]

[1] This custom was much used before the first pestilence, and is since somewhat changed. For John Cornwall, a teacher of grammar, changed the method of instruction in the grammar-school, and (the) construing from

Doubtless this inevitable change was looked upon by many with much disfavor. The growing ignorance of a tongue which was widely used throughout Christendom, and seemed to have before it a great future, was regarded almost in the light of a calamity. Trevisa's remark, that the children in the grammar-schools knew "no more French than their left heel," was re-echoed in the alliterative poem of "Piers Ploughman," by Langlande, who is, in theory at least, supposed to represent the sentiments of the common people. In a passage inveighing against the general ignorance prevalent in his day, he says, —

> Gramer, the grounde of all, bi-gyleth now children;
> For is none of this newe clerkes, whoso nymeth hede,
> That can versifye faire, ne formalich enditen;
> Ne nought on amonge an hundreth, that an auctour can construe,
> Ne rede a lettre in any langage but in Latyn or in Englissh.[1]

French into English; and Richard Pencrich learned from him that manner of teaching, and other men from Pencrich: so that now, the year of our Lord a thousand three hundred four score and five, the ninth (year of the reign) of the second king Richard after the conquest, in all the grammar-schools of England children give up French, and construe and learn in English, and have thereby advantage on one side, and disadvantage on another. Their advantage is, that they learn their grammar in less time than children were wont to do; (the) disadvantage is, that now grammar-school children know no more French than their left heel knows: and that is harm for them, if they shall pass the sea and travel in strange lands, and in many (other) cases also Also, gentlemen have now much left teaching their children French."

[1] Grammar, the ground of all (studies), now leads astray children;
For there is no one of these new clerks, whoso taketh heed,
That can versify fairly, or compose in established form;[2]
And not one amongst an hundred that can construe an author,
Nor read a letter in any language but in Latin or in English.

[2] Either in prose? or alliterative verse?

Yet, in fact, this kind of instruction in French was far from being utterly abandoned at that period. Even as late as the reign of Henry VIII., at the time of the dissolution of the monasteries, it was still found taught in the conventual schools, — at any rate, in one case. A letter to Cromwell from John Ap Rice, one of the visitors of religious houses, relating to the monastery of Laycock in Wiltshire, mentions a form of French as still being used there which was certainly then used by no people to whom that tongue was a native speech. "The house," he says, "is very clean, well-repaired, and well-ordered: and one thing I observed worthy the advertisement (i.e. notice) there. The Ladies have their Rule, the Institutes of their Religion, and the ceremonies of the same written in the French tongue, which they understand well, and are very perfitt in the same. Albeit that it varieth from the vulgar French that is now used, and is much like the French that the Common Law is written in."

But more convincing evidence even than the change in the method of instruction in the schools, as to the general adoption of English by all classes, can be found in the act in regard to the pleadings in the law-courts, which was passed by the Parliament held at Westminster in 1362, the thirty-sixth year of Edward III. The preamble recites in full the reasons which led to the making of the statute; and, in spite of the verbiage usual in documents of this kind, most of it is well worthy quotation. "Because it is often shewed to the king," it said, "by the prelates, dukes, earls, barons, and all the commonalty, of the great mischiefs which have happened to divers of the realm, because the laws, customs, and statutes of this realm be not commonly known in the same realm, for that they be pleaded, showed, and judged in the French tongue, which is much unknown in the said realm: so that the people who do implead or be impleaded in the king's court, and in the courts of others, have no knowledge nor understanding of that which is said for them or against them by their serjeants and other pleaders; and that reasonably the said laws and customs shall be the sooner learned and known and better understood in the tongue used in the said realm, and by so much every man of the said realm may the better govern himself without offending of the law, and the better keep, save, and defend his heritage and possessions; and in divers regions and countries, where the king, the nobles, and others of the said realm have been, good governance and full right is done to every person, because that their laws and customs be learned and used in the tongue of the country: the king, desiring the good governance and tranquillity of his people, and to put out and eschew the harms and mischiefs, which do or may happen in this behalf by the occasions aforesaid, hath ordained and established by the assent aforesaid, that all pleas which shall be pleaded in his courts whatsoever, before any of his justices whatsoever, or in his other places, or before any of his other ministers whatsoever, or in the courts and places of any other lords whatsoever within the

But in the latter half of the fourteenth century a number of eminent writers in the native speech arose. Sir John Mandeville, after giving in Latin an account of his travels, and turning this into French, translated it again out of French into English about the year 1356; and the work is entertaining reading at this day. A few years later Langlande executed the first version of his famous alliterative poem, "The Vision of Piers Plowman," which was widely circulated. Toward the close of the century, Gower, after composing works in Latin and French, tried writing in English also, at the request, as he tells us, of King Richard II. But the two great authors of this time are Wycliffe and Chaucer; and their influence upon the language can not well be over-estimated. To the translation of the Scriptures, completed about 1380 by the former and his disciples, we owe that peculiar religious dialect, alike remarkable for simplicity, for beauty, and for force, which we still see preserved in the more modern versions of the Bible, and which renders the prose of that work distinct from every other existing form of English prose. It is only through this translation that Wycliffe can be said to have exerted a lasting influence upon our tongue. But what he did for the language of religion, Chaucer did for the language of literature. In his works men for the first time had great models in the native speech; and the dialect in which he wrote became the one universally employed in literature, largely in consequence of his writing in it. His genius it was that gave dignity to the speech in which it found manifestation. But in nothing is his foresight and wisdom more conspicuous than in the fact that he was the first man of learning to perceive the resources of the English language and the impropriety and gross folly of Englishmen writing in any other. He was, for his time, a great scholar; and his choice of his native tongue was not, like Wycliffe's, dictated by a desire to reach and affect through it all classes in the community, but by a profound confidence, not only in the power of expression it possessed, but in the future that lay before it. Nor was the authority of his name and example in this respect unnecessary. He died in 1400; and, for more than a century after his death, it was still a venturesome undertaking for an Englishman to write in English if he could write in Latin. A hundred and fifty years later, Roger Ascham, one of the greatest scholars of his age, wrote a book entitled "Toxophilus," first published in 1545. In his dedication of the work to the gentlemen and yeomen of his native land, he felt it necessary to apologize for having written it in the native speech. "If any man would blame me," said he, "either for taking such a matter in hand, or else for writing it in the English tongue, this answer I may make him: that, what the best of the realm think it honest for them to use, I, one of the meanest sort, ought not to suppose it vile for me to write. And though to have written it in another tongue had been both more profitable for my study, and also more honest for my name, yet I can think my labor well bestowed, if with a little hinderance of my profit and my name, may come any furtherance to the pleasure or commodity of the gentlemen and yeomen of England, for whose sake I took this matter in hand." And again, in his dedication to the king, Henry VIII., he says that it would have been easier, and fitter for his profession, to have written the book in Latin or in Greek. This is by no means an extreme case. In 1623, seven years after the death of Shakspeare, Bacon spent no small part of his time in turning his books, originally written in English, into Latin, with the avowed object of saving them for posterity; and in the dedication of the third edition of his Essays to the Duke of Buckingham, written in 1625, he says, "I do conceive that the Latin volume of them (being in the universal language) may last as long as books last." The immense incapacity of an author of the seventeenth century, and that author Bacon, to comprehend the future of his native tongue, is, perhaps, the highest tribute that can be paid to that great author of the fourteenth century who deliberately trusted his reputation entirely to it.

Debasement of Anglo-Norman French.— The second cause for the preference of English to French, which showed itself more and more during the fourteenth century, was a direct result of the loss of Normandy. At the time of the conquest, and for a long period following, there was no one tongue in Northern France recognized by all as the classic French language; but there were four great dialects of it, corresponding to four great political divisions, each with a literature of its own. One of these was the speech of Normandy, and this it was that in the eleventh century was carried over into England. But, during the centuries following, the power of the French royal house was steadily rising, and that of its great feudal dependents was as steadily falling. The dialect it employed was the dialect of its ancestral dominions, the Isle of France, in which Paris is situated; and, as it slowly extended its authority over the neighboring districts, it extended along with it the use of its own form of speech. As the French of Paris spread over the country, the tongues of the provinces, which had once been used in literature, sank gradually from the condition of dialects to that of *patois*. This was what took place in Normandy after its loss by the English crown. But, bad as the speech of Normandy might come to appear as compared with that of Paris, it would naturally seem far worse with that dialect after it had been transported to England, and cut off from direct communication with the same dialect on the Continent. Diverging more and more, as time went on, not merely from the speech of Paris, but even from the provincial speech of Normandy itself, it was, in consequence, subjected to a double degradation as the *patois* of a *patois*. This process of debasement began to show itself early, though doubtless at first only here and there. Walter Map, a writer of the twelfth century, tells us that at Marlborough there was reported to be a spring, of which he who tasted was sure to speak French afterward in a barbarous manner; so that from that time he who spoke that language incorrectly and inelegantly was said to speak French of Marlborough. Divergences naturally went on increasing during the two centuries following; and, while the French taught everywhere in the English schools would be certain to have a pretty uniform character, it was equally certain to deviate further and further from the French which had come to the front as the classic form of the language. Langlande refers contemptuously to the "French of Norfolk;" and Chaucer, in the Prologue to "The Canterbury Tales," introduces the prioress, who, as a fashionable woman, felt it incumbent to speak French, but was unable to speak what had then come to be regarded as pure French. He says, —

> And Frensch sche spak ful faire and fetysly,
> After the scole of Stratford atte Bowe,
> For Frensch of Parys was to hire unknowe.

In the Prologue to "The Testament of Love," written by a contemporary of Chaucer, and long imputed to him, there occurs a sentence which marks plainly the contemptuous opinion entertained by the French themselves of the debased Anglo-Norman dialect found in England. "In Latin and French," said the author, "hath many sovereign wits had great delight to endite, and have many noble things fulfilled; but certes there be some that speak their poesy matter in French, of which speech the Frenchmen have as good a fantasy as we have in hearing of Frenchmen's English."

General Adoption of English by all Classes. —All these agencies co-operated in bringing about the adoption of the native speech by all classes; yet at the end of the fourteenth century, while the success of English was well assured, its victory was even then far from complete. As was not unnatural, French, after it ceased to be necessary, came to be fashionable; and its use long survived its usefulness. It continued to be also, to a great extent, the language of official documents. Nearly all the letters of Henry IV., who reigned from 1399 to 1413, are written in it or in Latin; and indeed, in the early part of his reign, it almost seems as if it were not considered respectful to address him in English. A letter of the Scottish Earl of March, dated Feb. 18, 1400, offering his services to the English monarch, and entreating his support, contains an apology at the close for being written in the English language. "And, noble prince," says the earl, "mervaile yhe nocht that I write my lettres in Englishe, fore that ys mare clere to myne understandyng than Latyne or Fraunche."

But, during the whole reign of Henry IV. and his successor Henry V. (1413–1422), the marks of growing unfamiliarity with French rapidly accumulate. One of the most striking instances of this is to be found, indeed, in the very earliest part of the fifteenth century, in the case of the negotiations that took place in 1404, between France and England, in regard to the outrages committed by each nation at sea. Three of the ambassadors on the part of the latter power were

Thomas Swynborn and John Crofft, knights, and Nicholas de Rysshetoun, a professor of both the civil and the canon law. In a letter of Swynford and De Rysshetoun to the French Council, dated Sept. 1, 1404, they beg that the answer may be returned to them in Latin, and not in French, for the reason, as appears subsequently, that with the latter they were unacquainted. Again: in a letter of the 3d of October to the Duchess of Burgundy, Swynborn, Crofft, and De Rysshetoun state, that although the treaties between England and France had been wont to be drawn up in French by the consent of the temporal princes concerned in them, who did not understand Latin as well as French, yet all the letters missive that had passed between the contracting parties had been written in the former tongue, as being the common and vulgar idiom; and this custom they desire to have continued, for reasons that further on are distinctly given. For on the 21st of October, in acknowledging the reception of a communication from the French ambassadors, they complain of its being written in French, and state, that, for men unlearned as they were, it might as well have been put into Hebrew. It is a most striking proof of the general ignorance of French that had come to prevail in England, that ambassadors selected to carry on delicate and difficult negotiations, one of whom was a scholar by profession, should have been utterly unacquainted with the language of the people with which terms of settlement were to be made, — a language, moreover, which was still largely used in official documents in their own country. This ignorance kept on steadily increasing among all classes; and a necessary result was to substitute the native for the foreign speech in all the transactions of life, including, what is always the last to be changed, prescribed forms. It was sometimes the case that the higher orders changed their methods far sooner than those inferior to them in position. It was in the first half of the fifteenth century that many of the London guilds began to have their regulations translated from French into English, and to use the latter tongue in keeping their books. A curious entry in the records of the Company of Brewers, not only asserts directly that the greater part of the Lords and Commons were in the habit of having the proceedings in which they were concerned written down in the native language, but it moreover seems to say that direct influence was exercised by King Henry V. to substitute the use of English for French. Of the entry, which is in Latin, the following is a translation: "*Whereas*, Our mother-tongue, to wit, the English tongue, hath in modern days begun to be honorably enlarged and adorned: for that our most excellent lord, King Henry the Fifth, hath, in his letters missive, and divers affairs touching his own person, more willingly chosen to declare the secrets of his will; and, for the better understanding of his people, hath, with a diligent mind, procured the common idiom (setting aside others) to be commended by the exercise of writing; and there are many of our craft of brewers who have the knowledge of writing and reading in the said English idiom; but in others, to wit, the Latin and French, before these times used, they do not in any wise understand; for which causes, with many others, it being considered how that the greater part of the Lords and trusty Commons have begun to make their matters to be noted down in our mother-tongue, we also in our craft, following in some manner their steps, have decreed in future so to commit to memory the needful things which concern us."

At last, towards the close of the fifteenth century, the laws enacted by Parliament were for the first time expressed in English. They had, after the conquest, usually been published in the Latin; but in the reign of the first Edward (1272–1307), at the very time the French was beginning to lose its hold upon the nation, it was introduced into the statutes. In these it gradually supplanted the Latin, and by the end of the fourteenth century that tongue was no longer used in legislative enactments. At the end of the fifteenth century, French, in turn, had given way to the English, and the triumph of the popular speech was complete.

CHAPTER V.

PERIODS IN THE HISTORY OF THE ENGLISH LANGUAGE, AND THE CHANGES WROUGHT IN IT BY THE NORMAN CONQUEST.

WHAT was this popular speech, which, at the end of the fourteenth century, was for the first time manifesting its capability of becoming the vehicle of a great literature? It was certainly not the Anglo-Saxon. Between that and. it had taken place a divergence even more profound and wide-reaching than that which marks the separation of French from its parent Latin. The tongue spoken or written by an Englishman of the tenth century would have been as unintelligible to an Englishman of the fourteenth as it is to an Englishman of the nineteenth. In the course of those four hundred years the language had not simply suffered modification, or undergone development, it had experienced revolution. Nor was this popular tongue precisely that which is found in the literature of to-day; though the differences between it and our present speech are differences of degree, and not of kind; or, to make use of the same form of statement already employed, they are differences that have arisen from modification and development, and not at all from revolution. To bring out the general nature of the divergence in grammar and vocabulary that came into being between the English of the tenth and eleventh centuries and that of the fourteenth will be the aim of the present chapter.

The Language before the Conquest. — Up to the Norman conquest the linguistic situation may be thus described: A Low-Germanic tongue, usually called by those who spoke it *Englisc*, or English, but which by us is usually styled Anglo-Saxon, was the speech of all the Teutonic inhabitants of Great Britain from the Channel to the Frith of Forth. In it there existed several dialects; but one of these, the West-Saxon, had become the language of law and of literature, — the language in which the educated classes talked and wrote. Into this language there had been introduced in the course of centuries a slight number of Celtic and of Norse words, a much larger number of Latin ones. But, notwithstanding these additions, it continued to be — what it had been, not merely as regards grammar, but also as regards vocabulary — essentially a Teutonic tongue.

The Language after the Conquest. — With the introduction of Norman-French, this state of affairs underwent a change. It was not that the Anglo-Saxon ceased to be a spoken tongue, or even a written one; but it did cease to be a cultivated one.

One result of this was, that the West-Saxon dialect sank speedily from its position of supremacy, and in process of time fell to the level of the other dialects which it had itself supplanted. The inevitable effect was, that the popular speech was left to run its own course, without any restraining influence whatever Each district had words and forms, and syntactical constructions, and methods of pronunciation, of its own, which were little known or used outside of its borders. All was in confusion; and changes necessarily took place rapidly. This was something that is always sure to occur when a cultivated tongue comes to be used exclusively by the uneducated or the partially educated; for it is a speedy result that no standard of authority exists anywhere in it, which is felt to be binding upon all. The influence of the old literature is gone; and as yet no great authors have risen to establish methods of expression to which the speech of the better class will be made to conform. There are in it but few books written, and there are but few persons to read those that are written. Learned almost wholly by the ear, and scarcely at all by the eye, the language is specially subject to the phonetic and linguistic changes of all kinds that rude and ignorant men may bring about by modifying pronunciation, by confounding declensions and conjugations, by disregarding syntactical laws, in short, by all the numerous processes of decay and regeneration to which a living tongue is subject by the very fact of its being a living tongue. To all these influences the native speech was exposed, with little check, after the conquest; and it at once entered, in consequence, upon a series of rapid and violent changes.

These changes were of several kinds; but there were two principal ones. One of them was the loss of inflections in the native speech; the other, the introduction into it of French words. The latter is a direct result of the conquest; the former, only an indirect one. For, even in the Anglo-Saxon period, the process of stripping the speech of its inflection had already begun to show itself to a slight extent; and it has taken place on a large scale in the case of other Teutonic peoples, whose languages have been subject to none of the influences that follow subjugation by a foreign race speaking a foreign tongue. What the introduction of the Norman-French into England, and its use there by the higher classes, did, was to abolish any standard of authority for the native speech. It was thereby speedily thrown into a chaotic condition; all orderly development was prevented; the abandonment of inflection, which to some extent was certain to come some time, was rapidly hastened. Moreover, there can be little doubt that an additional result was the giving up of inflections on a scale that would never have taken place had the language been left subject only to the influences that could have affected it in a country largely cut off by its position from contact with foreign nations. These are indirect consequences only; but they were the first to exhibit themselves, and are therefore the first to demand our attention.

The changes, indeed, that took place, as a result of the conquest, indirectly in the inflectional system and directly in the vocabulary, of the English tongue, were so numerous and great that it has been customary to give the language during several centuries different names. It is of itself a convincing proof of the confused and varying character of our early speech, that scarcely any two scholars have agreed upon the titles or dates of the periods which they have adopted. This is not at all to be wondered at. Scientific precision in such respects is not attainable in even the most cultivated and stable tongues. Dates in the history of a language are convenient for reference: they are worth nothing for accuracy of statement. Men do not use one form of speech one year, and a different form the following year. This, which is true of any tongue, no matter how marked the changes, is especially true of the earlier stages of our own, in which the changes were not merely rapid, but in which they were unequal in different parts of the country. The language of the north of England advanced much more quickly toward Modern English than the language of the south; and a statement, in consequence, which would be true of the one, might be grossly false of the other.

Periods of the English Language.—It is, accordingly, to be borne in mind that the titles and dates about to be given are in themselves of no authority, and are used mainly as a matter of convenience; that the same terms, when employed by others, may not and often do not mean the same things; that other divisions, and an entirely different nomenclature, will be found in other works treating upon this same subject. With this understanding it is only necessary to add that the following will be the names and limits of the periods into which, in this volume, English is divided.

I. The Anglo-Saxon period will embrace that form of the language spoken from the first coming of the Saxons and Angles — that is, from the middle of the fifth century — to the middle of the century following the Norman conquest, — that is, to the year 1150.

II. The Early English period will embrace the form of the language spoken between 1150 and 1350. When a further subdivision of this is rendered desirable, the first half of it, the century from 1150 to 1250, will be spoken of as the Semi-Saxon, or Late Anglo-Saxon: the second half of it, the century from 1250 to 1350, will be called the Old English.

III. Middle English will include the form of the language used between 1350 and 1550.

IV. Modern English will be the name given to the language as spoken from the middle of the sixteenth century to the present time.

The following schedule represents, accordingly, the nomenclature of the periods, with their limits, as employed in this volume: —

I.	Anglo-Saxon			450–1150
II.	Semi-Saxon, or Late Anglo-Saxon	1150–1250	Early English	1150–1350
	Old English	1250–1350		
III.	Middle English			1350–1550
IV.	Modern English			1550–

Literature of the Early English Period.— Of the literature of the Anglo-Saxon period, a slight account has already been given. In the Early English period there were composed a large number of works, many of which still exist only in manuscript. To a great extent they are translations from the French, or a working-over of French productions. As regards their subject-matter, they may be divided into the following classes: 1. Religious works, including legends of saints and martyrs. These may be said to begin with the Ormulum (life of Christ, made up from the Gospels, by an Augustinian monk named Ormin or Orm), Hali Meidenhad (Holy Maidenhood), and the Ancren Riwle (Rule of Anchorites). All of these belong to the Semi-Saxon period. Later there are series of homilies and homiletic treatises, both in prose and verse. In the Old English period may be mentioned, as among the most important works, Dan Michel's "Ayenbite of Inwit" (Remorse of Conscience), in the Kentish dialect, the "Handlyng Synne" by Robert of Brunne, "The Pricke of Conscience" by Richard Rolle de Hampole, and versions of the histories, or parts of histories, contained in the Bible, such as

"Genesis and Exodus," and the "Cursor Mundi," an account of the world founded upon the Old and New Testaments, with legends interspersed drawn from every quarter. To this list, imperfect as it is, may be added a large number of lives of saints and martyrs, both in the Semi-Saxon and Old English periods. 2. Romances and legendary history. These may be said to begin with the "Brut," a poem composed by Layamon, a Worcestershire priest, which gives an account of the legendary history of Britain from its occupation by a mythical Brutus (a great-grandson of Æneas) and his Trojan followers, down to its partial conquest by the Saxons. Among the metrical romances of the Early English period, "King Horn," "Havelok the Dane," several legendary poems founded upon the life of Alexander the Great, and varying widely from real history, may be regarded as representative specimens. 3. Histories, partly fabulous, it is true, but not so deemed by their authors. These belong to the Old English period exclusively, and consist of works in verse by Robert of Gloucester and by Robert Manning of Brunne. The latter is a translation from the French of Pierre de Langtoft. Both of these treat of the history of Britain from the legendary coming of Brutus to a period near their own time; the former ending with the accession of Edward I. in 1272; the latter, with his death in 1307. 4. Shorter poems, some of which are of a satirical nature, but most of them purely lyrical. The most conspicuous among these are "The Land of Cokaygne," the "Ule and

Nihtegale" (the Owl and Nightingale), and a series of lyric poems of a political, devotional, or social nature. The works in all these classes are of the highest value to the student of the language; but it is only those of the last class that have any claim whatever to literary excellence, and these are comparatively few in number.

One feature worthy of mention, that characterizes the Early English period, is the tendency to abandon alliteration, and substitute for it final rhyme. In Anglo-Saxon verse instances of rhyme are only occasional, and probably often purely accidental: at any rate, it is only in a piece of eighty lines that it is deliberately employed throughout, and in that it is mixed with alliteration, with the result that no modern scholar has been successful in getting any coherent meaning out of the poem, or rather of putting any into it. Alliterative verse did not die out till the sixteenth century; but the only conspicuous work composed in it, "The Vision of Piers Plowman," belongs to the fourteenth. Its inferiority, indeed, to rhyme as an instrument of expression, led to its abandonment by all the Teutonic nations at comparatively early periods in their literary history.

Changes in Grammar between Anglo-Saxon and Middle English.—A more detailed account of the changes that took place in the grammatical structure after the conquest will be found in another place: here only a slight summary can be given. Comparisons can necessarily be made only between periods which have a standard literature of their own, not exhibiting the peculiarities of individual writers, but the universal characteristics of the cultivated speech. In this particular case the comparison must be made, accordingly, between the literary West-Saxon and that dialect of English which was employed by the great writers of the fourteenth century, and by them made the language of all our literature. Of these, Chaucer, as the greatest of all, may be taken as the representative of the rest. It is, however, to be borne in mind that whatever may be the limits fixed upon for the periods in the history of any tongue, assertions made in regard to them can only be true generally: they are always subject to specific exceptions. For illustration, *its*, as the genitive of the neuter pronoun of the third person, is a characteristic of Modern English as contrasted with the earlier speech in which *his* was the form employed. Yet, while this is true generally, it is so far from being true specifically, that *his* can be found where we should now use *its*, for a hundred years after the Modern English period begins.

Let us begin, then, with the modifications which the inflectional system underwent. These are first brought to our knowledge by certain orthographical changes which took place in consequence of a change in pronunciation. Two of them are of special importance. One is of the weakening into *e* of the vowels *a*, *o*, and *u* of the terminations. Thus, in Anglo-Saxon, *-an* is the regular ending of the infinitive: it was soon after the conquest weakened into *-en*. 'To tell,' in the eleventh century was *tellan:* in the twelfth century it became *tellen.* So, in like manner, *oxa*, 'ox, became *oxe; oxan*, 'oxen,' became *oxen; stânas*, 'stones,' and *stôlas*, 'stools,' became *stanes* and *stoles; denu*, 'den,' became *dene.* This was a change that was certain to happen in English, as in the other Teutonic languages, had the Norman-French never set foot in Britain. All the effect produced by their coming was to hasten its general adoption; and during the twelfth century it did become generally established. The second change was the dropping of the final *n*, — a peculiarity which the Northumbrian dialect, as has been seen (p. 37), exhibited at an early day. This, however, was much slower of general adoption than the weakening of the vowels *a*, *o*, and *u;* but, as it continued to extend itself more and more, the result of the two changes working together was to make the final *e* the one termination of the Middle English which represented nearly all the terminations of the Anglo-Saxon that had been preserved at all; so that in the study of this one ending is involved the study of nearly the whole grammatical inflection of that period. It was, moreover, largely due to the steady reduction of all terminations to this single one, that the confusion sprang up in usage, which, in turn, led, to a great extent, to the rejection of inflection altogether. What there was left of it in the fourteenth century, compared with Anglo-Saxon, can be stated very briefly.

In the noun, the two leading declensions of the Anglo-Saxon (the vowel and the consonant, or the strong and the weak), with their several subordinate declensions, had been reduced to the one inflection seen in the masculine noun of the vowel declension. The singular, as in Modern English, had a distinct form only for the genitive case; the ending being *-es*. All the cases of the plural were alike; the termination being, as now, the same as that of the genitive singular. This *-es* of the genitive singular and of the plural usually formed a distinct syllable in pronunciation, at least in monosyllabic nouns.

The adjective, which in Anglo-Saxon was very rich in inflections, had been nearly stripped of them altogether. The plural was generally distinguished from the singular by the addition of *e*, — a distinction which necessarily could not be made when the singular itself ended in that letter. With the disappearance of the terminations had nearly disappeared, also, the difference between the two original declensions of the adjective, — the definite and the indefinite; though a trace of the former continued to manifest itself in the addition of *e* in certain cases to the singular.

The personal pronouns and the interrogative *who* (A. S. *hwa*) were somewhat more fortunate in preserving their inflection. They retained a distinct form for the case which we now call the objective; and this was founded upon the original dative, the original accusative having been given up. The dual number of the pronouns of the first and second persons was entirely lost. In the case of the pronouns of the third person, some of its forms had been abandoned, and their places were supplied from the original demonstrative pronoun now represented by *that.* Pronouns which had inflections resembling those of the adjective were stripped of them in the same manner as they.

In the case of the verb, while the distinction between the two leading conjugations still continued to exist as now, the barriers between the subordinate conjugations under each had been generally broken down. Again: the verbs of the strong or old conjugation — that is, verbs like *drive, drove,* which add nothing to form the preterite, and suffer vowel change — had in vast numbers passed over to the weak conjugation, that is, to verbs like *light, lighted,* which take an additional syllable (or letter) to form the preterite. The inflections, to some extent, were still retained; thus, for illustration, *they tell* was *they tellen* or *they telle.* The use of compound verb phrases, such as *I have told, I shall tell,* had been vastly extended; and in particular, at this very time, the employment of *do* and *did* with the infinitive — as in *I do give, I did give* — was just beginning to be adopted generally.

A consideration of these statements shows that Middle English differs but slightly in its grammatical structure from the English of to-day. In fact, no small proportion of the difficulty that the modern reader at first encounters in examining the literature of this period is due merely to difference of orthography.

A passage from Chaucer in the original spelling, and in modern spelling so far as it can be employed, will illustrate better than pages of description the essential likeness, and the extent of the unlikeness, that prevail between the language of the fourteenth century and that of the nineteenth; and when compared with the specimens of the English of the Anglo-Saxon period, found on pp. 25, 27, 28, will show clearly how wide was the chasm that separated the language of the fourteenth century from that of the eleventh.

In the modernized version of the following passage from "The Canterbury Tales" the pronunciation of syllables no longer sounded is marked by the sign \`; the accentuation of syllables not now accented is marked by the sign ′; while the insertion of a hyphen between syllables shows that they are all to be pronounced.

"In tholde dayes of the Kyng Arthour,
Of which that Britons speken greet honour,
All was this land fulfild of fayerie;
The elf queene with hir joly compaignye,
Daunced ful ofte in many a grene mede;
This was the olde opinion, as I rede.
I speke of manye hundred yeres ago;
But now kan no man se none elves mo.
For now the grete charitee and prayeres
Of lymytours and othere hooly freres,
That serchen every lond and every streem,
As thikke as motes in the sonne beem,
Blessynge halles, chambres, kichenes, and boures
Citees and burghes, castels hye and toures
Thropes and bernes, shipnes and dayeryes,
This maketh that ther been no fairyes.

For ther as wont to walken was an elf,
Ther walketh now the lymytour hym self,
In undermeles and in morwenynges,
And seyth his matyns and his hooly thynges
As he gooth in his lymytacioun.
Wommen may go now saufly up and doun,
In every bussh or under every tree;
There is noon other incubus but he."

"In th' oldè dayès of the King Arthoúr,
Of which that Britons speakèn great honoúr,
All was this land fulfilled of fa-e-rý;
The elf queen, with her jolly company,
Dancèd full oft on many a greenè mead;
This was the old opinion, as I read.
I speak of many hundred years ago;
But now can no man see none elvès mo.
For now the greatè charity and prayérès
Of limiters [1] and other holy frérès,
That searchèn every land and every stream,
As thick as motès in the sunnè-beam,
Blessing hallès, chambers, kitchenès, and bowers,
Cities and boroughs, castles high and towers,
Thorpès [2] and barnès, shipnès [3] and da-i-riés,
This maketh that there ben no fa-i-riés.
For there as wont to walkèn was an elf,
There walketh now the limiter himself,
In undermelès [4] and in mórwènýngès, [5]
And saith his matins and his holy thingès
As he goth in his lim-i-ta-ti-ón.
Women may now go safely up and down,
In every bush or under every tree;
There is none other incubus but he."

[1] A begging friar, assigned a certain limit for begging. [2] Villages. [3] Stables. [4] Afternoons. [5] Mornings.

Change in the Vocabulary.—Such is a brief outline of the changes that took place in the inflectional system of the English tongue. Many of them would doubtless have happened had there been no Norman conquest; but to that event were certainly due both the rapidity with which, and the extent to which, they were carried out. But the second great change we have to consider was no indirect result: this was the introduction of foreign words into the vocabulary, a process which, in certain respects, has transformed the character of our speech.

The coming of the Normans into England brought two languages into close geographical connection. French was the speech of the higher classes; English, that of the great body of the people: yet for two centuries these tongues existed side by side, without the latter borrowing words, to any extent, from the former. It is not necessary to assume that this state of things was due to any hostility between the races, or to the disinclination on the part of the conquered people to use the language of their conquerors. They did not employ any new words because they did not need them: the existing stock of terms was amply sufficient to convey all the knowledge they sought to impart, or to express the few new ideas to which they gave birth. Certainly the fact of little borrowing cannot be disputed. The "Brut" of Layamon was composed nearly a hundred and fifty years after the conquest: it is a poem containing thirty-two thousand short lines, and yet there are in it hardly a hundred words of Norman-

French origin. The proportion is even less in the "Ormulum," — a composition of about the same date, and containing nearly twenty thousand short lines. The number of French words adopted into English speech naturally became more and more as time went on; and at every period since its introduction it has always varied with the nature of the subject-matter; but, down to the end of the thirteenth century, the additions that had come from this source to the native speech formed only a small percentage of the whole.

It was in the latter half of the Old English period — that is, from 1300 to 1350 — that a great change took place in this respect. It was during those years that the French-speaking population of the island may be said to have generally abandoned their original tongue, and to have adopted that of the mass of the people. It was natural that they should bring into the speech they had made their own many of the words most familiar to them, especially those descriptive of their ways of life, and expressive of thoughts and feelings peculiar to themselves. This was, indeed, the case to a remarkable extent. During the half-century referred to, a vast multitude of words came from the French into the English: what had been left of the grammatical inflection was Teutonic; but the vocabulary from this time assumed that mixed character which has ever since been one of its marked peculiarities. Even in the earliest writers of the Middle English period, the foreign words constitute one-half of the whole number they employ; and the proportion has remained essentially unchanged from that time to the present. Such a statement is, of course, based upon the special glossary of an author in which a word that occurs but once in his writings counts for as much as one that is used by him a thousand times; not upon the frequency of the occurrence of Teutonic or of Romance words in particular pages.

This vast accession of French words is technically called the "Latin of the Third Period;" but it is widely different in character from any accession the language had previously received; for it entered into and modified the whole frame-work of expression, and profoundly influenced the course which the language was to take in reference to future additions to its vocabulary. Other Teutonic tongues may make use of Romance words: the English must make use of them, even in denouncing them. This is an essential distinction, which may be disregarded, but cannot be denied; and it had its origin in that change in the nature of the language which was a direct result of the vast irruption of French terms in the fourteenth century. Has this change been a benefit, or an injury? This question has given rise to much controversy, and is, from its nature, one that can never be settled to the satisfaction of all. In this place it is only important to point out the principal losses which the speech suffered as a consequence of the alteration in its character.

Losses of Middle English as compared with Anglo-Saxon. — Let us first consider the loss of native words. Language is always economical, and is not long disposed to retain terms and expressions of which it has no real need. When, therefore, two different words — the one of Anglo-Saxon, the other of French origin, but both meaning precisely the same thing — came to exist side by side, one of two results was almost certain to happen: either both were retained, and a distinction was made in their signification, or if no such use could be made of both, or, as a matter of fact, was not made, one of them was almost certain to be dropped. In a large number of cases in the speech of the fourteenth century, it was the native word that was rejected, and the foreign one that was retained. It is probably an under rather than an over estimate to assert that more than one-half of the Anglo-Saxon vocabulary has been lost to Modern English; and the place of it has necessarily been supplied, whether for good or ill, by importations from alien sources.

A second and more serious blow to the resources of the language was the loss of a large number of formative prefixes and suffixes, by the addition of the former of which the meaning of the word was modified, and by that of the latter the word itself was changed from one part of speech into another. In these elements the original speech abounded, and possessed, in consequence, almost unlimited power in the creation of new terms from native roots. Thus from the Anglo-Saxon *flôwan*, 'to flow,' seven new compounds were formed by the addition of various prefixes, of which seven, only one, *oferflōwan*, 'to overflow,' survives with us. In a similar manner, from the verb *sittan*, 'to sit,' fifteen new verbs were formed, of which not a single one is to be found to-day, though their places are in part supplied in this case, as in others, by joining separate particles to the verb, forming such expressions as, *sit by*, *sit on*. And, even in some instances where a prefix has been retained in certain words, the power of employing it to form new ones has been given up. Thus *with* is still found in *withdraw*, *withhold*, *withstand*, but we no longer think of prefixing it to other verbs; whereas, originally, it could have been compounded with almost any verb, and was actually compounded with about thirty. Again: the Anglo-Saxon was comparatively rich in formative suffixes, by the appending of which one part of speech was changed into another. For illustration: In Modern English the adding of the suffix *-er* to the verb *do* changes it into the noun *doer;* the adding of *-ness* to the adjective *black*, changes it into the noun *blackness;* the adding of *-y* to the noun *snow* changes it into the adjective *snowy*. Many of these formative suffixes belonging to the ancient tongue the modern tongue has lost; though here, to some extent, it has supplied their places by borrowing from the French, the Latin, and the Greek.

The third loss was in the power of forming self-explaining compounds. In this respect the Anglo-Saxon rivalled the modern German. Thus *carpenter* could with them be expressed by *treow-wyrhta*, 'tree-wright,' or 'worker in wood;' *butcher*, by *flǣsc-mangere*, 'flesh-monger,' or 'dealer in flesh;' *library* by *bōchūs*, 'book-house;' and hundreds of illustrations could easily be given of the facility and freedom with which men then employed the power of combining familiar words to form new ones. Many of these compounds went out of use in the fourteenth century in consequence of words with an equivalent meaning having been taken from the French. The mere loss of these was not in itself so serious a detriment, however, as the indisposition, which sprang up in consequence, to form or to employ self-explaining compounds whose places could be readily supplied by borrowing. This indisposition, not to say aversion, can be plainly traced in the history of the language from the beginning of the Middle English period to the present time. Thus, for illustration, the Anglo-Saxon *sunnen-stede* appears in Early English, and later as *sun-stead*, that is, the sun's stopping-place; and was used to denote that part of the ecliptic in which the sun is farthest from the equator. In lieu of this, we now go to the Latin *solstitium*, formed of two words similar in meaning to the corresponding English ones, and from it derive the term *solstice*. By this we certainly lose something in picturesqueness and force of expression, though we may possibly gain in precision. Or an illustration of a later period can be employed. A certain liquid substance exuding in various ways from the earth needs a name. Seen oozing from the crevices of a rock, it is naturally called *rock-oil*, a term, to all appearances, sufficiently definite to distinguish it from all other kinds of oil. Yet, instead of using this, we go to the Latin *petra*, 'rock,' and *oleum*, 'oil,' and *rock-oil* appears as *petroleum*,—a word, the meaning of which must be learned before it is understood. Processes like these are constantly going on, and in the case of scientific words they may be considered necessary; for it is of the utmost importance that a technical term should convey to the minds of all one idea, and but one idea,—that its signification should be imposed upon it, and not be suggested by it. This power of forming self-explaining compounds can, however, hardly be said to be lost: it is rather a power held in abeyance, dwarfed by disuse, but by no means destroyed.

These changes may seem to have seriously impaired the value of the language. To a certain extent it may be admitted that they have been detrimental; but they have been far less so than they appear. It would, indeed, be a mistake to suppose that there have not been great gains made, as well as great losses suffered. If one method of expression is denied language, another is speedily found to take its place. The giving up of numerous Anglo-Saxon formative endings, by which words were changed from one part of speech into another, has been largely and perhaps wholly counterbalanced in Modern English by the facility with which the simple words themselves now pass from one part of speech to another. Thus *black* is an adjective; but it is used likewise as a noun and a verb. Again: *stone* is a noun; but it is also a verb, and may be used with the attributive sense of an adjective, as, for instance, in *stone house* and *stone jar*. The wide employment of the substantive in the manner last designated, which forms one of the most striking peculiarities of Modern English, far more than offsets any loss due to the lack of facility in forming self-explaining compounds. Moreover, if many words belonging to the Anglo-Saxon have disappeared from the tongue now spoken, their places have been more than supplied by importations from foreign sources; and these have now become so thoroughly identified with the words that have come from the original speech, that, in a large number of cases, no one but the special student is conscious of any difference in their origin. It is only prejudice or ignorance that will deny that these importations have added immensely to the resources of the language, especially in its power of representing delicate shades of thought, and the higher and more complex relations which exist between the conceptions of the mind. In this respect the borrowed words stand in decided contrast to the native ones, to which latter is mainly left the representation of all deep feeling. The language of the reasoning faculties is, in consequence, largely different with us from the languages of the emotional faculties, with the advantage to the former, that it gains by this in precision, and to the latter, that it gains in vividness and power. There results, indeed, from the union of the foreign and native elements, a wealth of phraseology and a many-sideness in the English tongue, which give it in these respects a superiority over any other modern cultivated speech. German is strictly a pure Teutonic speech; but no native speaker of it claims for it any superiority over the English as an instrument of expression, while many are willing to concede its inferiority. At any rate, the character of the language, whether for good or ill, was fixed for all succeeding time at the beginning of the Middle English period. We may grieve over it, or we may rejoice over it; but we cannot change it. What it then became under the hand of the great writers who moulded it, that it has since continued essentially to be, and that it will be certain to remain so long as it lasts, in its present form, as a spoken and written speech.

CHAPTER VI.

THE THREE DIALECTS OF EARLY ENGLISH, AND THE RISE OF THE MIDLAND.

It has already been remarked that the dialect in which Chaucer wrote became the language of literature, and has remained as such until this day. What was this dialect? How came it to be employed by him? What was its relation to other dialects, or to the ancient tongue from which, in a certain sense, it may be said to have descended? To make the answer to these questions clear, it will first be necessary to recapitulate at this point, briefly but connectedly, what has been said elsewhere, but in scattered passages.

Of the various dialects existing during the Anglo-Saxon period, that is from 450 to 1150, the West-Saxon was the one that attained to literary supremacy. Enough exists of the form of language spoken in the ancient kingdom of Northumbria to make it certain that the speech of the north of England varied in many respects from that of the south. But, as the West-Saxon is the only one of the earliest English dialects that can be said to have both maintained and preserved a literature, it is for us the literary Anglo-Saxon, the only remaining type of our tongue in its original classical form. But from this position of supremacy the Norman conquest had the speedy effect of displacing it. Its special forms and inflections, its peculiarities of grammatical construction, could not be long looked upon as the standard of correct writing and speaking. Such a standard could only be maintained by an educated class; and the attention of the educated classes was from this time turned exclusively, either to Latin or to French. The West-Saxon, as an inevitable consequence, sank to the level of the other dialects: it had no longer any special pre-eminence of its own. Henceforward he who wrote in the native language wrote in that form of it with which he was most familiar. He wrote in the dialect of the district of country in which he had been brought up, or in which he dwelt; and, with nothing existing anywhere that could be regarded as authority, the forces that tend to bring about diversity of speech were sure to gain strength more rapidly than those which tend to bring about uniformity.

The Three Early English Dialects. — During these centuries, therefore, — the twelfth, the thirteenth, and the fourteenth, — it is to be borne in mind that there was in no sense a national language. There existed a number of dialects, each one of which had as much right as any of the others to be called the English language. The points of similarity were naturally far greater in number and in importance than the points of dissimilarity; but, for all that, the latter were sufficient to make the variations observable by all, and especially the difference between the speech of the north and that of the south of England. This at once came to the surface as soon as the pressure was withdrawn that had brought all the previously existing dialects under the supremacy of the West-Saxon. It had existed from the earliest period; but it only became prominent when both were brought to a common level of comparison by sharing in a common degradation. But little more than half a century had passed after the conquest, when the chronicler William of Malmesbury asserted that the speech of the Northumbrians, especially at York, sounded so rude and harsh to the men of the South, that the latter were scarcely able to understand it. Similar testimony to this divergence is borne by Giraldus Cambrensis, a scholar who flourished not much later. About 1194 he finished a work in Latin, giving an account of Wales; and in it he incidentally pointed out that the language of Southern England was more ancient in its character than that of the northern parts, and much closer to the original tongue as preserved in writing.

Upon this point we have again precise and positive testimony from Higden, the writer of the first half of the fourteenth century who has already been quoted on this question of language. He asserted distinctly the existence of three leading dialects in his time. These are his statements, as translated by Trevisa: —

"Also Englysch men, theygh hy hadde fram the bygynnyng thre maner speche, Southeron, Northeron, and Myddel speche (in the myddel of the lond), as hy come of thre maner people of Germania; notheless, by commyxstion and mellyng, furst with Danes and afterward with Normans, in menye the contray longage ys apeyred, and some vseth strange wlaffyng, chyteryng, harryng and garryng, grisbittyng. [By these five words Trevisa translates the Latin *boatus et gorritus*] . . . Also, of the forseyde Saxon tonge that ys deled a thre, and ys abyde scarslych with feaw vplondysch men, and ys gret wondur; for men of the est with men of the west, as hit were vndur the same party of heuene, acordeth more in sounyng of speche than men of the north with men of the south; therfore hyt ys that Mercij, that buth men of Myddel Engelond, as hyt were parteners of the endes, vndurstondeth betre the syde longages, Northeron and Southeron, than Northeron and Southeron vndurstondeth eyther other."[1]

The extant writings of these periods bear ample witness to the truth of Higden's statement. There were, especially during the thirteenth and fourteenth centuries, and even earlier, three great divisions of English speech, with differences so pronounced, that the dwelling-place of a man within certain limits could

[1] "Also Englishmen, though they had from the beginning three kinds of speech, Southern, Northern, and Midland speech (in the middle of the land), as they came from three kinds of people of Germany, nevertheless, by mixing and mingling, first with Danes and afterward with Normans, in many the native language is corrupted, and some use strange babbling, chattering, growling and snarling, teeth-grinding. . . . Also, in regard to the aforesaid Saxon tongue, that is divided into three, and has remained [in use] with [a] few back-country men, there is great wonder; for men of the East with men of the West, as it were under the same portion of heaven, agree more in the sound of [their] speech than men of the North with men of the South. therefore it is that the Mercians, that are men of Middle England, as it were partners of the ends, understand better the border languages, Northern and Southern, than either Northern or Southern understands the other."

be immediately told by his language. The distinction is traceable now without difficulty in the works that have been handed down; but it was as fully recognized then. Chaucer, for illustration, wrote in the Midland dialect of the eastern counties: in so doing he regularly forms the third person singular of the present tense of the verb in *-th*, the plural in *-en* or *-e*. But in "The Reeve's Tale" he introduces two characters who are described as coming from a town "far in the north;" and the special peculiarities of that dialect are designedly represented in the forms they use. In the language put into their mouths the third person singular of the present tense ends in *-s*, as generally in Modern English: the plural has likewise the same termination. Other characteristics of the speech of the North, or of certain varieties of it, occur frequently, such as *I is*, *thou is;* the use of *a* for *o*, as in *ga*, *ham(e)*, *hald nat*, *sang;* of *til* for *to;* of *sal* for *shall;* and others might be mentioned. These were differences that could not be disregarded by a writer of that time. The divergence, indeed, was not only generally recognized, it was also so deeply marked, that works composed in either of the two extreme dialects required to be translated into the other in order to be understood. A well-known early English poem, the "Cursor Mundi," already mentioned, was written about the end of the thirteenth century in the language of the North. One story in it was taken, however, from a work composed in the dialect of the South; and the author of the "Cursor Mundi" speaks of the latter in words which would almost lead one to think that he looked upon it as a foreign tongue; for, after mentioning his authority, he goes on to say, —

> "In a writt this ilke I fand,
> Himself it wroght I understand.
> In Suthrin Englijs was it drann,
> And I haue turned it till vr aun
> Langage of the northren lede,
> That can nan other Englis rede."[1]
>
> *Lines* 20059–64.

Geographical Limits of the Three Dialects. — The geographical limits of these divisions of English speech may be roughly stated as follows: the Northern dialect was the lineal descendant of the Northumbrian dialect of Anglo-Saxon, and it covered about the same extent of territory; that is, the region stretching from the Humber on the south to the Frith of Forth on the north, and bounded by the Pennine Mountains on the west. It was, however, during the fourteenth and fifteenth centuries, and later, constantly making its way still farther to the north, in Scotland. The Midland dialect occupied the central counties from the Humber to the Thames, and the district west of the Pennine chain; and the Southern stretched from the Thames to the English Channel, with a portion of the western counties north of the Thames. It is not

[1] "In a writing this same [thing] I found;
He himself composed it, I understand.
In Southern English was it composed,
And I have turned it to our own
Language of the northern people,
That can read no other English."

to be understood that there were not variations, and great variations, within these lines: it is only to be said that the differences within the great divisions were slight compared with the resemblances. The Midland dialect, however, as seen in the speech of the eastern and the western counties, was in some points so dissimilar that it is often divided into the East Midland and the West Midland.

It was the language of the North and that of the South, as is stated by Trevisa, that stood the farthest apart. Between these two wavered the dialect of the Midland counties; sometimes and in some places inclining to the one, at other times and in other places inclining to the other. Each one of the three called itself the English speech, but did not deny the title to the others. Scotch was then the appellation given to the tongue of the Celtic inhabitants of Northern Britain. Its modern sense, as applied to one variety of our language, was not then known. But one important thing these dialects had in common. The influx of French words into their vocabulary was about the same in each, and occurred at about the same period. On whatever other points they differed, here they agreed. The Norman conquest did not bring Scotland under the sway of a foreign race, nor were the Scottish Lowlands parcelled out among a body of nobles who spoke a strange tongue; yet French words penetrated at about the same time, and to about the same extent, not only into the English spoken on both sides of the Humber, which divided the Northern dialect from the Midland, but also into the English spoken on both sides of the Tweed, which divided the two kingdoms. In the fourteenth century the language of Barbour, the Archdeacon of Aberdeen, shows as much the trace of French influence as does that of his contemporary Chaucer, the comptroller of the port of London. The introduction into our tongue of the Romance element was in no sense peculiar to the speech of any one dialect or any one district of country: it was a general linguistic movement, which extended to every place where English was spoken at all.

The great radical distinction between the speech of the North and of the South was, that the latter was extremely conservative in holding on to its grammatical inflections; while the former let them go rapidly. The language of the South may, perhaps, be spoken of as more especially the descendant of the West-Saxon dialect, the classical Anglo-Saxon of our fathers; yet it was far from adhering to it so closely that great variations did not speedily arise. It exhibited, for instance, in course of time, peculiar pronominal forms, such as *is*, *his*, *hes*, meaning 'them,' for which there is nothing corresponding to be found in the monuments that have been preserved of the earliest speech. Still it clung as firmly as it well could to the original forms and inflections; and whatever it gave up, it gave up reluctantly. We have no such means for tracing the linguistic history of the North as we have that of the South; for, from about the end of the tenth century to the end of the thirteenth, no works were written in the language spoken in or descended from that spoken in the ancient Northumbria; or, if written, they have not been preserved. But it is evident that the development of the Northern dialect was in the sharpest contrast to that of the Southern. It abandoned its inflections without hesitation. The works produced in it in the fourteenth century show, that, in its rejection of grammatical form, it had even then frequently gone farther than the English we use has now, or, at any rate, had shown a disposition to go farther. One or two illustrations are all that will be needed at this point. The ending *s* of the genitive is often dropped: *man saul* appears for 'man's soul.' So is the ending *s* of the third person singular of the present, and the *ed* of the preterite, seen in such expressions as *he think*, 'he thinks,' and in *he cumand*, 'he commanded.' In fact, in the fourteenth century the Northern dialect had moved so far to the form now exhibited by Modern English, that a work written at that time, if printed in the existing orthography, would present but few and slight difficulties to the ordinary reader, so far as inflections and grammatical constructions are concerned.

It was in respect to slowness or swiftness of change that the great characteristic difference manifested itself between the speech of the North and of the South. In some cases as a result of this, in others entirely independent of it, the two dialects showed marked divergences: these were partly orthographical, partly lexical, partly grammatical. A few illustrations will be given to make this statement perfectly clear; those peculiarities being chosen by preference which have maintained themselves in Modern English. First, as regards orthography. The Southern dialect was inclined to use the letter *v* for *f*, a tendency which was unknown to the North; thus the Anglo-Saxon *fox*, a 'fox,' and *fixen*, a 'female fox,' became in the Southern dialect *vox* and *vixen;* and Modern English has retained the original form of the one, and the altered form of the other. Again: the South was apt to turn the Anglo-Saxon *c* into *ch*, especially before the vowels *e*, *i*, and *y*, and at the end of a syllable; whereas this letter was represented in the North by its equivalent *k*, the sound of which the Anglo-Saxon *c* had under all circumstances. Accordingly the Anglo-Saxon *cyrice*, 'church,' became in the Southern dialect *chirche*, in the Northern *kirk*, still preserved in the Scottish; the Anglo-Saxon *cernan*, 'to churn,' and *cist*, a 'chest,' became in the South *chirne* and *chist*, and in the North *kirn* and *kist*, the two latter of which are also retained in the dialectic speech of the North, including the Scottish. Again: the Anglo-Saxon *sēcan*, 'to seek,' appeared respectively in the speech of the two regions as *seche(n)* and *seke(n)*. In the simple verb we now use the Northern form, but in the compound *beseech* we follow the South. As regards lexical differences, the Northern dialects adopted a number of Scandinavian words, brought in by the invasion and settlement of the Norsemen. Comparatively few of these found their way into the South; though some of them were adopted into the speech of the Midland dialects, especially in those counties which had shared in the conquest of the Danes, and in this way they have been transmitted to Modern English. The Northern local dialects naturally retain them in somewhat large numbers; as, for one instance that will do for many, the word *gar*, 'to cause,' may be adduced. This comes directly from the Norse verb *göra*. As regards grammatical differences, besides the general tendency of the North to drop inflections altogether, and the South to retain them as long as possible, there was one very marked characteristic difference. The plural of the present tense of the verb in the Northern dialects either ends in *-s*, or drops the termination entirely; in the Southern it ends in *-th*, the former following in the ending in *-s* the old Northumbrian dialect, the latter the West-Saxon. *Men say* would therefore be represented respectively by *men says* and *men sayeth*. These peculiarities lasted down in the literary language to a comparatively late period, though in modern editions the text is, in this respect, silently changed whenever possible. The usage can be seen in the following illustrations: —

> O father Abraham, what these Christians are
> Whose own hard dealings *teaches* them suspect
> The thoughts of others.
>
> SHAKSPEARE, *Merchant of Venice*, act i. scene 3.

A board groaning under the heavy burden of the beasts that *cheweth* the cud. — FLETCHER, *Woman-Hater*, act i. scene 2.

Another marked difference was the preference exhibited by the Southern dialect for plurals in *-en* in the case of nouns. This was based upon the Anglo-Saxon plural in *-an*, of which *oxen* in Modern English is the only genuine survival. But the termination was added in the Southern dialect to many nouns which etymologically had no right to it: it was even given sometimes to those ending originally in *-as*, of which the representative was strictly *-es*. On the other hand, the Northern dialect had scarcely any plurals in *-en* at all, nearly all nouns forming their plurals in *-es* or *-s*.

Between these two dialects stood that of the Midland counties, not merely in respect to position, but in respect to language also. It partook, to a large extent, of the peculiarities of each; while in some particulars it was independent of both. It is hard to affirm or to deny that it is a direct descendant of the West-Saxon. If we maintain the former view, we shall have to admit that some of its distinguishing characteristics must have come from a dialect or dialects existing in the Anglo-Saxon period, which, however widely employed in colloquial speech, left no trace of itself or of themselves in written literature. On the other hand, it follows so closely, in many respects, the West-Saxon, that, if not directly derived from it, we must assume for it a descent from some dialect having very near relationship with that tongue.

Thus, as we have seen, in the early part of the fourteenth century three great dialects existed in Britain, each calling itself English, each possessing a literature of its own, and each seemingly having about the same chance to become the representative national tongue. Of these three it was the Midland that became the language of literature, — the language we speak and write to-day; and its supremacy has involved, as one result, the degradation of the other two, with all their varieties, to the condition, in general, of local *patois*, maintaining themselves as the speech of the rude and uneducated only, and destined, with the greater spread of education, to ultimate extinction. Several circumstances concurred to give predominance to the Midland dialect. In the first place, it covered a larger extent of territory than either of the others. In particular, the strength of the Northern dialect as a rival was much weakened by the fact that no small portion of the region in which it was spoken had from an early period been separated from England, and been placed under the rule of the king of the Scots. In the second place, the Midland was the speech of the district in which the two universities of Oxford and Cambridge were situated; and all the powerful linguistic influences that flowed from these two great centres of higher education were constantly at work to extend the supremacy of the form of speech heard in them. These influences were, moreover, aided by the fact that this dialect was in its nature a compromise between the two found on each side of it, and could, therefore, be much more readily adopted by both than could either by the other. In the third place, there is little doubt that the Midland was the speech mainly employed at the court and the capital, as the French was gradually displaced from its position as the language of social intercourse. All of these contributed to give it special prominence as the dialect destined to become the representative one of the whole nation. Yet, powerful as these various agencies were in themselves, they were insufficient to establish its supremacy over the rest, and cause them to sink into subordinate positions, of which not only others would be conscious, but which would be acknowledged by themselves. No really national language could exist until a literature had been created which would be admired and studied by all who could read, and taken as a model by all who could write. It was only a man of genius that could lift up one of these dialects into a pre-eminence over the rest, or could ever give to the scattered forces existing in any one of them the unity and vigor of life. This was the work that Chaucer did. He it was that first showed to all men the resources of the language, its capacity of representing with discrimination all shades of human thought, and of conveying with power all manifestations of human feeling. His choice of the Midland, or rather the fact of his writing in it, raised it at once into a position of superiority which was never afterwards disputed. His productions, scattered everywhere, unconsciously affected the speech of all who read, and were consciously looked upon by all who set out to write as the authoritative standard of expression. The words and grammatical forms he used, the syntactical methods of construction he followed, became the oncs generally adopted by his successors. With him, indeed, began the exercise of that great conservative restraint which literature throws about language, which arrests all sudden changes, and which, so long as it operates unimpaired, renders revolution or anarchy in the speech an impossibility.

It has already been stated that the Midland dialect was not altogether uniform; and that it has been divided into that of the Eastern and of the Western counties. It was in the former of these that Chaucer wrote. To speak with absolute precision, it is therefore to be said that the cultivated English language, in which nearly all English literature of value has been written, sprang directly from the East Midland variety of the Midland dialect. To that it owes the forms of its words and its leading grammatical characteristics, though in these respects it has likewise been influenced in particulars by the speech both of the North and of the South.

The Scotch Dialect. — But, while these three dialects were in use in England, it was the Northern alone that was spoken in Scotland; and, as the Scotch is the only dialect of English that can be said to have a literature of its own, a brief account of it is here in place. This Northern dialect had in that country gradually spread itself on every side from its original centre in the South, had crossed the Forth, and, steadily pressing back the Celtic tongues, had in the fourteenth century made its way along the coast as far as the Moray Firth. The political separation of England and Scotland, at a period when no literary standard existed anywhere, would of itself have been almost certain to develop, in process of time, differences in the speech of both, even had it been precisely the same in the beginning. But a special cause increased a divergence that was in any event sure to take place to a certain extent. While, in the one country, it was the Midland dialect that became the ruling one, in the other it was the Northern,—the only one known there at all. Accordingly the literary language in Scotland had a linguistic development in some measure independent of that found south of the Tweed. At the same time, it is not to be forgotten that Scotch, as an epithet applied to speech, meant originally the Erse of the Celtic inhabitants; that what we call the Scotch tongue, or dialect, is really English, and, moreover, that it was invariably called English by the men who wrote in it during the fourteenth and fifteenth centuries, and generally by those who wrote in it during the sixteenth. It was then, however, sometimes designated as the Scotch tongue, as opposed to the English; but after the union of the two countries by the accession, in 1603, of James to the English throne, it sank from its independent position, and came to be considered and called the Scotch dialect of the English language.

Scotch literature may be said to begin with John Barbour, Archdeacon of Aberdeen, who died in 1395, but finished in 1375 a long historical poem called "The

Bruce," in which he celebrated the deeds of Robert Bruce. It has been several times printed, and contains between thirteen and fourteen thousand lines. He was followed, in the beginning of the fifteenth century, by Andrew of Wynton, prior of the monastery of St. Serf, in the Isle of Loch Leven, who wrote in nine books the "Orygynal Cronykil of Scotland." Of the works attributed to James I., who reigned nominally from 1406 to 1437, and actually ruled the country from 1424 to 1437, the only one certainly known to be his is "The Kinges Quhair," a poem of nearly fourteen hundred lines, in praise of the daughter of the Earl of Somerset, who afterwards became his wife. In the latter half of the fifteenth century the legendary exploits of Wallace were celebrated in a poem of nearly twelve thousand lines, attributed to Henry the Minstrel, or Blind Harry as he is commonly called. A number of poetical compositions were produced also at this time by Robert Henryson of Dunfermline. Among his writings may be mentioned a collection of thirteen fables, and "The Testament of Cresseid," a sequel to the Troilus and Cressida of Chaucer. The greatest name of all this early period is William Dunbar, who flourished from about 1460 to about 1520, and whose works were both numerous, and varied in their character. Contemporary with him was Gawin Douglas, Bishop of Dunkeld, whose most famous production was his translation of Virgil. But perhaps the poet of the sixteenth century who was then most popular, and continued to be so down even to the last century, was Sir David Lyndsay. His works are specially remarkable as having exerted great influence in helping forward the cause of the Reformation. The later literature in the Scotch dialect, after the union of the crowns, is very rich, particularly in ballad and lyric poetry, and is much of it of an order of merit to which the literature before the union can rarely lay claim. This latter, indeed, has received much praise from some; but to most readers the works belonging to it are apt to seem uninteresting, and they are certainly very long. In spite of the excellence of occasional passages, and even of occasional poems, it must be said of early Scottish literature, that, taken as a whole, it requires patience to read it, and patriotism to admire it.

The particular variety of the Northern dialect which was adopted in literature while Scotland remained an independent kingdom was that spoken in Edinburgh and its neighborhood. This was naturally affected somewhat by the Celtic speech, with which it came into close contact; and the long alliance with France introduced into it from that tongue a large number of words never used, either in conversation or in writing, south of the Tweed. The influence of Chaucer, both on style and manner of treatment, is, however, very noticeable in the compositions of several of the early Scotch poets; and it is a signal illustration of the power over the development of a language exerted by an author of great genius, that many forms characteristic of the Midland or Southern dialect, but foreign to the Northern, were introduced from his works into the variety of the latter dialect in which early Scotch literature was composed, though they seem never to have maintained themselves there. The superiority of English literature could not, indeed, fail to make itself felt in the case of tongues so nearly allied. Still, had the two countries continued to be separate nationalities, differences in the speech would have become thoroughly established; and in the Island of Great Britain there would have been two sister languages as distinct from one another as are, for instance, Spanish and Portuguese. But the union of the two crowns at the beginning of the seventeenth century reduced the Scottish, from the position of a tongue independent of the English, to that of a dialect of it. Having no longer any common literary standard within its borders, it speedily diverged into a number of local dialects, each of which has peculiarities of its own due to its surroundings, and all of which, when used in literature, have been largely affected by the influence of the standard English. No small share of the poetry composed in what is called the Scotch dialect is Scotch rather in name than in reality: it is literary English clothed in Scottish spelling, and rendered only a little more strange by the introduction of a few provincial words. Of course, in such a statement, it is only the written language that is considered, not the spoken; for the Scotch pronunciation varies widely in some respects from that of the classical tongue. But this adoption of forms and grammatical constructions belonging to the English of literature shows, that, even in this peculiar home of the Northern dialect, the Midland has, here as elsewhere, proved too powerful for its ancient rival.

CHAPTER VII.

CHANGES IN THE MIDDLE ENGLISH PERIOD (1350–1550).

It is with the Middle English period that English literature in the limited but strictly proper sense of the word may be said to begin. The production of writings of a character so high as to be recognized everywhere as an authoritative standard of expression could not fail to have an immediate effect upon the future of the language. It was the one great result of the influence now brought to bear upon it, that, from the end of the fourteenth century, our tongue has pursued an orderly development. It suffers changes, and, indeed, constant changes, both in grammar and in vocabulary: if it did not, it would no longer be a living speech. But these changes take place within certain well-defined limits; they require the consent of vast numbers, sometimes of generations; they are spread over great spaces of time. The conservative and restraining influence of literature over language necessarily grows more powerful with every successive century, because literature itself is read and studied by constantly increasing numbers. The changes that have taken place during the five hundred years that have gone by since the beginning of the Middle English period bear not the slightest comparison, in either extent or importance, with those that took place during the two hundred years before that period. How comparatively insignificant the former are has already been fully exemplified in the extract which has been given from Chaucer, with the ancient spelling in one case preserved, and in the other case with it modernized.[1] An examination of these shows clearly that it is the difference of orthography, far more than the difference of vocabulary and of construction, that makes the language of the fourteenth century seem difficult.

English, therefore, from this time forth, enters upon an entirely new history. Its changes during the various periods since have been changes in degree, but never in kind. In order to comprehend clearly the character of the transitions through which it has gone during the past five hundred years, it is necessary to have well in mind one or two principles that underlie the development of language. It has already been pointed out, that, in the speech of rude and ignorant men, grammatical changes take place rapidly; whereas, under ordinary circumstances, few new words are added to the vocabulary. This fact becomes very noticeable when a cultivated tongue ceases to be used

[1] Pages 79, 80.

any longer by the educated, and is heard only from the mouths of the illiterate. The variations which spring up under such circumstances are easy of observation, because we have an ideal standard preserved by which to compare the present with the past. But the precise reverse of this condition of things is true of any language in which is embodied the spoken and written speech of a cultivated people. In it no sudden alterations can be made in the grammar, because great literary models have given permanent form and character to that which already exists. Nor can violent alterations be ever made without a revolution mighty enough to upset the language itself in its existing form. While, therefore, in a cultivated speech, changes in inflection and syntax do take place, they invariably take place slowly and on a small scale; and, if they happen to attract observation at the time, they never succeed in establishing themselves without a struggle. On the other hand, the vocabulary is constantly increasing. The domain of knowledge is always widening; and new terms are constantly needed to express the new facts which the many-sided activity of the race has gathered, and the new ideas it has conceived. An existing vocabulary, therefore, cannot for any long period satisfy the demand made upon it; or, in other words, a living tongue can never become what is called fixed until the men who speak it get to be intellectually dead. There is, in consequence, an absolute necessity resting upon every generation, either of developing new words from existing roots, or of imposing new senses upon words already in use, or of borrowing strange words from foreign tongues; and in modern languages it will be found that these three agencies are in active operation side by side.

From the beginning of the Middle English period till the present time, aversion to grammatical change, with consequent slowness in its adoption, and fondness for new or foreign words, and facility in their formation or introduction, have been especially characteristic of our tongue. During the first two centuries the former feeling had the least influence; during the last three the latter has made itself more conspicuous. The composite character of the vocabulary had been established by the middle of the fourteenth century; by the end of it the language had received and assimilated nearly all the words it has ever taken from the Old French. During the fifteenth century there was not very much addition from any quarter. It was not until the close of the Middle English period that new words began to come in in large numbers, and then, as a general rule, they were taken directly from the Latin. This smallness of addition to the vocabulary was mainly due to the failure of the intellectual movement that had begun so auspiciously in the latter half of the fourteenth century. Chaucer died in 1400; but he left no successors to his genius or his authority; and, for one hundred and fifty years after his death, literature was in a state of collapse. As, therefore, the lexical changes were slight, it is the grammatical changes that are for us, during this period, the matter of chief importance.

In these the two counteracting influences that literature exerts over language began to show themselves at once. One of them is the tendency to produce uniformity, the other the tendency to arrest all change; no matter in either case whether the result is to be desired or to be deplored. From the conflict of these opposing agencies the grammatical forms of the language came out at the end of the Middle English period what we now find them. The reduction to uniformity that was then effected has never since been disturbed: the anomalies that were then left in our speech have remained with us still. Here the most important of the changes that took place are all that can be given.

Declension of Nouns.—In the writings of Chaucer a number of nouns still failed to form their plurals in *-s*, according to what had by that time become the regular ending. Some of them terminated in *-n*, either in strict accordance with the original Anglo-Saxon declension in *-an;* others had had that termination added by what had originally been a blunder, but which blunder had in his time become correct usage. By the middle of the sixteenth century all of the former class had passed over to the regular formation in *-s*, with the single exception of *oxen*. *Eyen* or *eyne* may also be found along with *eyes*, but then, as occasionally now, only in poetry; and the same statement is true of one or two other words. Of the latter class, *children* (A. S. *cildru*) and *brethren* (A. S. *brôthru*) and *kine* (A. S. *cŷ*) still retain an *n* to which etymologically they are not entitled; but, in the sixteenth century, the regular forms *brothers* and *cows* established themselves alongside, and have for most purposes supplanted the older plurals. So, again, in Chaucer, a number of nouns are found with the plural of the same form as the singular. They are usually descendants of the Anglo-Saxon neuter noun of the vowel-declension, many of which had the nominative and accusative plural the same as the nominative and accusative singular. Some of these also assumed the *s*. *Thing* and *year*, for illustration, were originally plural as well as singular; but they added during this period the final *-s*.

Declension of the Third Personal Pronoun. — The only change of importance in the pronoun that took place during the Middle English period was in the plural of the pronoun of the third person. In Chaucer this had *they* in the nominative, but, in the genitive and objective, *here* and *hem*, the descendants of the forms used in the Anglo-Saxon. In place of these, *their* and *them*, corresponding in form to the nominative, were substituted in the speech of all, as, even as early as the fourteenth century, they had been used in the speech of many.

Inflection of the Adjective. — At the beginning of the Middle English period the adjective had been nearly stripped of the numerous inflections it had possessed in the Anglo-Saxon. During the two centuries that followed, it lost the little it had retained. The use of the final *e*, to denote the plural and the definite declension in the singular, was abandoned altogether; and the adjective was left, as we now have it, without any inflection whatever. In its comparison the vowel-modification, which in some cases it underwent in Chaucer and his contemporaries, disappeared before the middle of the sixteenth century. *Long* and *strong* and *old*, at the beginning of the Middle English period, had for comparatives *lenger*, *strenger*, and *elder*; at the end of it, they had the regular forms, *longer*, *stronger*, and *older*, now in use; though the last-named word, *old*, still retained, as at present, both forms.

Inflection of the Verb. — The fact has already been mentioned, that, after the Norman conquest, the disposition became widely prevalent to drop the final *n*. But, though this was always in operation, it had not, even in the time of Chaucer, been carried out to a complete result. In his writings the infinitive of the verb, and the plural number of both the present and the past tenses of the indicative, end in *en* or *e*; thus we have *to hopen* or *to hopè*, *they hopen* or *they hopè*, and *they hopeden* or *they hopede*. In the case of the past tense it is not at all unfrequent, also, to have the final *e* dropped in pronunciation: it sometimes happened in the case of the other two parts of the verb that have been mentioned. This tendency to drop the *n*, which had been the prevailing one in the fourteenth century, became almost universally established in the fifteenth. Ben Jonson in his English Grammar asserts, that, until about the reign of King Henry VIII. (1509–1547), present plurals were found in *en*. But, though they are found at that time, they lingered then, as they did at a later period, as survivals of the past, rather than as forms in living, current use. Along with the *n* gradually disappeared the final *e*. It was dropped universally during the fifteenth century in pronunciation: in some cases it was dropped in the spelling, and in other cases retained.

This same remark is also true of the final *e* of the noun, and, indeed, of all the other parts of speech in which it is found. In some cases the *e* was retained in the spelling after it had disappeared from the pronunciation, as in *love*, *fame*, and numerous other words, where its retention has been of no use. Again: it has been dropped both in spelling and pronunciation, as in *peyne*, pain, *trouthe*, truth, and *blisse*, bliss, and also in adverbs derived from adjectives, such as *brighte*, *lowe*, *faire*, *deepe*, in which, had it been retained, it would have had the one merit of distinguishing one part of speech from another.

There was, as may be inferred, a steady movement toward uniformity of inflection during the Middle English period. But, while this accomplished much, it did not succeed in accomplishing every thing. Anomalous forms still continued to exist. Though *sistren* and *doughteren* and *ton* had become *sisters* and *daughters* and *toes*, *oxen* and *children* had failed to pass over into *oxes* and *childers*; though the plural *hors* and *folk* and *year* and *thing* had become *horses*, *folks*, *years*, and *things*, *sheep* and *deer* had not become *sheeps* and *deers*. Nor did plurals whose form was due to vowel modification, such as *men*, *feet*, *mice*, *geese*, lose any of their numbers after the fourteenth century. The complete success of any radical movement to bring about an ideal uniformity was in a large number of instances counteracted by that conservative opposition to all change which is a marked characteristic of cultivated speech. This has been seen in the inflection of the noun; but it most conspicuously asserted itself in the conjugation of the verb. Here a movement toward uniformity which had been in active operation since the break-up of the Anglo-Saxon was finally arrested. Not only, indeed, was it arrested, but it may be said that a movement in the opposite direction started into being, though it has never been productive of important results.

There are in English, as in every other Teutonic tongue, two leading conjugations of the verbs, — one called the old, or strong, conjugation; the other, the weak, or new. The main distinction between them is easy of comprehension. The weak verb, to form the past tense, adds, or originally added, a syllable, in Anglo-Saxon, *de*, which, under certain circumstances, became *te*. In a very few cases, also, the vowel of its root was varied; thus, *drygan*, 'to dry,' formed a preterite *dryg-de; drȳpan*, 'to drip,' formed the preterite *drȳp-te; tellan*, 'to tell,' formed the preterite *teal-de; sēcan*, 'to seek,' formed the preterite *sôh-te*. On the other hand, the strorg conjugation added nothing to form the past tense, but the vowel of the root in every case underwent change; thus, *drinc-an*, 'to drink,' had in the first person of the preterite singular *dranc*, *glīd-an*, 'to glide,' had for the corresponding form of the preterite *glād*. For the three centuries immediately following the Norman conquest the distinction between these two conjugations was largely broken down; but the changes that resulted inured to the benefit of only one of them. Numbers of verbs originally having the strong inflection gave it up, and took the weak in its place. So many, indeed, of the Anglo-Saxon strong verbs had been wholly lost to the language by the beginning of the middle English period, furthermore, so many of those that were retained had become weak, and the general movement in that direction was so decided, that it seemed merely a question of time when the strong inflection would disappear entirely. But this movement received a check with the creation of a great native literature. In fact, the strong conjugation has lost nothing during the past three hundred years, and has lost but little during the past five hundred. One illustration will make this statement perfectly clear. "The Canterbury Tales" of Chaucer contain more than seventeen thousand lines of poetry: an examination of the strong preterites as found in the poetry of that work show that of them only the following twelve have in Modern English passed over completely or partially to the weak conjugation: —

Modern English Infinitives.	Preterites used by Chaucer.	Modern English Preterites.
1. carve,	carf,	carved.
2. gnaw,	gnew,	gnawed.
3. glide,	glod,	glided.
4. laugh,	lough,	laughed.
5. leap,	leep,	leapt.
6. quake,	quok,	quaked.
7. shape,	schop,	shaped.
8. starve,	starf,	starved.
9. swell,	swal,	swelled.
10. wash,	wessch,	washed.
11. wax,	wax,	waxed.
12. wield,	weld,	wielded.

The three following, again, had already, in Chaucer's time, begun to conform to the tendency, then prevalent, to pass over to the weak conjugation. It will be noticed that they have, with him, both weak and strong forms; like *thrive*, for illustration, which has the double preterites *throve* and *thrived*.

Modern English Infinitives.	Preterites used by Chaucer.	Modern English Preterites.
1. creep,	{ creep, crepte, }	crept.
2. sleep,	{ sleep, slepte, }	slept.
3. weep,	{ weep, wepte, }	wept.

Again: the four following verbs, inflected strong by Chaucer, have in Modern English both a strong and weak inflection, though, in the case of *climb* and *help*, the strong preterite is poetic or provincial.

Modern English Infinitives.	Preterites used by Chaucer.	Modern English Preterites.
1. climb,	clomb,	clomb, climbed.
2. crow,	crew,	crew, crowed.
3. heave,	haf,	hove, heaved.
4. help,	halp,	holp, helped.

On the other hand, four of the verbs inflected by Chaucer according to the weak conjugation have, by a kind of counter-movement, passed over to the strong, and are now inflected accordingly. Two of them, *grind* and *grow*, are strong in Anglo-Saxon; but the other two are weak. It ought to be added, that, in the case of *grind* and *grow*, Chaucer has the strong past participle in *en*.

Modern English Infinitives.	Preterites used by Chaucer.	Modern English Preterites.
1. grind,	grynte,	ground
2. grow,	growede,	grew.
3. stick,	stikede,	stuck.
4. wear,	wered(e),	wore.

Any such examination as this is in its nature partial and incomplete; but it is sufficient to prove the truth of the general statement made in regard to the influence of literature in arresting the transition of verbs from the strong to the weak conjugation.[1] This point,

[1] As Chaucer manuscripts vary to some extent in the form of the preterites of verbs, it may not be amiss to state that the results given above are based upon an examination of the Harleian MS. No. 7,334, edited by Thomas Wright.

indeed, needed to be presented sharply, because there is a common impression that the strong verbs are disappearing from our tongue. The impression, however, is an entirely mistaken one. None of the strong verbs that were left us at the end of the Middle English period, more than three hundred years ago, have since been lost, though, in a few cases, weak preterite forms have arisen since, or, rather, have perpetuated themselves alongside of the strong forms. In fact, the reverse of the common impression is the truth; for a few weak verbs have, in the Modern tongue, passed over to the strong conjugation. Even a certain number of anomalous verbs of the weak conjugation have successfully resisted the tendency, once prevalent, to inflect them regularly. *Reach*, to be sure, has given up its older preterite, *raught;* but, on the other hand, words like *teach*, *catch*, and *tell*, still prefer their preterites *taught*, *caught*, and *told*, to the forms *teached*, *catched*, and *telled*, which have at times been in use.

These were the main changes that took place during the Middle English period, as the result of the two influences that are always at work upon cultivated speech. One addition to the inflectional system of the verb, and one loss, are also to be noted as having characterized the history of the language during these two centuries.

The addition was in the shape of a new method to express the relation of present and past time. The phrases compounded of parts of the verb *be* and the present participle, such for illustration, as *I am going*, and *I was going*, had been in common use from the earliest period of the language. During the Middle English period were established, also, the phrases for the present and the past tense, formed by compounding *do* and *did* with the infinitive, as in *I do go*, *I did go*. They did not, to be sure, make then their first appearance in our speech; but it was not until the beginning of the fifteenth century that they became common, and not until the end of it that they became general.

The loss was the plural form of the imperative mood. Originally this mood had two distinct forms for the second person of the singular and for that of the plural; thus, in the Anglo-Saxon verb *helpan*, 'to help,' the form used in the imperative would always be *help*, whenever a single person was addressed; whenever more than one, the form would be *helpath*, which in later English would become and did become *helpeth*. In the fourteenth century the two forms had largely come to be confounded; and by the end of the fifteenth the plural ending (*e*)*th* had disappeared altogether.

The Middle English period saw, also, the final abandonment of the grammatical gender, and the substitution, in its place, of one corresponding to the natural distinctions of sex. This was the result of processes that had been steadily at work since the Norman conquest. In Anglo Saxon the gender of the noun depended not upon its meaning, but upon its termination, or method of inflection. Objects with life were, in consequence, sometimes neuter; while far more frequently objects without life were masculine or feminine. The early language presents us in this respect the same characteristic as the other tongues of the Indo-European family, such, for instance, as Latin, Greek, or the modern German. Thus, in Anglo-Saxon, *wíf*, 'woman,' 'wife,' was neuter. Again, *múð*, 'mouth,' and *tóð*, 'tooth,' were masculine; *tunge*, 'tongue,' and *nasu*, 'nose,' were feminine; *eáge*, 'eye,' and *eáre*, 'ear,' were neuter. It is evident that the system of denoting gender, whatever it may have been at the beginning, had now become a purely conventional one; and one great compensation for the loss of inflection was, that with it this system necessarily disappeared. A gender which depended upon differences of termination and declension could not continue to flourish after those differences had been swept away; and, when to this loss was added the still more important loss of the inflection of the adjective and the adjective pronouns, every method of denoting it was gone. The consequence was, that it was the meaning that decided the gender to which the noun should be ascribed; and this necessarily brought the gender into harmony with the real distinctions of sex. The breaking-down of the grammatical system began immediately after the conquest. The substitution of the natural system may be said to have been mainly effected before the beginning of the Middle English period; by the end of it, the change had become perfectly established. Since that time, it is only in the language of poetry, or of passion, affectionate or inimical in its character, that objects without life are personified, or objects with life are spoken of as things; nor would even this be possible, had not a few of the pronouns still retained a separate inflection for distinction of sex.

CHAPTER VIII.

MODERN ENGLISH.

Up to this time in the nomenclature of the periods of the English tongue, and in the dates assigned to them, there has been among scholars a wide diversity of usage. In regard to the latest period, however, there is a pretty substantial agreement. The beginning of Modern English is by most writers referred to the middle of the sixteenth century; by some it is specifically reckoned from the accession of Queen Elizabeth, which took place in 1558.

No dates can ever be given in the history of the development of any tongue, against which some objections cannot be brought. For convenience of reference, a further subdivision of Modern English is desirable. In this work it will be separated into the three following periods. The first extends from 1550 to the year of the restoration of the Stuarts in the following century, that is to 1660; the second, from 1660 to a point in the latter part of the eighteenth century, and in this the year 1789, the date of the breaking out of the French Revolution, affords a convenient terminus; the third period extends from 1789 to the present time. Though the divison is made primarily for convenience of reference, it will be found, that, on the whole, it is a satisfactory division for the historical treatment of both the language and the literature.

It has been pointed out in the previous chapter, that, in highly-cultivated tongues, changes in grammar always take place slowly; while changes in vocabulary, particularly in the nature of additions to it, meet with no opposition, or with comparatively little. In early speech, men think mainly of what they are going to say, not of the way in which they are to say it; and the hearer or reader likewise cares so much more for the matter, that he does not consciously give much heed to the manner. In later times all this is reversed. The vehicle of the thought has then become a subject of consideration independent of the thought; that is, language has begun to be studied for itself, as well as for what it conveys. When any tongue has reached this point of development, the opposition to change in established forms of expression is sure to become exceedingly powerful; for against such changes are arrayed all the authority of past usage, and all the prejudice in favor of what actually is existing, and has been found to do, though perhaps clumsily, the work demanded of it. In fact, it may be said that these changes never succeed in making themselves adopted, until the necessity for them is imperious enough to over-ride the protests of professional purists, and the feeling of dislike to innovation which becomes almost a second nature in the cultivated users of speech.

True as these statements are of any tongue, they are especially true of Modern English. While the lexical changes have been comparatively numerous, both in the meanings given to old words and in the actual introduction of entirely new words, the grammatical changes have been on a very limited scale. In the inflection of the noun there have been none at all; in the adjective there could be none, because, at the beginning of the Modern English period, it had already been reduced to the root form. In the pronoun and the verb there have taken place certain changes, and of these an account of the most important will now be given.

Inflection of the Pronoun.—The latter half of the sixteenth century witnessed the rise, or at least the general prevalence, of a confusion in the use of the nominative and objective cases of the personal pronouns and of the interrogative *who*, which in some instances has been perpetuated to our time in literature, and in many more still survives in colloquial speech. *Ye*, for illustration, in the language of Chaucer, invariably denotes the nominative; *you*, the objective; and this distinction will still be found observed in the authorized version of the Bible. But in the sixteenth century this distinction began to break down, and before the first period of Modern English was completed the two forms were used interchangeably for each other. At the present time the original nominative *ye*, though occasionally found, is practically supplanted by the form *you*, which originally belonged only to the dative and to the accusative. But, besides this, colloquial speech, and to no slight extent literature, have preserved and perpetuated to our time expressions in which *I* and *me*, *he* and *him*, *who* and *whom*, and several others, are confounded with each other, and furnish a vast field for never-ending discussions as to correctness of usage.

Of all the parts of speech the pronoun is the most adverse to the introduction of any new forms; yet to its limited number the close of the sixteenth century saw the addition of *its*. The genitive of *it* (originally *hit*) is etymologically *his*; but this is also the genitive of *he*. It was inevitable that confusion should arise in the use of this one form as applied equally to an object with life and to one without life, as soon as the system of grammatical gender had passed away. Confusion did arise; and expedients of all kinds were resorted to for the sake of securing clearness. Sometimes, as is the case in the English Bible, *of it* and *thereof* were used; sometimes *the* was employed, as in this example from Bacon, "that which retaineth *the* state and virtue;" and, more frequently still, *it* was used itself as a genitive. Both *the* and *it* were very commonly joined with *own*, making such phrases as *the own* and *it own*. The most usual method to avoid ambiguity was, however, to change the construction of the sentence. All these difficulties led to the formation of *its*. The first record of its appearance in print that has yet been found belongs to the year 1598; and its infrequency is made conspicuous by the fact that it appears but ten times in Shakspeare's works. With Ben Jonson it is much more common, and by the middle of the seventeenth century it had become thoroughly established; though the fact that Milton uses it but three times in his poetry, and rarely in his prose, shows that in the minds of some there was a prejudice still lingering against it. By the end of that century, however, its comparatively recent origin seems to have been entirely forgotten.

Inflection of the Verb. — In the verb the inflectional changes have been of more importance. One of them is purely special. This is the transition of the form *be* of the substantive verb from the indicative to the subjunctive mood. In Elizabethan English *they be* is found constantly alongside of *they are;* just as it is yet, in those two great conservators of archaic expression, — the language of poetry and of low life. In the latter it still occurs constantly, in the former occasionally; but it early began, in literary prose, to be confined to the subjunctive mood; and this has now become the established practice in the ordinary cultivated speech.

A second change has been the gradual substitution of *-s* for *-th* as the termination of the third person singular of the present indicative. In the Midland dialect of the eastern counties, from which literary

English directly sprang, this part of the verb ended invariably in *-th:* such was the practice of Chaucer and his contemporaries, and their very occasional use of the form in *-s* is due generally to the desire of accommodating the rhyme. On the other hand, this third person regularly ended in *-s* in the Northern dialect. From this dialect it began to make its way into literary English in the former half of the sixteenth century. The practice of employing it became more and more prevalent, and by the end of that century it is found, at least in some writers, full as frequently as the form in *-th*. During most of the first period of Modern English the terminations *-s* and *-th* flourished side by side, neither seeming to have any preference in popular estimation; but, toward the latter part of it, the former ending became the one generally used, and with the progress of time gradually displaced the other. That the termination *-th* did not die entirely is probably due to the influence of the English Bible. Though the authorized version of that work appeared as late as 1611, the language used in it belonged, as is well known, to the early portion of the preceding century. In it the ending is throughout in *-th:* it never, for instance, says *he makes*, but invariably *he maketh*. To this is due the preservation of the form, and the additional fact that it is now almost entirely confined to the language of religion.

There is nothing more supremely characteristic of our speech, especially in its later periods, than the extent to which it has developed the use of passive formations. In this respect it has gone far beyond any other cultivated modern tongue. The discussion of this belongs mostly to syntax, and needs here nothing beyond simple reference. But the tendency in this direction which the language has long manifested, has had, as one result, the addition, during the past hundred years, of entirely new verb-phrases, made up of the present and past tenses of the substantive verb, and of past participles compounded with *being*. The history of this presents a striking instance of the difficulty in which the decay of old forms leaves a language, and the ingenuity it displays in striking out new paths to expression.

Anglo-Saxon had no special form for the passive; and, to represent the present of that voice, it combined the past participle with the present tense of either the verbs *wesan* and *beón*, 'to be,' or the verb *weorðan*, 'to become,' preserved in early English in the form *worth(en)*. But the latter word, in process of time, disappeared from the language, and the tenses of the substantive verb became the only ones that were combined with the past participle to express the passive relation.

This it could easily do for the present tense, when the verb whose participle was used denoted a feeling which was in its nature continuous. 'The man is loved, is feared, is admired,' were expressions which presented no difficulty nor ambiguity; but, when the verb whose participle was used denoted a simple act, the combination of the passive participle with the present tense of the verb *be* had the effect of giving to the full verbal phrase, not the sense of something which was then actually taking place, but of something which had already taken place. It was a completed, not an existing action, which was signified by it. 'The man is shot, is wounded, is killed,' could not well be employed of any thing else than a finished result, not of an action going on to a possible result. And when the principal verb denoted, according to the context, as in many cases it did, sometimes a completed, and sometimes continuous action, another source of ambiguity was at once added.

One way taken to avoid the difficulty was to change the form of expression. In order to assert, for illustration, that an individual was in danger of violent death, inversions like 'they are killing the man' were introduced. In fact, either changing the expression, or the employment of various circumlocutions, became the common way of getting rid of the ambiguity. Another method, however, sprang up, though its use was comparatively limited: this was to join the present of the verb *be*, almost always when the subject was without life, to the verbal substantive in *ing*, governed by the preposition *on* or *in*. The preposition, in time, took the form of *a*, or, rather, was corrupted into it by slovenly pronunciation, and was then frequently joined directly to the substantive. In this way arose expressions like 'the house is a-building,' 'the brass is a-forging,' 'the dinner is a-preparing;' and from the substantive finally fell away the preposition, leaving the verbal phrase designed to denote the passive relation precisely the same in form as the verbal phrase compounded of the substantive verb and the present participle. The former, in fact, were necessarily limited in number; for it was rarely the case that a subject with life could be given to the verbal phrase representing the passive. In 'the house is building,' and 'the man is building,' it is obvious at a glance that the idea conveyed by *is building* is essentially distinct. Nor would the difficulty have been removed, had the preposition been retained. 'The man is a-eating' could not by any possibility be looked upon as a passive formation, and made to mean that the subject of the verb was the object of the action signified by the verbal substantive.

Some other method of expression was felt to be necessary: accordingly, in the latter half of the eighteenth century, a new verb-phrase, made up of the substantive verb and the compound past participle, came into being. Like the forms compounded with *do*, these phrases were confined to the present and preterite tenses. Their use speedily became common; and, though they met with vigorous opposition, they were found so clear in meaning, and so convenient in practice, that opposition was of no avail. They have been adopted by nearly every living writer of repute, and may now be considered thoroughly established. Double methods of expression, like 'the house is building,' and 'the house is being built,' will in some cases doubtless continue to exist side by side for a long time to come; but no new ones of the former kind will make their way into general use, while there is no perceptible limit to the spread of those of the latter.

These constitute the important inflectional changes that have taken place in Modern English. There are other grammatical changes, mostly syntactical in their nature, into which the limits of this work do not suffer us to enter. The character of them may be gathered from one or two illustrations. The form of the subjunctive mood still continues to exist in our tongue; but the use of that mood as conveying any shades of meaning distinct from that of the indicative passed away in the Middle English period. So, also, in the first period of Modern English, the double negative, as strengthening the negation, was abandoned under the influence of the Latin, in which two negatives make an affirmative; but, though given up in the cultivated speech, the original idiom exhibits all its early vitality in the language of low life. Questions like these, connected with the history of usage, would require a special work for their proper discussion.

It is in the vocabulary that the greatest changes have taken place, and are still taking place, in Modern English; though they have never been of such a kind and extent as to affect radically the character and continuity of the speech. In general terms, it may be said that the losses in words have been comparatively slight; while the gains have been numerous: but these gains are far from having been spread equally over the history of the modern tongue. The period from 1550 to 1660 is especially remarkable for the vast number of terms that came into the language, especially from the Latin, and to some, though to a much slighter degree, from the French, the Spanish, and the Italian. The disposition to introduce these foreign words had begun in the early part of the sixteenth century; but it did not get under full headway until the latter half. It was a natural result of the causes then in operation. It was a time of great activity and intense excitement. The intellectual impulse which had been set in motion by the revival of letters was still in its first vigor. It had rent the Christian Church into two hostile camps, using against each other, in defence of their dogmas, all the resources of the common learning of the past and the new learning that was coming in. A world hitherto unknown had been laid open to view, and fresh explorations were constantly bringing to light fresh facts. The rapid increase of knowledge and of the development of thought needed new words for their expression; and new words were accordingly introduced without stint or hesitation. The readiest resource at that time, of the English-speaking race, was the Latin; and there was scarcely a single author of that period who did not feel himself at perfect liberty to coin from it any terms which seemed to him to express more exactly the ideas he sought to convey. The consequence was, that vast multitudes of words came then into our tongue, large numbers of which have never been collected into our dictionaries, and perhaps, in some cases, have never had any existence outside of the written speech. Certainly many of them never came into general use, and no small proportion of them were probably confined to the individual authors who invented them. In conformity with the terminology previously used, this influx is often called the "Latin of the Fourth Period."

But, at the time of the restoration of the Stuarts, the intellectual impulse above mentioned had practically spent its force. The period from 1660 to 1789 was a critical rather than a creative age; and it added but a small amount to the English vocabulary. This state of things, however, was again broken up towards the close of the eighteenth century. A great political and humanitarian movement was in progress throughout Europe, which was attended, not merely with a social upheaval, but with a general intellectual movement, which presents many striking resemblances to that of the sixteenth century. As regards language, it has been followed by two results. During the past hundred years, our tongue has shown a marked tendency to go back to its older forms, and to revive a large number of words that have been kept alive only in the provincial dialects; and this is a tendency which the constantly-increasing attention paid to the study of English in its earlier stages will naturally accelerate. The second result is the introduction of a vast number of new words, which the rapid advance in every department of human investigation has rendered necessary. Many of these, to be sure, are nothing but revivals of terms which had previously been brought in during the sixteenth and seventeenth centuries, but had fallen into disuse; but much the larger proportion of them are entirely new coinages. Especially is this true in the manifold departments of modern science, in which every advance gives birth to a number of hitherto unknown words. These, in most instances, are taken from the Greek. To a large extent they are purely technical in their character; but, with the progress of the arts, a certain number are sure to pass into general circulation. Still, in spite of these vast accessions, very few old words that were ever in common use have been lost; nor do they, to any great extent, suffer change of meaning. The continued and indeed ever-increasing popularity of the great writers of Modern English is sufficient to prevent the terms they use from becoming obsolete, or the language itself to wander far away from the forms which they have made familiar.

The fact of English possessing, to a large extent, a double vocabulary — one composed of Teutonic, the other of Romance words — has given a marked character to the literature of various epochs. Still, at any time, a difference of terms employed will always be due to a difference of subject. It has already been pointed out, that the language of reasoning and philosophy, of intellectual processes of any kind, will always make extensive use of the Latin element; while, on the contrary, the language of feeling, in whatever shape manifested, will be mainly taken from the Teutonic element.

But, even in treating of subjects of a similar character, different writers living at the same time will vary widely in their choice of words. Moreover, it may be said that the literary speech has shown a constant tendency to oscillate between the two vocabularies. During the first period, from 1550 to 1660, the Latin influence was plainly predominant. It affected, not alone the words, but also the construction. The involved and stately sentences of Bacon, Hooker, and Milton, belong to a species of writing which is no more cultivated: indeed, it is only in the dramatists of the Elizabethan age, that any thing closely resembling modern prose can then be found. In the second period, the two elements of the vocabulary were, in the main, harmoniously blended, though during the latter part of it, under the influence of Johnson, a temporary re-action manifested itself in favor of the Latin. But this speedily passed away. On the other hand, during the last period of Modern English, and especially at the present time, a violent re-action in favor of the Teutonic element has set in; so that, in spite of the immense accessions to the vocabulary from the classical tongues, due to the progress of science, it is probably true that the proportion of words of native origin used by popular writers, as contrasted with those of foreign origin, is greater now than at any time during the past three hundred years. But the history of the language shows that there is nothing permanent about any of these movements, whether in favor of the Teutonic or of the Romance element of our tongue. Both are essential to the speech in its present form, and a marked preference for the one, to the exclusion of the other, can, at best, be never any thing more than a temporary fashion.

Settlement of the Orthography.—It was in the second period of Modern English, that the orthography became fixed. In the time of Chaucer it may fairly be described as phonetic; so that, as pronunciation varied in different parts of the country, the spelling necessarily varied with it. One of the results of the art of printing was to bring about uniformity on this point. It was, however, a result that was very gradually reached. The seventeenth century showed a marked advance toward uniformity over the sixteenth; and still more decided was the advance of the latter part of the seventeenth century over the earlier part. At the beginning of the eighteenth century the present orthography was pretty nearly established; though in regard to numerous words there was still wide diversity of usage. It was not until after the publication of Johnson's dictionary, in 1755, that the existing spelling can be said to have become universally received. That given by him to words has been the one generally followed by all later writers; and a deference has sprung up for it which is not justified by any thing in its character. Orthography was a matter about which Johnson was totally incompetent to decide; and, largely in consequence of the respect and even reverence paid still to that which he saw fit to employ, the spelling of English is probably the most vicious to be found in any cultivated tongue that ever existed. It is in no sense a guide to pronunciation, which is its only proper office; and, even for derivation (an office for which it was never designed), it is equally worthless, save in the case of words of direct Latin origin.

Wide Extension of English. — During the modern period of its history, English has been carried over a large share of the habitable globe, and the number of those who speak it is constantly increasing. Under conditions that existed in former times, this fact could be followed but by one result. Different tongues would have sprung up in different countries, varying from each other, and varying more or less from their common mother; and the differences would have constantly tended to become more marked with the progress of time. But there are two agencies now in existence that will be more than sufficient to prevent any such result. These are, first, the common possession of a great literature accessible to men of every rank and every country; and, secondly, the constant interchange of population that results from the facility of modern communication. Joined to these is the steadily-increasing attention paid to the diffusion of education, the direct effect of which is to destroy dialectic differences, and make the literary speech the one standard to which all conform. These agencies become year by year more wide-reaching and controlling. The forces that tend to bring about unity are now so much more powerful than those that tend to bring about diversity, and the former are so constantly gaining in strength, that any marked deviation between the language as spoken in Great Britain and in its Colonies, and in America, can now be looked upon as hardly possible.

This brings us directly to the discussion of a question with which the general history of English may properly conclude: What is to be the future of our tongue? Is it steadily tending to become corrupt, as constantly asserted by so many who are laboriously devoting their lives to preserve it in its purity? The fact need not be denied, if by it is meant, that, within certain limits, the speech is always moving away from established usage. The history of language is the history of corruption. The purest of speakers uses every day, with perfect propriety, words and forms, which, looked at from the point of view of the past, are improper, if not scandalous. But the blunders of one age become good usage in the following, and, in process of time, grow to be so consecrated by custom and consent, that a return to practices theoretically correct would seem like a return to barbarism. While this furnishes no excuse for lax and slovenly methods of expression, it is a guaranty that the indulgence in them by some, or the adoption of them by all, will not necessarily be attended by any serious injury to the speech. Vulgarity and tawdriness and affectation, and numerous other characteristics which are manifested by the users of language, are bad enough; but it is a gross error to suppose that they have of themselves any permanently serious effect upon the purity of national speech. They are results of imperfect training; and, while the great masters continue to be admired and read and studied, they are results that last but for a time. The causes which bring about the decline of a language are of an entirely different type. It is not the use of particular words or idioms, it is not the adoption of peculiar rhetorical devices, that contribute either to the permanent well-being or corruption of any tongue. These are the mere accidents of speech, the fashion of a time which passes away with the causes that gave it currency: far back of these lie the real sources of decay. Language is no better and no worse than the men who speak it. The terms of which it is composed have no independent vitality in themselves: it is the meaning which the men who use them put into them, that gives them all their power. It is never language in itself that becomes weak or corrupt: it is only when those who use it become weak or corrupt, that it shares in their degradation. Nothing but respect need be felt or expressed for that solicitude which strives to maintain the purity of speech: yet when unaccompanied by a far-reaching knowledge of its history, but, above all, by a thorough comprehension of the principles which underlie the growth of language, efforts of this kind are as certain to be full of error as they are lacking in result. There has never been a time in the history of Modern English in which there have not been men who fancied that they foresaw its decay. From the sixteenth to the nineteenth century on, our literature, whenever it touches upon the character of the vehicle by which it is conveyed, is full of the severest criticism; and its pages are crowded with unavailing protests against the introduction of that which now it hardly seems possible for us to do without, and, along with these, with mournful complaints of the degeneracy of the present, and with melancholy forebodings for the future. So it always has been: so it is always likely to be. Yet the real truth is, that the language can be safely trusted to take care of itself, if the men who speak it take care of themselves; for with their degree of development, of cultivation, and of character, it will always be found in absolute harmony.

In fact, it is not from the agencies that are commonly supposed to be corrupting that our speech at the present time suffers: it is in much more danger from ignorant efforts made to preserve what is called its purity. Rules have been and still are laid down for the use of it, which never had any existence outside of the minds of grammarians and verbal critics. By these rules, so far as they are observed, freedom of expression is cramped, idiomatic peculiarity destroyed, and false tests for correctness set up, which give the ignorant opportunity to point out supposed error in others; while the real error lies in their own imperfect acquaintance with the best usage. One illustration will be sufficient of multitudes that might be cited There is a rule of Latin syntax that two or more substantives joined by a copulative require the verb to be in the plural. This has been foisted into the grammar of English, of which it is no more true than it is of modern German. There is nothing in the usage of the past, from the very earliest times, to authorize it, nothing in the usage of the present to justify it, except so far as the rule itself has tended to make general the practice it imposes. The grammar of English, as exhibited in the utterances of its best writers and speakers, has, from the very earliest period, allowed the widest discretion as to the use either of the singular or the plural in such cases. The importation and imposition of rules foreign to its idiom, like the one just mentioned, does more to hinder the free development of the tongue, and to dwarf its freedom of expression, than the widest prevalence of slovenliness of speech, or of affectation of style; for these latter are always temporary in their character, and are sure to be left behind by the advance in popular cultivation, or forgotten through the change in popular taste.

Of the languages of Christendom, English is the one now spoken by far the largest number of persons; and from present appearances there would seem to be but little limit to its possible extension. Yet that it or any other tongue will ever become a universal language is so much more than doubtful, that it may be called impossible; and, even were it possible, it is a question if it would be desirable. However that may be, its spread will depend in the future, as it has in the past, not so much upon the character of the language itself, as upon the character of the men who speak it. It is not necessarily because it is in reality superior to other tongues, that it has become more widely extended than they, but because it has been and still is the speech of two great nations which have been among the foremost in civilization and power, the most greedy in the grasping of territory, the most successful in the planting of colonies. But as political reasons have lifted the tongue into its present prominence, so in the future to political reasons will be owing its progress or decay. Thus, back of every thing that tends to the extension of language, lie the material strength, the intellectual development and the moral character, which make the users of a language worthy enough and powerful enough to impose it upon others. No speech can do more than express the ideas of those who employ it at the time. It cannot live upon its past meanings, or upon the past conceptions of great men which have been recorded in it, any more than the race which uses it can live upon its past glory or its past achievements. Proud, therefore, as we may now well be of our tongue, we may rest assured, that, if it ever attain to universal sovereignty, it will do so only because the ideas of the men who speak it are fit to become the ruling ideas of the world, and the men themselves are strong enough to carry them over the world; and that, in the last analysis, depends, like every thing else, upon the development of the individual; depends, not upon the territory we buy or steal, not upon the gold we mine, or the grain we grow, but upon the men we produce.

If we fail there, no national greatness, however splendid to outward view, can be any thing but temporary and illusory; and, when once national greatness disappears, no past achievements in literature, however glorious, will perpetuate our language as a living speech, though they may help for a while to retard its decay.

PART II.

HISTORY OF INFLECTIONS.

CHAPTER I.

SOME FEATURES COMMON TO ALL THE TEUTONIC TONGUES.

1. HE who contrasts the English of the Anglo-Saxon period with the English of to-day is at once struck by the difference between the ancient and the modern tongue in respect to vocabulary and to inflection. It is with the latter alone that we have to do in the following pages; and the history of it is largely a record of abandonment of forms once deemed necessary, and of confusion in the use of those that were retained. Nevertheless, it would be a great error to suppose that loss or change of inflection is especially characteristic of the later life of our language as distinguished from the earlier. Even when our speech made its first appearance in a few written monuments of the seventh and eighth centuries, it had then already given up much that once belonged to it. The stripping of inflections from the English tongue had begun long before any productions which have been handed down had been composed in it. Many of the irregular forms

which are still found at this day owe their existence, and their apparently anomalous character, to changes which had taken place before a word of our language had been committed to writing; in periods, indeed, when we have not the slightest knowledge as to where even the men lived who spoke our speech.

2. But, without the aid of written monuments, how can we know this to be a fact? How can we be sure that forms once existed in our tongue which have never been preserved in its literature? The answer to these questions not only renders necessary an account of the characteristics of the inflections pervading the earliest period of English, but, to some extent, also an examination of certain features which are common to it with the other Teutonic tongues. Its precise relations to them, the grammatical peculiarities which distinguished them all, must be clearly comprehended, before the student can understand the reason of the general tendencies which have manifested themselves in the history of our inflection, or the origin of the particular anomalies which are still retained in it.

3. It has already been stated that English is a member of a family of languages, called the Teutonic or Germanic, which itself forms one branch of a still larger family, termed the Indo-European, or the Aryan.[1] All the tongues belonging to the latter have come from the same source, and are, therefore, more or less remotely allied to one another. But as no record of this one primitive Indo-European speech exists, as

[1] See introductory chapter.

no monuments of it have been preserved, from which its words and forms could be gathered, we are under the necessity of making out what these words and forms must have been, by a comparison, in accordance with certain scientific principles, of the languages that have been derived from this unknown original tongue. Words and forms which are common to all its descendants, it is very safe to say, must have existed in the parent-speech; though naturally they are more changed and disguised in appearance, the more remote they are from it in time. Looked at from this point of view, it may be said, that, as a general rule, the older the tongue, the more likely is it to bear a closer resemblance to the original from which it came. Accordingly, Sanskrit, with a literature going back to at least fifteen hundred years before Christ, is conceded to be much nearer, in its forms and inflections, to the primitive Indo-European, than any of its numerous sister-languages.

4. In the same manner, as regards that branch of the Indo-European family to which English belongs, there are in existence no monuments of that primitive Teutonic speech from which the members of that branch have descended. The words and forms constituting it can only be made out, in the same manner as in the case of the primitive Indo-European, by a scientific comparison of those found in the derived tongues. Necessarily the older languages of this branch, monuments of which have been handed down, are of the first importance; and of these the Gothic,

whose scanty literature goes back to the fourth century after Christ, must be regarded as presenting, on the whole, much the nearest likeness to that theoretical primitive Teutonic speech which is the common parent of all. But the other older languages belonging to this sub-family are also of importance. These are the Old High German, the Old Norse, and the three Low-Germanic tongues, the Old Saxon, including the Netherlandish, the Old Frisian, and that English of the earliest period which has had given to it in ordinary usage the name of Anglo-Saxon.

5. All of these tongues had many things in common; but loss of inflection not only characterized the primitive Teutonic as compared with the primitive Indo-European, but also characterized the members of the Teutonic branch as compared with their immediate parent. But some of these six oldest tongues retained more than others, the Gothic naturally far the most of any. Each one of them, however, clung to particular forms and inflections which the others had partly or wholly given up. Before considering the special later history of English, it is therefore desirable to point out some general resemblances which existed between it in its earliest form, and the sister-languages of the same Teutonic branch. Understanding the common basis from which they started, the later relations of each to the others not only become at once much clearer, but the later history of our tongue has light thrown upon it by the development which has characterized the others. We shall, in

this place, limit ourselves to the general features that characterize the inflection of the noun, the adjective, and the pronoun, in order to make plain the loss sustained by the primitive Teutonic as compared with the primitive Indo-European, and further the loss of the English as compared with the parent Teutonic. The characteristics of the verb, so far as they are examined at all, will be discussed by themselves.

6. Case. — The primitive Indo-European had eight cases. These were the nominative, the subject of the sentence; the accusative, the case of the direct object; the dative, the case of the indirect object; the genitive, the case of general relation, or the *of* case; the instrumental, the case denoting accompaniment and means, the *with* or *by* case; the ablative, the case denoting separation, the *from* case; the locative, the case denoting the place where any thing is or is done, the *at* or *in* case; and the vocative, or the case of address. All of these were originally distinguished by difference of ending. But the tendency showed itself, from the earliest period of which we have any record, to give up one or more of these case-forms, and either to supply the place left vacant by another case, governed by a preposition, or to make one case do the duty of another in addition to its own; thus, in Latin, the ablative was required to perform the instrumental relation, and, in Greek, the genitive the ablative relation. Of these eight cases the primitive Teutonic still retained six, though only four of them could be said to exist in full vigor. The two that were entirely lost from

this branch were the ablative and the locative. Two others, the vocative and the instrumental, maintained a lingering life. A special form for the vocative is found in the noun of the Gothic. The instrumental is occasionally but clearly seen in the singular of the noun and adjective in the Old High German and the Old Saxon, and in the demonstrative pronouns of all the early Teutonic tongues, save the Old Norse. It is likewise regarded by some as belonging to the Anglo-Saxon noun and adjective. But the remaining four cases are found in all the older languages of this branch, including, of course, Anglo-Saxon, and still survive in one of them, the New High German.

7. **Number.** — The primitive Indo-European had three numbers, — the singular, the dual, and the plural. In the Teutonic noun and adjective the dual had disappeared entirely; but, in the personal pronouns of the first and second person, it is found in all the six earlier languages of this branch, save that, in some of them, forms for certain cases are very rare, if not lacking entirely.

8. **Declension.** — There are two declensions of the Teutonic noun. But in every tongue belonging to this branch there were words which could not be classified under either, inasmuch as they were relics of declensions once of wide employment in the primitive speech, but gone out of use in the Teutonic. These words are accordingly so few in number as to be properly treated as anomalous. The two declensions actually existing are commonly called the vowel or

strong, and the consonant or weak declension; but in the older languages they underwent still further division. The vowel-declension was split up into three, according as one of the short vowels, *a* or *i* or *u*, was the final of the formative syllable, or itself the formative syllable, added to the radical syllable to make the stem; thus, for illustration, the Gothic word for 'fish' was in the nominative *fisks*. Of this the radical syllable was *fisk*, to which the short vowel *a* was added to form the stem *fiska*; and to this, according to a widely-received hypothesis, the demonstrative pronoun *sa* was appended, making an original theoretical form for the nominative, *fiskasa*, which was cut down to *fisks*, the form with which we are familiar. In Anglo-Saxon it underwent still further abbreviation, nothing but the radical syllable *fisc* being left in the nominative and accusative singular.

9. In each one of these subordinate declensions in *a*, in *i*, and in *u*, the nouns had different inflections, according as they were of the masculine, the feminine, or the neuter gender; so that, in the primitive Teutonic, there were probably nine different inflections belonging to the vowel-declension. But this system nowhere exists in its theoretical perfection, there being, for example, not a single neuter noun belonging to the declension in *i* in any one of the earliest Teutonic tongues; and there are numerous other indications that this system was losing everywhere its complex character. In particular in the Anglo-Saxon the declension in *a* had practically absorbed the declen-

sion in *u*, the special terminations of the latter having been abandoned, and those of the former having been substituted. There was, besides, but very little left of the declension in *i*, its words having largely gone over to the declension in *a*.

10. Again: of the primitive Indo-European consonant declensions, only the one in which the stem ended in *an* was retained in the Teutonic; of the others, but a few words remained. Accordingly the consonant declension is often called the declension in *n*. This became a favorite declension in the Teutonic tongues, and existed in full vigor in all the early ones. In them it had inflections somewhat distinct, according as the noun was masculine, feminine, or neuter, though these differences were by no means so marked as in the vowel declensions.

11. There is also a third declension, unlike either of the two just mentioned, which is found in pronouns and adjectives; but its origin and characteristics will be given further on (55). Besides these general features, common to the inflection of the Teutonic noun, adjective, and pronoun, there were certain peculiarities connected with the changes in vowels or consonants that need to be described here, for they have been perpetuated through all periods of English. They are not confined, however, to any particular parts of speech.

12. One of these is called **rhotacism**. This denotes the passing of the letter *s* into *r*,—a transition which was by no means uncommon in many of the

Indo-European tongues, and is familiarly exemplified in the Latin comparative of the adjective; as, for instance, *fort-ior*, *fort-ius*. Among the Teutonic tongues it was most widely employed in the Old Norse; but in Anglo-Saxon it was occasionally found, especially in the inflection of certain verbs. Modern English still preserves one trace of it in the imperfect of the substantive verb, which has for its singular *was*, but for its plural *were* instead of *wese*.

13. Far more conspicuous and important has been and is the part played by **vowel-variation**. This, as used in this work, will be employed to denote any change of vowel-sound, no matter from what cause arising, that takes place within the radical syllable. It will, therefore, denote alike the changes seen in inflection in such words as *man*, *men*, in *sell*, *sold*, in *thrive*, *throve*, and in the formation of new words from the same root, sometimes closely related in meaning, sometimes widely differing, as may be exemplified by *band* and *bond*, *grave* and *grove*, and numerous others. Two kinds of vowel-variation will be defined more specifically.

14. The first is **vowel-change** (German *ablaut*). This is especially seen in the change of the vowel of the radical syllable, by which the inflection of one class of verbs was and still is denoted. Familiar examples are *begin*, *began*; *thrive*, *throve*; *tear*, *tore*. This is so marked a characteristic of all the Teutonic tongues, including the English, that a short account of its origin is desirable.

15. In the primitive Indo-European the preterite was originally formed by simple reduplication. The verb was a mere root; and the idea of past time as distinguished from present was conveyed by the simple process of doubling the root. For instance, if the radical syllable *vid* meant *see*, *saw* would be expressed by *vidvid*. Joining these together, so as to make one word, and appending the personal endings, we have the primitive preterite tense. But in all the languages of our family, so many changes early occurred by the weakening or strengthening of vowels, that in none of them is the original simple reduplication preserved. In the primitive Teutonic, reduplication was, as in the other Indo-European tongues, the oldest method of forming the perfect; but Gothic, the oldest of all, has alone plainly preserved it, there being but faint traces of it left in the other languages of this sub-family. The Gothic has some forty verbs in which reduplication appears; but, even in that tongue, it had so far departed from the theoretical primitive type, that only the initial letter of the root was repeated with a constant vowel-sound denoted by *ai* (thus, present, *blanda*, 'blend,' preterite, *baibland*, 'blended;' present, *halda*, 'hold,' preterite, *haihald*, 'held;' present, *slêpa*, 'sleep,' preterite, *saizlêp*, 'slept'). But, in the other Teutonic dialects, the abbreviation had been carried still further. Not only was the final letter or letters of the reduplicational syllable dropped, but the initial letter of the radical syllable and, in some cases the vowel also of the radical syllable. The reduplicational and radical

syllables were thus united into one; and, in Anglo-Saxon verbs of this kind, the result of this contraction was a monosyllabic preterite with the diphthong *eô* running through both the singular and the plural. In some verbs there was a still further contraction to *ê*. Taking the three verbs above given, *blandan*, *healdan*, and *slǣpan*, we have, accordingly, in Anglo-Saxon, the presents, *blande*, *healde*, and *slǣpe*, the preterites, *bleônd*, *heôld*, and *slêp*.

16. This was not all. In many verbs an incidental effect of the reduplication had been to cause a change in the vowel of the radical syllable, either by weakening it or strengthening it. This change of vowel, originally a mere incident, became, in the course of events, systematized; and a natural result was, that it began to be looked upon as denoting of itself the preterite relation. When it came to be so regarded generally, the necessity of the reduplicated syllable to express past time disappeared, and the syllable itself was accordingly dropped. The vowel-change remaining constituted a method of conjugation which is one of the most striking peculiarities of the Teutonic branch of the Indo-European family. It is only these verbs which have dropped the reduplicated syllable that can be strictly said to have undergone vowel-change; but as, even in the verbs in which the reduplicational and radical syllables have been united into one, there has been a variation of vowel, resulting from contraction, the latter are also usually included in this class.

17. The second kind of vowel-variation is in this

work termed **vowel-modification** (German *um laut*). It is in Modern English exemplified in the inflection of a number of nouns, such as *man, men; foot, feet; mouse, mice.* It is not only widely different in its character from vowel-change, it is likewise widely different in its origin. It was not known to the Gothic; it is comparatively infrequent in Old High German; but in the other Teutonic tongues it is prevalent, especially in the Norse. In Anglo-Saxon it was principally caused by the influence of the vowel *i* of a following syllable.

18. Vowel-modification is the variation of sound produced in a radical syllable by the influence of a vowel in the syllable added, usually an added inflectional syllable. It is a noticeable fact, that, under certain circumstances, the vowel of an added syllable has often a tendency to modify the vowel of the syllable to which the addition is made. Before pronouncing the vowel of the first syllable, the thought of the vowel of the following one comes into the mind. Unconsciously there is an effort to bring about a similarity of sound; and the result is, that a sound is given to the vowel of the first syllable intermediate between the sound it had previously and the sound of the vowel in the syllable added. This is seen, for illustration, in the infinitive of some Anglo-Saxon verbs, in which the *a* of the added syllable has changed the *i* of the radical syllable into *e*. Thus, to the root *hilp*, if the termination *-an* of the infinitive be added, the infinitive itself becomes, not *hilpan*, but *helpan*, our 'help.'

19. But it was the influence of a following *i* that was most conspicuous in Anglo-Saxon in modifying the vowel of a preceding syllable; and the results of this influence are still to be seen in Modern English. It is not necessary to point out all the variations wrought by this vowel; only those which have been perpetuated will be mentioned here. The influence of the *i* of a following syllable changed *a* of the preceding to *e*, *ea* and *u* to *y*, *ó* to *é*, and *ú* to *ý*. One illustration will suffice. The Anglo-Saxon *fót*, 'foot,' has in the nominative and accusative plural *fét*, and also the same form in the dative singular. The change of *ó* to *é* in these cases of the noun is due to the influence of an *i*, which once belonged to them as an additional syllable, but which had come to be dropped. But, though the cause disappeared, the effect continued. Men retained in their speech the modification wrought by the vowel after the fact had been long forgotten that the vowel itself had ever been added.

20. This concludes all that is necessary to be said here of the features common to English with the other Teutonic tongues. Before entering, however, upon the later specific history of the inflection of our language, it is important to have clearly in mind the terminology here employed, and, though already given in full, it will bear repetition. The history of the language is in this work divided into four periods: the first, called the Anglo-Saxon, extending from the coming of the Teutonic tribes to the year 1150; the second, the Early English, extending from 1150 to 1350; the third, the

Middle English, from 1350 to 1550; and the fourth, the Modern English, from 1550 to the present time.[1] It is also to be remembered, that, during the Early and Middle English periods, the language both of literature and of daily life was divided into three great dialects, called, from their geographical position, the Northern, the Midland, and the Southern; and tha literary English is a descendant of the Midland, and the Scotch dialect belongs to the Northern.[2]

21. There is still another point which needs special consideration before entering upon the internal history of our tongue. This is the important fact, that, from the beginning of the twelfth century to the middle of the fourteenth century, — and the limits might be extended, — there was no such thing as standard English. Every thing, in consequence, was fluctuating and uncertain. No authority existed anywhere, as to the use of words and grammatical forms, to which all felt themselves obliged to submit. Every writer was, to a large extent, a law unto himself, and followed the special dialect of his own district in the lack of a generally recognized standard which could not be safely violated. But a tongue split up into dialects, and possessing nowhere binding rules for syntactical agreement and arrangement, nor authoritative methods of inflection, can hardly be said to have a history of any general orderly development of its own. The account which is given of it can never be much more than a classification of the differences of speech pre-

[1] See pp. 70, ff. [2] See pp. 91, ff.

vailing in different sections of the country, or a record of the peculiarities of grammar and vocabulary that characterize individual writers. This is especially true of our speech during the Early English period. In it, at that time, can be found the processes going on in full activity that destroyed the language of literature as seen in the tenth and eleventh centuries, and, likewise, the regenerating processes going on that were to develop the language of literature of the fourteenth and the following centuries. It is only between these clearly defined points that comparison can properly be made; and, even at the beginning of the latter period, the language of literature is rather in process of formation than actually formed. Still, after the break up of the classical Anglo-Saxon, the fourteenth century is the first period in which any thing can be called fixed, and in which, in consequence, any comparison can be made between the past and what is existing. In the conflicting usage of this time also, the Midland dialect is necessarily selected, to the exclusion of the other two, because from it Modern English strictly descended; and of the authors who wrote in the Midland, with more or less diversity of usage among themselves, the language of Chaucer is likewise necessarily selected as representative, not only because he was much the greatest of all, but more especially because his works had more influence on the future development of the speech than the works of all the others put together. The two points, therefore, selected in representing the forms prevalent in the early history of the language will be the tenth and eleventh centuries, — the period of the later classic West-Saxon dialect of Anglo-Saxon, — and the latter half of the fourteenth century, which witnessed the birth of Modern English literature in the strict sense of that phrase.

22. One further preliminary statement is necessary. The Anglo-Saxon alphabet consisted of twenty-four letters, which, with three exceptions, were borrowed from the Roman. Of these three one was merely a crossed *d*, and is represented by the forms Ð and ð: the other two were Runes. One of them is by German editors usually represented by *v*, by English editors by *w*. The other Runic letter was Þ þ. Both ð and þ are represented in Modern English by the combination *th*, which has two distinct sounds, — one seen in *thou*, *then*, *tithe*; the other, in *thin*, *three*, *death*. There is no distinct form for *j* from *i*; and though *k*, *q*, and *z* occur at times in the manuscripts, they did not represent sounds then, any more than now, which were not already represented by other letters, or by combinations of letters. The use of *k* for *c* became much more common after the Conquest. By the fifteenth century the employment of the two characters representing the two sounds now conveyed by *th* was entirely abandoned. Another character, ȝ, was in common use during the Early English period, and represents generally the Anglo-Saxon *g* at the beginning of a word; the Anglo-Saxon *h* at the middle or end of one; as Anglo-Saxon *geár*, Early English *ȝere*, Modern English *year*; Anglo-Saxon *niht*, Early Eng-

lish, *niȝt,* Modern English *night.* During the middle ages the letters of the Roman alphabet were changed into a variety of forms by the ingenuity of the monastic scribes; and the peculiar modification of this alphabet used in England is called black-letter. During the fifteenth and sixteenth centuries books were printed almost invariably in black-letter; but, in the first half of the seventeenth century, it was generally given up for the clearer, original Roman characters from which it had been taken.

CHAPTER II.

THE NOUN.

23. The following general statements may be made of the English noun during the Anglo-Saxon period. It had, —

1. Two declensions: the vowel, or strong, and the consonant, or weak. The former was limited mainly to stems which ended originally in *a* (8), although there were remains of those in *i* and *u*, especially the one in *i*. The latter was likewise mainly limited to the stems ending in *n* (10), fragments only of those in *r* and *nd*, and some other letters, remaining.

2. Two numbers: the singular and the plural.

3. Four cases: the nominative, the genitive, the dative, and the accusative. Many grammarians, following Grimm,[1] add a fifth, the instrumental, which they distinguish from the dative in the singular by marking for the former the final *e*, common to both, as long *ê*. There is no difference at all in the plural.

4. Three genders: the masculine, the feminine,

[1] Geschichte der Deutschen Sprache, 936. Compare sect. 55.

and the neuter. As will be seen by the examples, it is grammatical, not natural gender.

24. The following paradigms of the masculine noun *stân*, 'stone,' of the feminine *denu*, 'valley,' and the neuters *hors*, 'horse,' and *scip*, 'ship,' will exhibit the various inflections of the noun of the vowel-declension as commonly seen in the Anglo-Saxon They all belong to the declension in *a*; and the stems are *stâna*, *dena*, *horsa*, and *scipa*; but this vowel has in the various cases often been dropped altogether, or been weakened, or changed into other vowels.

I. Vowel Declension.

SINGULAR.

	Masculine.	Feminine.	Neuter.	
Nom.	stân,	denu,	hors,	scip.
Gen.	stânes,	dene,	horses,	scipes.
Dat.	stâne,	dene,	horse,	scipe.
Acc.	stân.	dene.	hors.	scip.

PLURAL.

	Masculine.	Feminine.	Neuter.	
Nom.	stânas,	dena,	hors,	scipu.
Gen.	stâna,	{ dena, denena,	horsa,	scipa.
Dat.	stânum,	denum,	horsum,	scipum.
Acc.	stânas.	dena.	hors.	scipu.

25. Nouns originally belonging to the other two vowel declensions, that is, those whose stems ended in *i* or *u*, had, even in the Anglo-Saxon, gone over

wholly or partially to the *a* declension. There were no small number of feminines, however, which belonged still to the *i* declension; but their forms had become largely confused with those of the prevailing declension in *a*. As none of them had any influence upon the later development of the inflection, their consideration is omitted here altogether.

26. The consonant, or, more specifically, the consonant declension in *n*, will be exemplified by paradigms of the masculine noun *oxa*, 'ox,' of the feminine, *tunge*, 'tongue,' and of the neuter, *eáre*, 'ear.' The stems are *oxan*, *tungan*, and *eáran*. But not only have the original case-endings usually disappeared; but, in some instances, the *n* also has been dropped, or the *a* weakened into *e*.

II. Consonant Declension.

SINGULAR.

	Masculine.	Feminine.	Neuter.
Nom.	oxa,	tunge,	eáre.
Gen.	oxan,	tungan,	eáran.
Dat.	oxan,	tungan,	eáran.
Acc.	oxan.	tungan.	eáre.

PLURAL.

	Masculine.	Feminine.	Neuter.
Nom.	oxan,	tungan,	eáran.
Gen.	oxena,	tungena,	eárena.
Dat.	oxum,	tungum,	eárum.
Acc.	oxan.	tungan.	eáran.

27. According to some one of the paradigms found

in sects. 24 and 26, the immense majority of all nouns were declined during the Anglo-Saxon period. There are a few exceptions, which will be referred to later. As between the vowel and the consonant declensions, there was not much difference in the number of substantives belonging to each in the Anglo-Saxon; and the foreign words that came in were inflected according to either. When ending in a consonant, these were usually inflected according to the vowel declension, and, when in a vowel, according to the consonant. This state of things did not perpetuate itself. It is evident, on even a superficial examination, that, of the six different inflections given above, Modern English has retained only that found in the masculine noun of the vowel declension, — the one represented by *stân*.

28. Still, for a century after the Norman conquest, these different inflections were kept up with a fair degree of correctness. The changes that took place, however, such as they were, involved, as an inevitable consequence, the confusion of the declensions. One of these was the general weakening into *e* of the vowels *a*, *o*, and *u* of the endings. This manifested itself, indeed, long before the Conquest; but the influence of the literary speech was sufficient to keep it under restraint. As soon as that was removed, this general weakening of the vowels made rapid headway. In consequence of it, *stânas*, for illustration, became *stanes*, *denu* and *dena* became *dene*, *scipu* became *scipe*, and *oxan*, *tungan*, and *eáran* became *oxen*,

tungen, and *earen*. So far then, as difference of inflection was denoted by difference of vowel in the endings, all distinction between number, case, and declension, had disappeared before the end of the twelfth century by the general use of *e* for the vowels previously employed.

29. This was not enough of itself, however, to overthrow the inflectional system of the noun: another change came in to break down the broad distinction previously prevailing between the vowel and the consonant declensions. After the middle of the twelfth century, there was a constant tendency toward their assimilation, from the arbitrary gains and losses that went on in the use of a single letter. This was *n*, which was of special importance from its terminating a large number of cases in the consonant declension. From these, however, it came, in the twelfth century, to be frequently dropped. This dropping of the final *n* had likewise manifested itself, as early as the ninth century, in the West-Saxon dialect, though then more especially in the infinitive and subjunctive of the verb, and in the definite adjective; but here, again, as in the case of the weakening of the vowels *a*, *o*, and *u* to *e*, the literary language had arrested the movement. Within a century after the Conquest, however, the process had again begun. Thus the genitive, dative, and accusative singular of *oxan*, *tungan*, and *eáran*, of the consonant declension, after passing through the intermediate stages, *oxen*, *tungen*, and *earen*, became frequently with the *n* dropped, *oxe*, *tunge*, and *eare*.

This brought them at once into complete similarity with many nouns of the vowel declension; but here, again, another element entered, to add to the confusion. It was not uncommon, in the uncertainty that sprang up, for an *n* to be added to the dative and accusative singular of nouns belonging to the vowel declension. Thus Anglo-Saxon *cyng*, 'king,' is a masculine noun inflected in the same manner as *stán*. Its dative and accusative singular should strictly have been, accordingly, in late twelfth-century English, *kinge* and *king* respectively. As a matter of fact, they both sometimes appeared as *kingen*. So confused, indeed, did usage become in the proper employment of these two declensions, especially in the plural number, that it is by no means infrequent to find the same word, in the pages of the same author, sometimes with the plural *es* of the masculine nouns of the vowel declension, or with the plural *en* of the consonant. In the south of England in particular, it almost seems as if the two terminations could be used indiscriminately; and double endings of the plural were certainly common there till the Middle English period.

30. Nor, indeed, was this all. A third plural form came into use, ending in *e*. It was derived from the weakened *a* or *u* of the feminine and neuter nouns of the vowel declension, or from the dropping of the *n* of the consonant declension. The same author, therefore, formed, at times, his plural with three different endings. Thus the two texts of the "Brut" of Layamon furnish, as plurals for the Anglo-Saxon mascu-

line noun *stán*, the forms *stanes*, *stanen*, and *stanè*, for plurals of the neuter noun *hors*, the forms *horses*, *horsen*, and *horsè*. Such a system as this, which was little more than the product of ignorance and confusion, had in itself no element of perpetuity. The process of simplifying inflection merely as a measure of relief went on rapidly, in consequence, though much more so in the North than in the South; and the simplification was usually attained by discarding inflection entirely. When, in the latter half of the fourteenth century, a new language of literature appeared, the inflection of the noun had been reduced to nearly its present state; and whatever of it had been preserved conformed to that of the Anglo-Saxon masculine noun of the vowel declension, represented in the paradigm of *stán*. As this inflection became the one finally established, its history requires a more detailed examination of the cases belonging to it and of the gradual adoption of the endings characteristic of them by nouns originally inflected differently.

31. As regards the singular, the fact, that, in this number, masculines and neuters of the vowel declension had precisely the same inflection, — as can be seen by comparing *stán* and *hors*, — had, doubtless, much to do with the universal adoption of the endings belonging to them; for these two declensions united embraced a very large proportion of the nouns of the language. In these the nominative, dative, and accusative came, in the time of Chaucer, to have the same form. The process generally took place after this

manner, in the case of words ending in a consonant. The dative and accusative singular early began to lose, and by the fourteenth century had practically lost, all distinction of form in the following two ways: either the dative sometimes dropped a final *e* to which it was entitled; or, secondly, and far more commonly, the accusative assumed a final *e* to which it was not entitled. Thus the dative and accusative came to have the same form, sometimes ending, sometimes not ending, in a final *e*. The same word, indeed, was not only treated in this respect differently by different authors, but differently at different places in the same manuscript. Thus, for illustration, the dative and accusative of the Anglo-Saxon *scip* would, in Early English, be represented in both cases, sometimes by *ship*, and sometimes by *shipe*.

32. But the assimilation did not stop at this point. In Anglo-Saxon the form for the nominative and accusative was alike in the case of the masculine and neuter nouns of the vowel declension, and it was natural that this should continue. When, therefore, the accusative assumed an *e* which did not belong to it, the inevitable result was, that this *e* should be added likewise to the nominative. This would have been pretty certain to happen if no other influences than those already mentioned had been brought to bear; but, as a matter of fact, very powerful ones from other quarters aided to hasten the accomplishment of this result. This was the fact that the nouns belonging to all the other declensions, which had begun to conform

to the inflection of the masculine noun, had, by the weakening of the final vowel and the dropping of the final *n*, brought about the assimilation of the nominative, dative, and accusative. An examination of the changes through which *denu* and *oxa* went will make this perfectly clear. *Denu* had in Anglo-Saxon its dative and accusative *dene:* the weakening of the final *u* to *e* made its nominative of precisely the same form, *dene*. So *oxa*, which in Early English became *oxe*, had originally for dative and accusative *oxan*, which first became *oxen*, and then *oxe*. The result was, that, by the beginning of the Middle English period, the nominative, dative, and accusative of all nouns, had become the same in form. Occasional instances do occur of a regular dative form distinct from that of the nominative and accusative; but they were merely scattered survivals of a distinction that was generally disregarded.

33. The genitive singular, however, of the masculine and neuter nouns, remained constant to the ending *es*. More than this, the termination began, from the commencement of the Early English period, to encroach upon the genitives of the other declensions. These were *e* of the feminine nouns belonging to the vowel inflection, and *an* of all the nouns of the consonant inflection, which *an* also early became *e* by the dropping of the *n*, and the weakening of the *a*. For a long time genitives in *e* from these two sources continued to be used; and they are still found as late as the literature of the latter half of the fourteenth cen-

tury. But even then they were far from common; and, in the following century, *e* as a genitive ending died out entirely, and *es* was everywhere employed for all nouns, no matter what their origin.

34. In the plural the process of simplification was even more thorough. It is especially to be noticed, that, in this number, the one termination which was common to all nouns of whatever declension was the very first to give way. This was the *um* of the dative, which has left an occasional relic of itself in Modern English in the *om* of a few adverbs derived from nouns, such as *whilom*. It might naturally be expected that this particular ending, from the very universality of its use, would be the last to be given up; yet its early abandonment is susceptible of an easy explanation. Even in the Anglo-Saxon monuments of the ninth century this ending *um* frequently appeared as *on;* and the same statement is true of the centuries that followed. Within the hundred years after the Conquest, this *on*, from *um*, not only was much more common than its original, but its vowel underwent the weakening that overtook all the vowels of the endings, and the termination became *en*. This, in the case of nouns of the consonant declension, gave it the same forms as the nominative and accusative plural, the *an* of whose terminations had been weakened into *en* also. In the confusion that soon sprang up in the use of the two leading declensions by the dropping or appending of the final *n*, all distinctive character was taken away from this ending as

specially belonging to the dative plural; and it adopted the form universally that was found in the nominative and accusative, whether it was *es* of the vowel declension or the *en* of the consonant.

35. The genitive plural held out longer as a distinct termination. At least one form of it, *ene* or *en*, lasted down to the end of the fourteenth century, though it cannot be called at any time common. This *en*(*e*) is derived from the regular Anglo-Saxon genitive plural of all the nouns of the consonant declension, though it was sometimes seen in the feminine nouns of the vowel. But, when used in the Early English period, it was not limited to either of these; thus, in the phrase *Christe kingene kynge*,[1] 'Christ, King of kings,' the word *king*, which is etymologically a masculine noun of the Anglo-Saxon vowel declension, receives this termination. But from the very outset, after the breaking up of the inflections of the original tongue, the form of the genitive plural showed a tendency to assimilate itself to those of the nominative and accusative; and, by the beginning of the Middle English period, this had become the almost universally accepted rule.

36. The endings of those two cases, the nominative and accusative plural, as has already been stated, were usually either *es*, from the *as* of the masculine vowel declension, or *en*, from the *an* of the consonant declension. Had these been kept sharply distinguished, and confined to the nouns to which they properly belonged, they would, doubtless, have both lasted to our time.

[1] Langland's Piers Plowman. Text B, passus 17, 105 (about 1377).

but, in the absence of any standard of authority, they were confused with one another, and often applied at different times to the same noun, at the mere fancy of the writer. This is particularly true of the Southern dialect. Language, however, is too economical in the use of its material to permit long the employment of such double forms on any extensive scale. One of them had to disappear, and in our tongue it was the plural in *en*. In this simplification the Northern dialect, as usual, led the way; and one of the great points of contrast between it and the speech of the South was in the scarcity of the forms in *en*, in the one, as compared with their frequency in the other. Indeed, to this form the Southern dialect clung with so much tenacity, that there is little question that a large number of nouns with this ending would have been now in constant use, if that dialect had been the parent of Modern English, instead of the Midland. Not only did the speech of the South give to the same noun two plurals, — one in *es*, and the other in *en;* but it was as apt to give the termination *en* to Anglo-Saxon nouns of the vowel declension as to those of the consonant.

37. The Midland dialect, as usual, followed a path between the two extremes, but in this respect was influenced much more by the example of the North in discarding the termination in *en*. By the latter half of the fourteenth century, the ending *es* had become established as the regular form.[1] In Chaucer, the

[1] There were orthographic variations of this, due to difference of pronunciation, such as *is*, *ys*, *us*; but they do not need to be considered here.

representative author of the literary speech, we find the plural regularly terminating in *s;* and the only relics of the original plurals in *an* to be found in his writings are *asschen*, 'ashes;' *assen*, 'asses;' *been*, 'bees;' *eyen*, 'eyes;' *fleen*, 'fleas;' *flon*, 'arrows;' *hosen*, 'hose;' *oxen*; and *ton*, 'toes;' and of these the modern plurals in *s* are also to be found employed by him in the case of *ashes*, *bees*, and *toes*. To this list may be added *schoon*, 'shoes,' which in Anglo-Saxon, however, belonged generally to the masculine vowel declension, though it had occasionally plural forms of the consonant. This use of *s* as the regular termination of the plural, then firmly established, was never after subjected to change. It ought to be added, that the third plural in *e*, already described (30), had died out entirely; at least, in the confused use of final *e*, which had now become current, it was no longer recognizable as distinct from the neuter forms which are now to be described.

38. In examining the paradigms of the neuter monosyllabic nouns of the vowel declension (24) one fact becomes apparent: this is, that such of these nouns as had the radical vowel long by nature, or by position before two consonants, did not assume *u* in the nominative and accusative plural. Accordingly, these cases had the same form as the corresponding cases of the singular, as can be easily seen in the inflection of *hors*. Most of these nouns came gradually, during the Early English period, to conform to the declension of the masculine nouns, and assumed the termination

es in the plural. Occasionally some of them assumed *e*, the weakened form of the *u* final of the plural of neuter nouns of the same declension, whose vowel was short; but this was not often the case. In Chaucer's time the vast majority had accepted the plural in *s*, though some, such as *thing*, and *hors*, and *folk*, and *year*, were still in a state of transition, exhibiting double forms for the plural, — one ending in *s*, the other precisely resembling the singular. Others, again, held on to the ancient inflection, and apparently suffered no change; for, as the nominative singular was apt, in such instances, to have assumed a final *e*, it is, of course, impossible to say whether *e*, when it occurs in the plural, is to be considered, in any particular instance, as a plural termination, or a mere inorganic addition to the word.

39. Comparing, therefore, the literary language at the beginning of the Middle English period with that prevalent during the Anglo-Saxon period, it will be observed, that, in the centuries which intervened, the four cases of the noun, which in the singular had to a greater or less extent been distinguished by differences of form, had now been reduced to two. Again: in the Anglo-Saxon plural, the nominative and accusative had never had any distinction of form; but there had been special forms for the genitive and dative. These had now all been reduced to one, and that one was, with a very few exceptions, the form ending in *s*. Accordingly, the paradigm of the Anglo-Saxon *stán*,

which had now become the general representative of the noun inflection, was the following: —

	Singular.		Plural.
Nom., Dat., and Acc.	ston *or* stone,	*All Cases.*	stonès.
Genitive.	stonès.		

It is evident at a glance that this is practically the Modern English declension. The few slight changes that have since occurred are nothing, as will be seen, but a natural development of the tendency that had already brought the inflection of the noun to this point. The later history of the inflection will clearly show that the main differences between our declension to-day and that of the fourteenth century are all due to a more hurried pronunciation, and that other differences are apparent and not real, inasmuch as they are differences in the representation of the sounds, and not in the sounds themselves.

40. At the beginning of the Middle English period, nouns which had originally ended in a vowel almost invariably ended in *e;* and this *e*, we have seen, was frequently assumed by nouns which originally ended in a consonant, and were, therefore, not strictly entitled to it. But, between the fourteenth and sixteenth centuries, this final *e*, whether etymologically belonging to the word or not, disappeared from pronunciation. In the lawless and capricious spelling of the language that sprang up after the invention of printing, the retention of this final *e* in the orthography came to be a mere matter of accident. The words given in the

Anglo-Saxon paradigms are sufficient to serve as examples. Of the modern representatives of these, *stone* and *horse* now terminate in an *e*, to which they are not strictly entitled; *tongue* has retained, while *den* and *ear* have dropped, the *e* to which they are entitled; and *ox* or *oxe* in modern orthography sometimes receives it, and sometimes not. Again: *ship*, which in Early English frequently appeared as *shipe*, *schipe*, has gone back, as regards the ending, to its original form.

41. As the dative and accusative have come to be precisely alike in form in both nouns and pronouns, the name of "objective" is generally given by modern grammarians to the case expressing the relations of direct and indirect object, formerly expressed by the two. The indirect relation is, to be sure, usually indicated by a preposition with the noun; but it is not so invariably. In such a sentence as, 'He gave the boy a book,' *boy* denotes the original dative of the indirect, and *book* the original accusative of the direct object.

42. In the former half of the Middle English period the *es* of the genitive singular and of the plural commonly appeared as a distinct syllable, as in *stonès* in the example given above. This was sometimes not the case, however; and *s* itself is often found added in Chaucer, instead of *es*, to polysyllabic words, those, in particular, that ended in a liquid, as, for illustration, *naciouns*. But, by the beginning of the Modern English period, the final *es* had ceased to be pronounced

as a separate syllable, save in those cases where the nature of the word still requires it to be sounded, as in *foxes*, *horses*. The dropping of the unpronounced *e* was a result that usually followed. In the seventeenth century the practice of distinguishing the genitive singular from the plural came into vogue by placing an apostrophe before the final *s* of the former; but it was not till the eighteenth century that this became fully established. The still further distinction was then made of placing an apostrophe after the *s* of the genitive plural; so that, for example, the genitive singular *boy's*, and the genitive plural *boys'*, though spelled and pronounced alike, are in reading easily recognized as different. The genitive case has likewise come to be so limited in usage as to express ordinarily the relation of possession, and, in consequence, most grammarians give it the title of "possessive." This is, however, an unfortunate name; for, while this is the relation it expresses principally, it is by no means the one it expresses exclusively.

The plural form of nearly all nouns had come, in the fourteenth century, to be precisely the same as that of the genitive singular; and the later history of the one differs in no respect whatever from the later history of the other. When the *e* of the genitive ending was dropped, it was dropped in the endings of the plural: when it was retained in the former, it was also retained in the latter. The account just given of the one, therefore, involves that of the other.

43. This completes the history of what may be

called the regular inflection of the noun. It now remains to consider the comparatively few words, which, in spite of the pressure always at work to produce uniformity, have steadily resisted the tendency to go over to the declension which in the fourteenth century had become the standard one. These belong to four classes; and in all of them it is the method alone of forming the plural that distinguishes their inflection from the rest.

44. The first of these embraces the neuter monosyllabic nouns already spoken of (38) as exhibiting no difference of form between the nominative and accusative singular and plural. While most of these had gone over to the ordinary inflection in *s*, a few held out, and to this day have remained faithful to the original inflection. These are *deer* (A. S. *deór*), *sheep* (A. S. *sceáp*), *swine* (A. S. *swín*); and to these may, perhaps, be added *neat* (A. S. *neát*), though this is usually a collective noun. *Thing*, during the Middle English period, conformed to the regular declension, as did several others, though they often showed a disposition to exhibit double forms for the plural, — one with, and one without, *s*. But the tendency has always been toward the exclusive adoption of the regular inflection by these words. Yet, even in the Early English period, there had come into the language a number of words from Romance sources, which followed in their declension the native words that underwent no change in the plural; and, though most of these have now become regular, there are still several, both from foreign and

from native sources, that continue to show two forms for the plural. They usually denote number, measure, weight, or length of time; and with some of them, such as *brace*, and *sail* in the sense of 'vessel,' as 'fifty sail,' the regular form in *s* is unusual. In general, however, it may be said that the modern language shows an increasing preference for the plural in *s*. But there continue to be many words, such as *pair* and *pairs*, *score* and *scores*, *couple* and *couples*, in which the frequency of the form either with or without *s* varies with individual usage.

45. The second class includes a few nouns, which, in the English of the Anglo-Saxon period, invariably underwent vowel-modification (17) in the nominative and accusative plural, and have in some cases transmitted these modified forms to the English of our day. This was originally due, as has been explained, to the influence of a following vowel; and, while the vowel once following has been dropped, the vowel-modification wrought by it remains. In the instances about to be cited, it was an *i* that has disappeared, which brought about the variation of *ô* to *ê*, of *û* to *ŷ*, of *u* to *y*, and of *a* to *e*. In the Anglo-Saxon their variations were limited to the words of the following list, in which the nominative singular and plural are placed side by side: —

Singular.		Plural.	Singular.		Plural.
bôc,	*book*,	bêc.	gôs,	*goose*,	gês.
brôc,	*breeches*,	brêc.	tôð,	*tooth*,	têð.
fôt,	*foot*,	fêt.	cû,	*cow*,	cŷ.

Singular		Plural.	Singular.		Plural.
lûs,	*louse*,	lŷs.	burh,	*borough*,	byrh.
mûs,	*mouse*,	mŷs.	turf,	*turf*,	tyrf.
man,	*man*,	men.			

That this modification of the vowel was not in itself a sign of the plural is at once made clear by the fact, that, in Anglo-Saxon, the dative singular had in these words precisely the same form as the nominative plural.

46. Of these nouns, *book*, *borough*, and *turf* had gone over, by the end of the fourteenth century, to the regular inflection of the plural in *s*. In the Modern English *breeches*, however, the original vowel *ô* of the singular has been abandoned; and along with the exclusive use of the word in the plural, with its regular plural sign, the modified vowel *ê* of the original plural has been retained. Accordingly, it is from *brêc*, and not from *brôc*, that the present word has been directly derived. The transition took place during the Early English period. The etymological plural of *cû* was retained in the speech of the North, and is still found in the *kye* of the Scotch dialect. But another plural form, *kine*, had come in before the end of the fourteenth century, and became established in the language of literature. Its origin will be discussed in the remarks upon the third class (48). This, in turn, though it has never died out, was obliged, during the Modern English period, to give way in common use to the regular form *cows*. The remaining six, *foot*, *goose*, *tooth*, *louse*, *mouse*, and *man*, have remained un-

changed, in respect to vowel-modification, during all the periods in the history of the language, though sporadic instances occur, in which the regular ending *s* appears, particularly in the case of *foot*, which has shown at times, especially in the Early English period, a plural in *s*, with the vowel unmodified.

47. In the third class are embraced the few nouns which still exhibit the ending in *n*, once common to half the substantives of the language. It has already been stated, that, in the long conflict between the vowel and the consonant declensions, the former had triumphed; and of the ten words belonging to the latter, that are used by Chaucer (37), three are likewise to be found with plurals in *s*, clearly showing that the transition to the regular form was going on. It continued to go on with unabated vigor after his death; and, by the beginning of the Modern English period, the only genuine historical plural in *n* that was universally used in prose and poetry was *oxen*, for, while *eyen* and *shoon* continued to be employed, they were looked upon, then as now, merely as poetic forms. Of the vast number of nouns originally belonging to the consonant declension, *ox* is the solitary survival in Modern English, and even that, in the singular number, conforms to the vowel declension. It is to be added that *hosen*, which Chaucer used, dropped its *n*, but did not add an *s*.

48. At the same time, during this long conflict, the consonant declension did not fail to add some words to its numbers. In fact, in the Southern dialects, many

nouns, as we have seen, belonging to the vowel declension, formed their plural in *n*. Still the literary language in the latter half of the fourteenth century almost entirely discarded this termination; though, as might be expected, there is a slight difference of usage in the writings of different authors. Taking Chaucer as the representative of this period, the following statement can be made in regard to these forms. There are six words, as employed by him, which still continue to show in the plural a final *n* derived from the plural of the consonant declension. Three of them — *brother*, *sister*, and *daughter* — belong strictly to neither of the two leading Anglo-Saxon declensions, but to a group called *r*-stems, of which there were a few survivals in the Teutonic tongues. The other three, it will be noticed, exhibit irregularities. The Anglo-Saxon form, the Early English intermediate forms, and the Middle English form of the plural, are here given side by side; though there are numerous orthographic variations of the two latter, which will not be noticed here.

Anglo-Saxon.	Early English.	Middle English.
brôðru,	brothre, brethre,	bretheren.
dôhtru,	dohtere,	doughtren.
sweostru,	sustre,	sustren.
cildru,	childre,	children.
fâ, *hostile*,	fo,	fon.
cŷ,	kye,	kyn.

Of these words, *children* is the only one that has clung to the plural in *n* exclusively. *Kine*, while still retained, has given way, in common use, to the regular form, *cows;* and in the sixteenth century *brothers* was developed alongside of *brethren*, and in the seventeenth century became the form generally employed. The language still retains the two plurals, but makes a slight distinction, ordinarily, in their meaning. The *e* of *brethren* is perhaps an intrusion from the dative singular, in which the vowel *ó* was modified into *é*, just as *fót* became, in that case, *fét*. The other words, *daughter*, *sister*, and likewise *foe*, which was originally an adjective, gave up the *n* before the beginning of the Modern English period, and assumed *s* in its place.

49. There now remains the fourth class to be considered, — that of the foreign nouns that have been imperfectly Anglicized, and still retain, in consequence, the plural they had in the tongue from which they were taken. Naturally the endings are very diverse. Most of these words have been introduced during the Modern English period; many of them are terms connected with the natural or physical sciences. A large number of them are therefore technical in their character; and of all of them, it is true, that, at first, they are only employed by the educated. So long as their use was limited to this class, they underwent no change. The original plural, no matter what might be its ending, was rigidly retained. But no sooner did they cease to be purely technical than they were at

once affected by the tendency of the language to strive after uniformity. With many of them, in consequence, the English plural in *s* either superseded the foreign plural altogether, or became established alongside of it. As illustration of the former, *omens* has driven out the original plural *omina*, once in use, and *dogmas* has almost entirely taken the place of *dogmata;* while, on the other hand, *formulae* and *formulas* may be said to be equally common, though, in technical works, the former is perhaps preferred. There is, indeed, little question that all these words that come to be generally employed would go over to the regular form, and be fully Anglicized, were it not for the influence of the literary language, which in many cases makes the foreign plural perfectly familiar to all. The plural *genera*, from *genus*, for example, is so firmly established that *genuses*, from present appearances, can have no hope of ever being adopted. The same statement is also true of the Latin nouns in *is* whose plural ends in *es*, such as *ellipsis*, *ellipses*, *hypothesis*, *hypotheses*, *oasis*, *oases*, and others; though here the perpetuation of the original form has been materially aided by the difficulty of pronouncing what would be the Anglicized form.

50. It is natural, however, that, in many of these nouns, double forms should be produced, and indeed continue to increase as the words pass more and more from technical into common usage. The uneducated, or rather those not specially educated, cannot be expected to know the foreign plurals; and the substi-

tution of the English plural sign *s* gets rid, by an easy process, of all doubts and difficulties. Consequently we have *apparatus* and *apparatuses*, *radii* and *radiuses*, *phenomena* and *phenomenons*, *vortices* and *vortexes*, *virtuosi* and *virtuosos*, and numerous other double forms. In some cases there is a difference of meaning between these two plurals, as, for instance, between *genii* and *geniuses*, *indices* and *indexes*. In this respect the word *stamen* reverses the usual order of things; for while, in science, the Anglicized plural *stamens* is the form employed, it is the foreign plural *stamina* that is heard in the language of common life. But this is doubtless due to the fact that men have largely forgotten that the latter form has any singular connected with it.

51. For it is clear that the use of foreign plurals is certain, in some cases, to result in confusion. The great majority of men who speak English cannot be expected to be familiar with any speech but their own; and when endings are introduced of whose force they are ignorant, it is impossible that they should in every instance use them with exact propriety. Such terminations are in the nature of exceptions to a general rule, and the exceptions are but few which men will take the trouble to learn. It is too much to ask of those whose acquaintance with language is limited only to their own, or even to the modern tongues, to feel that *stamina* and *effluvia* and *errata* are real plurals: the fact, if known to them at all, must be learned in each particular case. Under such circumstances, mistakes in usage

are almost sure to arise. Perhaps no more striking illustration of this can be found than in the history of the two words *cherub* and *seraph*. Their respective plurals in the Hebrew, from which they were borrowed, were *cherubim* and *seraphim;* and these forms naturally were the ones first used for that number. But the language also developed the regular English form, *cherubs* and *seraphs*, giving the words, as in several other instances, two plurals. At this point, confusion came in. *Cherubim* and *seraphim* were not felt to be plurals, and the result was, that they were treated as singulars; and, being looked upon as singulars, they themselves, though really plurals, received the English plural sign *s* in addition. Consequently *cherubims* and *seraphims* came into wide use; and this corruption was thoroughly established in the language before the Middle English period. How firmly fixed it had become is evident from the fact that these are the forms generally, if not invariably, employed by the translators of the English Bible, though they were, of course, acquainted with the Hebrew.

52. Of these four classes of nouns, the plural of which varies from the regular plural, this only remains to be said: whenever the genitive is employed, they assume an *s*, after the manner of the ordinary inflection. This, in a few instances, renders the genitive plural different from the nominative plural. In the case of the nouns which undergo vowel-modification, that variation causes necessarily the genitive plural to differ in form from the genitive singular. These com-

plete all the exceptions to the regular inflection that Modern English presents outside of purely euphonic ones, such as the dropping of the sound of *s*, and sometimes of its sign, in the genitive of words which themselves terminate in the sound of *s*, as may be illustrated by such phrases as "for conscience' sake," and the like.

CHAPTER III.

THE ADJECTIVE.

53. The English noun, in the course of its history, has been largely stripped of its inflections; but its losses bear little proportion to those of the adjective. To a certain extent, the same influences operated upon both. Together they underwent the changes that were brought about by the weakening of the vowels *a*, *o*, and *u* to *e*, and the dropping of the final *n*; and the results which followed in the one case took place likewise in the other, and do not need to be repeated. But the losses of the adjective at even an early period were far more extensive than those of the noun, as the confusion of the declensions was also much greater. With the former part of speech, inflection has now entirely disappeared. One unchanged form has taken the place of the manifold ones originally used to express, not merely the distinction of gender, number, and case, but also of declension.

54. During the Anglo-Saxon period the adjective

was distinguished by the possession of the following characteristics: —

1. Two declensions.

2. Forms differing, to a great extent, for the three genders, — the masculine, the feminine, and the neuter.

3. Two numbers, the singular and the plural, with marked differences of forms for each.

4. Four cases, — the nominative, genitive, dative, and accusative. To these most grammarians add a fifth, the instrumental, which, in the paradigms found below, is put down as a secondary form of the dative, corresponding to the dative of the masculine and neuter nouns of the vowel declension of the noun. Those who regard these forms as belonging to the instrumental make the final *e* long *ē*, as in the similar case of the noun (23).

Rich as the adjective evidently was in inflection during the Anglo-Saxon period, it is evident that even then it had suffered losses. The vowels *a*, *i*, and *u*, may all have been added to the stem of the adjective as to that of the noun (8) in the primitive Teutonic; but even in the earliest of the Teutonic languages, the Gothic, the stems in *i* had disappeared, if they ever existed. Stems in *u* were still to be found in that tongue; but in the Anglo-Saxon they had given way entirely to stems in *a*, which had become universal.

55. The Teutonic adjective differs from the adjective of most of the other languages belonging to the

Indo-European family in two respects. The first is, that every adjective is declined in two different ways; and the second is, that one of these declensions is distinct from that of the noun. This latter declension is, according to a view widely adopted, based upon the addition to the adjective stem of a demonstrative pronoun which has fully united with it. This pronoun does not exist in any of the Teutonic tongues, save as it is thought to be detected in the terminations of the adjective, but is deemed to be the Sanskrit relative *yas*, *yâ*, *yad*, which, in the primitive Teutonic, had assumed the force of a demonstrative, and been appended to the adjective (with whose form it finally melted), instead of standing before it. One name of the declension in which this is seen is, therefore, the "pronominal."

56. The other declension is also called sometimes the "nominal" or noun declension, because its forms correspond with those found in the corresponding masculine, feminine, and neuter nouns of the consonant declension in *n* of the noun. Besides these, the terms "strong" and "weak" are applied to the two inflections; but there are, in addition, other names, derived from the use of the adjective, which will be the ones employed here. The adjective was usually declined according to the consonant or weak declension, when the substantive which it qualified was made definite, by connecting with the qualifying adjective the definite article, or a demonstrative or possessive pronoun; but, when the adjective was simply used

alone, the substantive was, as a consequence, indefinite, and the adjective was inflected, in such cases, according to the pronominal or strong declension. Hence have arisen the terms "definite" and "indefinite" as applied to the inflection of the adjective. This peculiar, and it must be said useless, characteristic of the primitive Teutonic, has wholly disappeared in English, but still survives in Modern German. The following paradigms of the adjective *blind*, 'blind,' inflected both ways, will show the forms of the language as they are generally found in the writings of the tenth and eleventh centuries. But during the Anglo-Saxon period itself there was a good deal of sloughing off of the terminations of the adjective in the indefinite declension, thereby reducing them to the same form. Thus the nominative and accusative plural would be ordinarily in the language of the eighth century, *blinde*, *blinda*, *blindu*, for the masculine, feminine, and neuter respectively, instead of the one form here given, *blinde;* and survivals of the earlier usage constantly make their appearance in the later Anglo-Saxon.

57. Indefinite (Pronominal or Strong) Declension.

	SINGULAR.			PLURAL.
	Masculine.	Feminine.	Neuter.	All Genders.
Nom.	blind,	blind,	blind,	blinde,
Gen.	blindes,	blindre,	blindes,	blindra,
Dat.	blindum, blinde,	blindre,	blindum, blinde,	blindum,
Acc.	blindne.	blinde.	blind.	blinde.

58. **Definite (Nominal or Weak) Declension.**

	SINGULAR.			PLURAL.
	Masculine.	Feminine.	Neuter.	All Genders
Nom.	blinda,	blinde,	blinde,	blindan,
Gen.	blindan,	blindan,	blindan,	blindena
Dat.	blindan,	blindan,	blindan,	blindum
Acc.	blindan.	blindan.	blinde.	blindan.

59. As an illustration of the use of these declensions, 'a blind man' would be, in Anglo-Saxon, *blind man;* 'of a blind man' would be *blindes mannes;* whereas, making the substantive definite by connecting it with the demonstrative pronoun, 'that blind man' would be *se blinda man;* and 'of that blind man' would be *þæs blindan mannes.*

60. A glance at these paradigms is sufficient to show how rich in inflection the English adjective was in the Anglo-Saxon of the tenth and eleventh centuries, though even then it had lost many of the endings which two centuries before had belonged to it. Down to the twelfth century this fulness of inflection was retained; but the same confusion that overtook the noun during the centuries following the Conquest befell the adjective also. The two declensions of the adjective are still retained to this day, as has been said, in Modern High German. In English this variation of inflection was one of the first things to go. By the end of the second century after the Conquest the distinction between the definite and the indefinite adjective had not only everywhere broken down, in

some places it had disappeared entirely; but the confusion that sprang up in consequence did not result in giving exclusive ascendency to any one particular inflection, as in the case of the noun: it had rather the effect of causing the terminations to be abandoned altogether. In a general way, it may be said, that, in the fourteenth century, the plural of monosyllabic adjectives ended in *e*, and was distinguished from the singular by that termination, and that this was the most that then remained of the once extensive inflection of this part of speech. So, for illustration, *blind* would be used for all cases of the singular, *blinde*, for all cases of the plural. But necessarily this distinction could not apply to adjectives which ended in *e*: it had even then ceased to apply to adjectives of more than one syllable. It was, moreover, further weakened by the fact that many adjectives which originally ended in a consonant had, like the noun, assumed a final *e* to which they were not entitled; and, in consequence, the ending of the singular was the same as that of the plural. By the end of the Middle English period the distinction between the two numbers was utterly swept away, and the unchanged radical form of the adjective was, as now, the only one employed. Remains of the definite declension also existed in the fourteenth century, especially in the assumption of the final *e* by adjectives preceded by the definite article and demonstrative pronoun. Thus, 'the blind man' would be generally written and pronounced *the blindě man.* But before the beginning of the Modern English period all traces of adjective inflection of any kind whatever had disappeared completely. A relic of the definite declension, perhaps the only one, is still seen in the form *olden* (A. S., *ealdan*) in phrases such as 'the olden time;' but in such an expression *olden* is, tc modern feeling, simply a correlative form of the adjective *old*, and not an oblique case of it, as originally it was.

61. The history of the participle declension does not differ from that of the adjective. It also was inflected both ways in Anglo-Saxon, and shared throughout in all the losses suffered by the latter.

Comparison.

62. Comparison, being really a matter of derivation, and not of inflection, does not strictly find a place in a history of the latter. It is convenient, however, to follow the usual method, and so treat it.

In all of the Indo-European tongues certain suffixes were added to the radical of the adjective to form the comparative: to form the superlative, a secondary suffix was added, usually to the suffix of the comparative. These suffixes underwent much change of form in the various languages; but their general resemblance and common descent are apparent in all.

The suffixes almost universally employed in the Teutonic to form the comparative were *is* and *ôs*: to these another suffix, *ta*, was added to form the superlative. But in every one of the Teutonic tongues, save the Gothic, the *s* of the comparative had suffered rhotacism (12), as it did usually in Latin (cf. *alt-us*, *alt-ior*, *alt-ius*); and the forms employed were, in consequence, *ir* and *ôr*. In the superlative, however, the change of *s* to *r* did not take place; and the original forms of the suffixes were therefore *ista* and *ôsta*.

63. In Anglo-Saxon, moreover, the *i* or *ô* of the suffix was dropped in the comparative. In many words, however, the vowel-modification produced by the *i* (19) continued to remain, and, in some instances, transmitted the modified form to a later period. Thus *lang*, 'long,' *strang*, 'strong,' under the influence of the vowel which had come to be dropped, became *lengra* (for *lengira*) and *strengra* (for *strengira*.) In a similar manner, *eald* or *ald*, 'old,' became in the comparative either *yldra* or *eldra*. But, as the vowels *i* and *ô* of the suffixes were dropped, the simple letter *r* was consequently all that was added to form the comparative; and, as adjectives in this degree were invariably inflected according to the definite declension, the termination of the nominative was therefore always *ra* and *re*. In the superlative, the final *a* of both suffixes was dropped, and the *i* of the ending *ist* was usually weakened into *e*. The comparison of the adjective in the Anglo-Saxon period may, in consequence, be fully seen in the following examples:—

blind,	*blind*,	blind-r-a,	blind-ôst.
brâd,	*broad*,	brâd-r-a,	brâd-ôst.
strang,	*strong*,	streng-r-a,	streng-est.
eald,	*old*,	yld-r-a,	yld-est.

64. In the Early English period the *i* and the *ó*, which had been dropped in the Anglo-Saxon, were resumed in the comparative; but there sprang up confusion in the use of the two vowels, and the *i*, it is to be added, was invariably weakened into *e*. The same adjective would appear in the comparative and superlative degree, sometimes with the suffixes *ore*, *ost*, sometimes with *ere*, *est*. A representative comparison of the adjective during this transition period would be the following: —

blind,	{ *blind-ere*,	*blind-est* (*e*).
	{ *blind-ore*,	*blind-ost* (*e*).

The forms with the vowel *e* became steadily predominant, and by the fourteenth century were almost invariably employed. The final *e* of the comparative was also at that time frequently dropped in spelling, as it had been in pronunciation; and by the beginning of the Modern English period it had disappeared altogether, leaving the comparison precisely in the situation in which it is at present.

65. The modification of the vowel seen in *strang*, 'strong,' *strengra*, 'stronger,' *lang*, 'long,' *lengra*, 'longer,' and other words, lasted down to the fourteenth century, and later; but in the Middle English period it disappeared from the language entirely, with the single exception of *old*, which still clings to *elder* and *eldest*, the representatives of the original comparison, although it has developed, and commonly uses, the more strictly regular forms, *older* and *oldest*.

66. In the "Ancren Riwle," a work written about

1220, the first recorded instance of a comparison by means of adverbs is found in the phrase *the meste dredful*. This comparison by means of the adverbs *more* and *most* is rare in the thirteenth century; but in the fourteenth it made rapid progress. Since that time it has steadily increased in use, flourishing side by side with the suffixes in *er* and *est*. In the case of polysyllabic adjectives this method of comparison is now much the more common one, few late English writers employing forms like Bacon's *honorablest*, Shakspeare's *sovereignest*, or Milton's *virtuousest*, *exquisitest*, *excellentest*. But the tendency to give up the employment of such formations is not due to their being improper, but to their being difficult to pronounce.

67. The existence of two methods of comparison enabled English to gratify that disposition to make use of double comparison to which all the Teutonic tongues have manifested an inclination. This was introduced in the fourteenth century, and for the next three centuries was largely employed. In the latter part of the sixteenth century, and the beginning of the seventeenth, when it was by many regarded as an elegancy of style, it was perhaps the most prevalent. Expressions like 'the *most unkindest* cut of all ("Julius Cæsar," act iii. scene 2), 'the *most straitest* sect of our religion' (Acts xxvi. 5), 'my *most dearest* nephew' (Sir Thomas More's "Edward V."), are to be found scattered through the pages of numerous writers of the Elizabethan age, and earlier. By Ben

Jonson this is spoken of as "a certain kind of English Atticism, or eloquent phrase of speech, imitating the manner of the most ancientest and finest Grecians, who, for more emphasis and vehemency's sake, used so to speak." This usage died out in the seventeenth century, but has been occasionally employed by English poets of the present time. The assertion, however, so frequently made, that adjectives expressing the highest possible degree of a quality, like *chief*, *supreme*, *perfect*, are not subject to comparison, whether logically correct or not, is not merely utterly at variance with the usage of the best writers of all periods of English, but with that of the best writers of both ancient and modern cultivated tongues.

68. The English irregular comparison seen in *good*, *bad*, *much*, and *little*, goes back to the earliest times, and indeed is common to all the Teutonic languages. The irregularity consists in the fact that the comparative and superlative are derived from a stem different from that of the positive. Moreover, in *worse* (A. S. *wyr-sa*) and *less* (A. S. *lǣs-sa*) the change of *s* to *r* (62) did not take place. *Lesser* is a double comparative, as is also *worser*,—a form common in the Elizabethan period, but now rarely employed. There has frequently been a disposition shown to compare these adjectives regularly. *Gooder* and *goodest*, *badder* and *baddest*, are occasionally to be met with in our literature, though they cannot be called common; and *littler* and *littlest* are forms frequently found in the English dialects, and sometimes make their appearance in the literary speech.

69. There are relics of still other suffixes of comparison to be found in Modern English; as, for instance, that of *ma*, seen in such words as *foremost* and *utmost*. In Anglo-Saxon, *for-ma* meant 'foremost,' and *úte-ma* meant 'utmost;' but even then the superlative force of the suffix *ma* began to be felt as weak, and *est* was added, thereby forming the strengthened double superlatives *fyrmest* and *útmest*. This double superlative suffix *mest* appears in Modern English as *most* in several words besides these; such as, *midmost*, *southmost*, the *o* having been substituted for *e* as a consequence of *mest* being confounded with the adverb *most*, used to express the superlative.

CHAPTER IV.

THE PRONOUN.

70. THE pronoun is usually divided into four classes, — the personal, the demonstrative, the interrogative, and the relative; to these is added frequently a fifth class, called the indefinite, comprehending a number of words which occupy a position half way between the noun and adjective, and sometimes partake of the nature of both. As they received the inflection of one of these two parts of speech, their later history is involved in that of the noun and adjective, and does not demand attention here. It is different with the words belonging to the four other classes. These have a history of a somewhat exceptional character. Ordinarily the discussion of the pronoun begins with the personal; but as, in the later development of the English language, some of the forms of the demonstrative have gone over to the personal, it is expedient in this case to begin with the former.

The Demonstrative Pronouns.

71. The only two genuine demonstratives in Modern English are *that* and *this* with their respective plurals.' But in the earliest period of the language they had a fulness of inflection of which there has been but little survival in the present tongue. Each of them will require separate consideration.

72. The following is the inflection in Anglo-Saxon of the demonstrative represented in Modern English by *that:*—

	SINGULAR.			PLURAL.
	Masc.	Fem.	Neut.	All Genders.
Nom.	se,	seô,	þæt,	þâ.
Gen.	þæs,	þæ̂re,	þæs,	þāra. þǣra.
Dat.	þām,	þæ̂re,	þām,	þâm. þæ̂m.
Acc.	þone.	þâ.	þæt,	þâ.
Inst.			þŷ, þê.	

Besides varying forms of the other cases not given here, the nominative masculine and feminine singular sometimes presented the forms *þe* and *þeô* for *se* and *seô;* and the former were apparently the older of the two. The transition of the nominative singular feminine, and of the whole plural, into the pronoun of the third person, will be discussed farther on (82).

73. In the twelfth century, the inflection began to fall away; but, as usual, there was, in this respect, the

widest difference between various sections of the country. By the beginning of the Middle English period, the forms were reduced to *that* for the singular, which, as is evident, was derived from the neuter nominative and accusative. The plural was represented by *tho*, the Anglo-Saxon *þá*. All the other forms had either disappeared, or been put to other uses. Nor was *tho* itself for the plural common. In Middle English the plural sign *s* was added to this form, making it *thos*, or, as it came usually to be spelled, *those;* and this has since remained the regular plural. By many, however, *those* is derived from the plural of the pronoun *þes* (76). The Northern dialect of the thirteenth century shows a plural *thas*, meaning 'those;' but in this, as in so many other cases, that dialect probably preceded the Midland in adding an *s* to the original form.

74. The instrumental *þé* or *þý*, however, continued to remain in use with the comparative of the adjective, and in the form *the* it is still constantly employed in Modern English, as it in fact has been during every period in the history of the tongue. In such phrases as "the more, the better," *the* is often falsely explained as an article; whereas it, in fact, is nothing more than a relic of the lost instrumental case of the demonstrative pronoun.

75. But the definite article does owe its origin to this demonstrative. In the Anglo-Saxon period this use of it is frequently exemplified, though many cases occur when it is hard to decide whether the word is

really the article or the pronoun. In the twelfth century the form *se* died out, and the correlative form, *þe*, took its place; and, from that time on, *the* and *that* became the general representatives of the article, being, in fact, used indifferently with nouns of any gender. As such they both remained down to the fifteenth century; though, in the Early English of the South, forms derived from the other cases were occasionally to be found. Especially is this true of *þen* or *then*, from the accusative *þone*, as may be seen by the following example: —

Then wey he nom to Londone, he and alle his.[1]

The and *that*, however, were the usual articles for several centuries. But the use of the latter as a demonstrative, as a relative, and also as a conjunction. had insensibly the tendency to cause *the* to be preferred as the article, not only for the sake of greater definiteness, but to relieve the other word from being too much over-worked. So, during the Middle English, *that* ceased to be used any longer as an article. Certain phrases in which it had once been so employed continued, however, to survive long after any such general employment of it had been abandoned. This is true, especially of the phrases *that oon*, and *that other*, meaning 'the one,' and 'the other.' In these the final *t* of the *that* was often transferred to the following word, giving us *the tone* and *the tother*, — expressions which are not uncommon in Elizabethan English, and,

[1] He took the way to London he and all his (Robert of Gloucester, vol. i. p. 364).

indeed, are occasionally met with now. In fact, the word *tother* is often used alone, and, when so used, is generally written with an apostrophe, *t'other*, as if the *t* were a contraction of *the*, instead of being in its origin the final letter of *that*.

76. The following is the paradigm of the Anglo-Saxon demonstrative pronoun whose representative in modern English is *this*: —

	SINGULAR.			PLURAL.
	Masc.	Fem.	Neut.	All Genders.
Nom.	þes,	þeôs,	þis,	þâs.
Gen.	þises,	þisse,	þises,	þissa.
Dat.	þisum,	þisse,	þisum,	þisum.
Acc.	þisne.	þâs.	þis,	þâs.
Inst.			þeôs, þŷs.	

77. Even less of this word has survived than of the foregoing. It is the neuter nominative and accusative that has alone remained of the singular; and the dropping of the other forms not only took place early, but had been completed by the close of the thirteenth century, though sporadic examples of some of them can be found later. In the fourteenth century, only the form *this* is found in the singular: the plural is represented by *this*, *thise*, or *these*, derived from the singular form. It was the last that gradually supplanted the two others, and became in Middle English the regular plural, which it has ever since remained. The form *this*, however, continued to survive, and, as

a plural, is not uncommon in Elizabethan English; as, for illustration, "Meaning to aid thee in *this* Turkish arms" (Marlowe's Tamburlaine, part ii. act i. sc. 3. 8vo of 1592); "What needs *this* long suggestions in this cause?" (Greene's James IV., act iii. sc. 3); "*This* high promotions" (*Ibid.*, act i. sc. 2); "In *this* semicircles" (Battle of Alcazar, act i. sc. 1). But it is far more common in certain expressions such as "this twenty weeks," "this hundred pounds," which are still in use, and are now ordinarily explained on syntactical grounds, which do not require *this* to be regarded as a plural.

78. Besides this, there were in Anglo-Saxon certain other words which are commonly reckoned as demonstrative pronouns. They are compounds of *líc*, 'like:' one of them is *ylc*, 'same,' which lasted down to the fifteenth century in the literary language as *ilk*, and then died out of common use; but it was preserved in the speech of the North, and is made somewhat familiar to us by its frequent occurrence in the poetry written in the Scotch dialect. Another of these demonstratives was *þylc*, 'that same,' 'that,' which in Early English usually appeared as *thilke*, and in Middle English died out entirely. Another compound, *þyslíc*, 'such,' was far from common even in Anglo-Saxon, and disappeared early; but such was not the case with *swilc*, which, after passing through many intermediate forms of spelling, varying with pronunciation, among which are *swilche*, *swulche*, *sulche*, *swiche*, *siche*, and *soche*, finally settled upon one of them,

suche, and has been retained in Modern English in the form *such*. Of these four, *ylc* followed the definite adjective-declension in Anglo-Saxon; the other three, the indefinite; and they all naturally shared in the fate that overtook these inflections. Besides these, *same* and *yon* are often reckoned as demonstratives in Modern English; but in the earliest period of the language they were used only as adverbs, and their employment as pronouns made its first appearance in the dialect of the North.

The Personal Pronouns.

79. The following are the forms of the pronouns of the first, second, and third persons, as found in Anglo-Saxon. The third person, which in its origin was a demonstrative, is the only one that distinguishes gender, and that in the singular alone.

FIRST PERSON.

	Singular.	Dual.	Plural.
Nom.	ic,	wit,	we,
Gen.	mîn,	uncer,	ûser,
Dat.	me,	unc,	ûs,
Acc.	mec,	uncit,	ûsic,
	me.	unc.	ûs.

SECOND PERSON.

	Singular.	Dual.	Plural.
Nom.	þu,	git,	ge,
Gen.	þîn,	incer,	eôwer,
Dat.	þe,	inc,	eôw,
Acc.	þec,	incit,	eôwic,
	þe.	inc.	eôw.

THIRD PERSON.

	SINGULAR.			PLURAL.
	Masculine.	Feminine.	Neuter.	All genders.
Nom.	he,	heó,	hit,	hi,
Gen.	his,	hire,	his,	hira,
Dat.	him,	hire,	him,	him,
Acc.	hine.	{ hí, heó. }	hit.	hi.

80. Comparing these forms with those found in Modern English, it is evident at once that the personal pronouns have retained more of the original inflection than either the noun or the adjective. It is they and the interrogative *who* that alone continue to make a distinction in form between the nominative and objective cases. Moreover, whatever losses they suffered, they suffered them before the Middle English period; and certain general statements can be made in regard to their forms as seen in Anglo-Saxon, and as contrasted with those exhibited by them even in Middle English.

81. The most noticeable thing is the fact, that in this, the earliest form of the language, the pronouns of the first and second persons still continued to retained the dual number. It had died out of the noun, the adjective, and the verb; but in Anglo-Saxon, as in the other early Teutonic tongues, it still survived in these two pronouns. But in it, as likewise in the others, it showed signs of giving way. Even in the ninth and tenth centuries it was not unusual to strengthen

the dual forms by one of the words meaning 'both' or 'two.' The nominative dual *wit*, meaning 'we two,' received not unfrequently the word *begen* or *bu*, 'both,' as in the following line: —

> Ne forlæte ic þe, þenden *wit* lifiað *bu*.[1]
>
> CADMON'S *Genesis*, *l.* 2256

Instances also occur in which *bu*, 'both,' and *twa* or *tu*, 'two,' are together added to the form of the dual. As the number was by no means essential to expression, its fate was sealed as soon as the force originally belonging to it was felt to be going. It survived the Norman conquest, and lasted down to the beginning of the thirteenth century; but it was never in any sense common. In the thirteenth century it disappeared entirely.

82. The second fact to be noticed is, that the feminine nominative singular of the third person, and all the forms of the plural, have been entirely supplanted by the corresponding forms of the demonstrative pronoun *se*, *seó*, *þæt* (72). This transition began to take place during the Early English period, but was not fully completed till the fifteenth century. It unquestionably owed its origin to the desire of distinguishing between the forms of the pronoun, which had frequently come to be the same for different genders, cases, and numbers. The form *he*, for example, sometimes represents in Early English the modern masculine *he*, the feminine *she*, and the plural *they*; and likewise *him* or

[1] I shall not desert thee while we two both live.

hem stands for the modern masculine *him*, the neuter *it*, and the plural *them*. The resort to the demonstrative was not unnatural, and took place for the plural certainly as early as the latter part of the twelfth century: for the feminine singular the substitution of the form *she*, derived from *seó*, for the original *heó*, seems to have taken place later. As usual, in all these movements the Northern dialect led the way; but the triumph of the newer forms was a very slow one. Two sets of forms, indeed, lasted side by side for centuries; and, even in the Middle English, *here* and *hem* are still used by Chaucer for the oblique cases of the plural; while he employs *thei* or *they* for the nominative. *Their* and *them*, however, became universally adopted towards the close of the fifteenth century, as they had long before been the prevailing forms. The old objective *hem* has left a relic of itself in modern speech in the contraction *'em*, which, in books printed in the first part of the seventeenth century, often appears as *'hem*, as if it had been contracted from *them*, and were not itself the original form. The vulgar use of *them* in such phrases as *them books* seems to be a relic of the ancient adjectival use of this demonstrative pronoun.

83. The third point to be marked is that the original Anglo-Saxon accusative has disappeared, and the modern objective case is derived, not from it, but from the dative; that is to say, *me* comes, for example, from the dative *me*, and not the accusative *mec; him*, from *him*, and not from *hine; her*, from *hire*, and not from *hi*

or *heó*. The only exception to this is to be found in the neuter pronoun of the third person, in which the modern form *it* has been derived from the accusative, and not the dative. Yet how universal was the preference for the latter case is made clear by the fact, that, when the plural of the demonstrative *se* was introduced into the pronoun of the third person, it was the dative *þám*, 'them,' and not the accusative *þá*, that was adopted for the objective. This disuse of the accusative began early. Even in Anglo-Saxon the strengthened forms *mec*, *þec*, *úsic*, and *eówic*, were largely discarded for *me*, *þe*, *ús*, and *eów*, which were the same as the dative; and the former died out immediately after the Conquest, if, indeed, they can be said to be existing at the time of it. The accusatives of the third person lasted longer; but early in the twelfth century they were sometimes supplanted by the dative, and, by the close of the thirteenth century, they had almost universally been abandoned. In the neuter pronoun the dative form *him* and the accusative *hit* or *it* were both for a long period in use: indeed, instances of the former occur late in the sixteenth century. But much before that time, under the increasing tendency to regard *him* as belonging exclusively to the masculine, the use of *it* for the neuter became general.

84. Besides these general statements, certain special changes are to be noted in the form of the pronouns. In the first person, *ic* often passed, in Early English, into the form *ich*, and, toward the latter part of it, more and more into the form *i*. It was generally written

for a long while with a small letter; but, during the Middle English period, a capital was employed to designate it, probably for the sake of distinguishing it from the prefix *i* of the passive participle (201), as *i-ronne*. The preposition *in* not infrequently appeared also as *i*, and this may have conduced to the speedier adoption of the distinguishing form. In the first part of the Early English period the genitives of the first and second personal pronouns often dropped their final *n*, and accordingly exhibited the double forms *min* and *mi*, *thin* and *thi*. The neuter *hit* came at the same time under the influence of a tendency which has been very powerful in all periods of the language, and dropped its initial *h*. Still both *it* and *hit* flourished side by side for several hundred years; and while, after the fourteenth century, the former became more common, the latter did not die out entirely till the sixteenth. A form *ha* or *a* for *he* made its appearance at the beginning of the Early English period, and, though still found in the provincial dialects, is only of importance here from the fact that it is constantly employed by the Elizabethan dramatists, and put into the mouths of the highest as well as the lowest characters. A relic of it is preserved in the interjection *quotha*, that is, 'quoth he.'

85. At the beginning of the Middle English period the following paradigms of the personal pronouns exemplify the usage of Chaucer, its representative author. In all cases where varying forms in equally common use exist, and there are numbers of such, those most

closely resembling Modern English have been selected.

	FIRST PERSON.		SECOND PERSON.	
	Singular.	Plural.	Singular.	Plural.
Nom.	I,	we,	thou,	ye,
Gen.	{ min, mi, }	oure,	{ thin, thi, }	youre.
Objec.	me.	us.	thee.	you.

THIRD PERSON.

	SINGULAR.			PLURAL.
	Masculine.	Feminine.	Neuter.	All genders.
Nom.	he,	she,	{ hit, it, }	they,
Gen.	his,	hire,	his,	here,
Objec.	him.	hire.	{ hit, it. }	hem.

86. That the Middle English personal pronoun is about the same as the Modern English, save in certain forms of the third person, is evident at a glance. *Their* and *them* took the place of *here* and *hem* in the fifteenth century, as has been stated. But, up to the seventeenth century, *his* remained as the genitive of both the neuter and the masculine, just as the dative for both had for a long period been *him*. But by the end of the fifteenth century the *h* had become generally discarded from *hit*, and, in consequence, *his* did not seem so properly the genitive of *it* as of *he*. As the disposition grew in strength to regard *his* as belonging exclusively to the latter, various methods were resorted to in order to avoid employing it as a neuter

One of the earliest of these was to use *it*, without any inflection, as a genitive; and this occurs certainly as early as the fourteenth century, and was common during the fifteenth and sixteenth. The creation and gradual adoption of the form *its* has already been told, and need not be here repeated.[1] Before the Restoration of the Stuarts, in 1660, it had become firmly established in the language; and, at the end of the seventeenth century, most men, doubtless, supposed it had always been in existence. Milton is the principal writer of the middle of the seventeenth century who exhibits any reluctance in using it. As is well known, it is found but three times in his poetry, and then only where it is almost essential to clearness. It, however, was sometimes used by him in his prose.[2]

87. One thing to be especially marked in the paradigms given of the Middle English personal pronouns is, that there is no confusion between the nominative and objective. In Chaucer's writings — and the same thing is true of his contemporaries — *ye* and *you*, for example, are never confounded. The former is invariably the case of the subject; the latter, the case of the object. Occasional instances of confusion between the two cases have been pointed out in writings of the fourteenth and fifteenth centuries; but they are so few in number, that it is more reasonable to attribute them to blunders by the copyists than to intention on the part of the author. No such statement can be made after the beginning of the Modern

[1] Pages 129, 130.

[2] *E.g.*, Areopagitica, Arber's reprint, p. 71.

English period. In the middle of the sixteenth century the distinction between the nominative and objective began to break down. In fact, if the language of the Elizabethan drama represents fairly the language of society, — and we can hardly take any other view, — the widest license in the use of the personal pronouns prevailed. *Me, thee, us, you, him, her,* and *them* were often treated as nominatives; while the corresponding nominative forms were frequently, though not so commonly, treated as objectives. Modernized editions of the authors of that period do not in this respect represent justly the usage of the time, as in all or nearly all of them changes in the text are silently made. In the case of *ye* and *you* this confusion has become permanently established in the language; and *you*, the representative of the original dative and accusative, has now become the regular form for both nominative and objective. *Ye* is also still used, but likewise indifferently in the two cases, and with comparative infrequency in either. In the other pronouns the original distinction has gradually re-asserted itself, and is, perhaps, more strongly insisted upon now than at any period since the sixteenth century. But there still continues, in regard to these forms, the widest conflict of usage and opinion. Colloquial phrases, such as, *between you and I*, have been handed down from the time of Queen Elizabeth; while the expressions, *It is me, It is him, It is her,* have been pretty steadily in use since that period, and frequently by the best writers. It is to be added that the expressions, *It is I*, *It is he*, and the similar ones are not older than the fifteenth century. The form in Anglo-Saxon was, for example, *I am it* (*ic eom hit*), and this continued to be employed down to the time mentioned.

88. It has already been remarked that the Anglo-Saxon genitives *mīn* and *þīn* frequently dropped their *n* in the Early English period. Precisely corresponding in form to these genitives were the adjective pronouns *mīn* and *þīn*, which had a full set of inflections, according to the indefinite declension, but which also dropped the final *n* at the same time. Corresponding to the genitive plurals, also, were the adjective pronouns *ūre* or *ūser*, 'our,' and *eówer*, 'your.' The corresponding adjective pronoun of the third person was *sīn*; but, even when Anglo-Saxon was committed to writing, it had died out nearly, as the original third personal pronoun itself had died out wholly, and been replaced by the demonstrative *he*. *Sīn* occurs not often under any circumstances, and almost wholly in poetry, though it is not unknown to prose.[1] Its loss has been a serious disadvantage to the precision and clearness of the language; for while its place was taken in Anglo-Saxon by the genitives *his*, *hire*, and *hira* of the third personal pronoun, it was not filled.

89. These genitives of the first and second personal pronouns were, therefore, the same in form as the nominative singular of the corresponding possessive pronouns during the Anglo-Saxon period. But, as

[1] *E.g.*, Blickling Homilies, p. 125, l. 21.

then the former were governed directly by verbs or prepositions, while the latter had full adjective inflections, the distinction between them was in most cases apparent. But when, on the one hand, the genitive became more and more confined to the expression of the possessive relation, and was no longer made the object of verbs and prepositions; and when, on the other hand, the adjective inflection of the possessive pronoun had entirely disappeared, — then the distinction between the two classes became rather nominal than real. Whether the same word should be regarded as the genitive of the personal pronoun, or itself as the possessive adjective pronoun, depended mainly upon definition. The genitive, especially in the plural, lasted down, to be sure, to the end of the fourteenth century, in phrases in which there could be no doubt as to its being a personal pronoun, such as, *at oure alther cost*,[1] meaning "at the cost of us all;" or, *I am yowre aller hed, I am yowre aller hele*,[2] that is, "I am the head of you all, I am the salvation (*heal*) of you all." But such expressions as these, comparatively infrequent then, have not been preserved in Modern English: hence many grammarians consider the genitive of the personal pronouns as no longer existing, terming these forms, wherever they occur, possessive adjective pronouns. In either case their history is the same.

90. The contracted forms *mi* and *thi*, for *min* and

[1] Chaucer: Canterbury Tale, Prologue, l. 799.
[2] Langlande's Piers Plowman, text B., xix. 468.

thin, made their appearance at the end of the twelfth century, and were at first used indifferently. Subsequently, in the Middle English period, a custom sprang up of using *min* and *thin* before words beginning with a vowel or silent *h*, and *mi* and *thi* before consonants. This was observed, with a fair degree of regularity, up to the latter half of the sixteenth century, after which it became largely a matter of individual choice. In process of time *my* and *thy*, as they had then generally come to be spelled, were used almost exclusively before nouns. and *mine* and *thine* when standing alone in the predicate, except in a few phrases, such as 'mine host,' that had survived the general abandonment of the ancient usage. The *e* of *mine* and *thine* is, of course, inorganic, and may have come from its being used to distinguish, after the manner of the adjective inflection, the plural from the singular.

91. The restriction of *mine* and *thine* to the absolute construction in the predicate was undoubtedly aided, to a great extent, by the creation of the forms *oures*, *youres*, and *hires*, 'hers,' and *heres*, 'theirs,' and their confinement to this same employment. Originally the pronoun, when used absolutely in the predicate, had simply the form of the genitive of the personal pronoun, or the nominative of the possessive; and this was the prevalent practice, not only in the Anglo-Saxon period, but during the Early English period also, at least in the Midland and Southern dialects. For example, the sentence 'the land is *ours*' would in the thirteenth century have appeared as 'the land

is *oure*.' The feeling, that, in such constructions, the pronouns were really genitives of the personal pronoun, and not possessive adjectives, seems to have been the ruling one. But as, by the fourteenth century, *s* had become the common termination of the genitive of all nouns, and was the termination of *his*, the masculine and neuter genitive of the third personal pronoun, this letter was at last added by a false analogy to the other forms, and, early in the Middle English period, *oures*, *youres*, *hires*, 'hers,' *heres*, 'theirs,' took their place alongside of the earlier *oure*, *youre*, *hire*, and *here*. The former, therefore, are strictly double genitives. They first made their appearance in the speech of the North, but, in the fourteenth century, became thoroughly established in the literary language of the Midland dialect. For a time they flourished side by side with the forms without *s*, which etymologically were more correct; but in the fifteenth century they displaced the latter altogether, and are now the ones exclusively in use in the construction mentioned. When *their* was adopted as the genitive of the personal pronoun, in place of *here*, it also added an *s* in such cases, like the others.

92. This result did not happen, however, without a struggle. Other forms existed, which have left traces of themselves, in the language of the uneducated, to this day. The old *n* declension, both of the noun and adjective, still survived in the fourteenth century in certain parts of the country, and was, as we have seen, applied to words which had no right to it in

Anglo-Saxon. Various dialects, consequently, especially of the South of England, instead of forming, in these cases, a double genitive in *s*, formed one in *n*; so that, in place of *oures*, *youres*, *hires*, and *heres*, we had the forms *ouren*, *youren*, *hiren*, *heren* (i.e., their'n). To this the analogy of *mine* and *thine* unquestionably contributed. These are not infrequent in the Wycliffite version of the Bible, made about 1380. In consequence, during the latter half of the fourteenth century, the genitive of the personal pronoun, when used in the predicate, can be found in three forms,— without any ending, with the ending *s*, or with the ending *n*. The following examples will show this clearly:—

> I wil be *youre* in al that ever I may.
>
> CANTERBURY TALES, *line* 13,176.
>
> My gold is *youres*, whanne that you lest.
>
> IB., *line* 14,695.
>
> But the erthetilieris seiden togidere, This is the eire; come ye, sle we hym, and the eritage schal be *ourun*.—MARK xii. 8.

The forms in *n*, however, speedily disappeared from the language of literature, though they have exhibited a marked vitality in the language of low life. Here, again, whenever *their* took the place of *here*, *their'n* was formed, after the analogy of the other forms in *n*, by those who employed the latter. In fact, this was sometimes extended to *his*, giving us *hisen* or *his'n* as a collateral form. These forms in *n*, it is to be added, are often falsely explained as contractions of *our own*, *your own*, *her own*, and so forth.

93. In Anglo-Saxon the simple personal pronouns were constantly employed also as reflexives; and this use of them has lasted down through all periods of the language to this day. But the reflexive sense of these words was also made often more emphatic in the early tongue by the addition of the forms of the adjective *self* to the corresponding forms of the personal pronouns; thus the dative *himself* would be in Anglo-Saxon *him selfum;* the accusative, *hine selfne.* During the Early English period the adjective *self* lost its inflections, and, both then and later, was, in these combinations, often looked upon, in consequence, as a substantive. In its simple form *self* it was at first usually added to the dative of all the personal pronouns; but in process of time, while, with the pronouns of the third person, it was joined with the objective, with the pronouns of the first and second persons it was joined to the genitive; or, perhaps, it would be more correct to say it was treated as a substantive, with which agreed the possessive adjective pronouns corresponding to the genitive of the pronouns of the first and second persons. This took place before the beginning of the Middle English period, and has since remained unchanged, though forms like *his self* and *me self* respectively, occasionally occur much later even. The only modification that for a long time took place was the frequent adding of the inflectional syllable *en*, giving such forms as *myselven, himselven.* This termination, however, did not denote the plural, which was not developed till near

the end of the Middle English period: 'themselves, for illustration, during nearly the whole of the fifteenth century, would be represented either by *hemself* or *themself*. But in the first half of the sixteenth century the plural ending *s* was added to the forms which were plural in signification. The strengthened form of the reflexive is generally used now when the pronoun is the direct object of the verb; but, when it is the object of some preposition accompanying the verb, the simple form is more common, thus we say, 'he laid himself down,' rather than 'he laid him down,' and, on the contrary, 'he looked about him,' rather than 'he looked about himself:' but both expressions have been constantly employed from the earliest period.

94. There remains one usage the consideration of which belongs more strictly to syntax than even the one just mentioned; but, as it is of some importance as connected with the disuse of certain forms of the verb, it will receive a slight notice at this point. This is the general abandonment in English of the singular pronoun of the second person, and the substitution of the plural in its place. In this respect our tongue does not differ from the other cultivated tongues of modern Europe; but, in its avoidance of this particular form, it has gone far beyond them all. In them it is the language of superiority, or affectionate intimacy; with us it is, outside of its employment in poetry, limited, for all practical purposes, to the language of prayer. This result has been reached gradually. The

Anglo-Saxon, like the Greek and the Latin, never used, in addressing an individual, any thing but the second person of the singular; and this continued to be the case for nearly two centuries after the Conquest. The substitution of the plural *ye* and *you* in such cases made its appearance towards the close of the thirteenth century; but it was then not merely little in use, it was restricted to narrow and well-defined limits. When so substituted, it was generally, if not invariably, employed as a mark of respect in addressing a superior. In the fourteenth and fifteenth centuries the use of the plural steadily increased, and in the sixteenth century it became the standard form of polite conversation. All this led to the greater disuse of *thou;* and, as *thou* was almost the only subject the second person of the verb ever had, the disuse of the pronoun led indirectly to the comparative disuse of this form of the verb, and, in some instances, to changes that were due to the lack of familiarity with the proper form in consequence of this disuse.

The Interrogative Pronouns.

95. In the Anglo-Saxon period the interrogative pronouns were *hwa*, 'who;' *hwæt*, 'what;' *hwilc*, 'of what sort;' and *hwæðer*, 'which of two.' During the twelfth century the words which had originally begun with the combination *hw* changed their form, and were spelled with *wh;* and this has from that time remained the universal practice. Of these four

interrogatives, *hwilc* and *hwæðer* had a full set of adjective inflections according to the indefinite declension, varying therefore with the gender. On the other hand, *hwa* was used both as a masculine and a feminine, the special feminine form which belonged to the primitive Teutonic having disappeared from the Anglo-Saxon and from the other sister-languages, with the exception of the Gothic. Of course, *hwæt* is strictly the neuter of *hwa*.

96. In Anglo-Saxon, *hwa* and *hwæt* have the following inflections: —

	Masculine and Feminine.	Neuter.
Nom.	hwa,	hwæt,
Gen.	hwæs,	hwæs,
Dat.	hwam,	hwam,
Acc.	hwone.	hwæt,
Inst.		hwŷ.

97. In general it can be said that this pronoun has had the same history essentially as the personal pronouns, especially the pronoun of the third person. In the Early English period the dative *hwam*, 'whom,' supplanted the accusative *hwone* in the masculine, as *him* did *hine*. As *him* gradually became confined to this gender, and the accusative *hit* or *it* took its place in the neuter, so *whom* came, even earlier, to be used only of persons, and the accusative *what* was alone used when objects without life were mentioned. Again: just as *his* lost its original neuter sense, and was replaced by *its*, so *whose* has been limited to persons; and, when inquiry is made in regard to things,

we now employ in place of it *what* or *which*, with the preposition *of*. So, also, in the sixteenth century, the same confounding of the nominative and objective cases that occurred with the personal pronouns occurred also with this interrogative. *Whom* is sometimes used where strict grammar requires *who*; but far more frequently was *who* used where *whom* would be the form expected. This is especially true of the Elizabethan period. In the dramatic writings of that time sentences such as these —

> *Who* have we here? — PEELE'S *Edward I.*
>
> *Who* do you take me to be? — GREENE'S *George a-Greene.*
>
> I see *who* he laughed at. — JONSON'S *Every Man in his Humor.*

are of constant occurrence; and the frequency with which they are used by writers of every grade is clear proof that they were not felt to be improper. Nor has this usage of *who* for *whom* been limited to this period. It may be said to have characterized the colloquial speech of England from the latter half of the sixteenth century to the present time, if the language of conversation has been justly represented in the literature which purports to reproduce it.

98. *Hwilc* was represented in the dialects and subdialects of Early English by various forms, such as *whilk*, *whulk*, *wuch*, *wich*, and *which*, the last of these becoming in Middle English the established form in the language of literature. Like *such* (78), it is a compound of *lic*, 'like,' and it was originally inflected according to the indefinite declension of the adjective,

and the history of its forms is included in the history of that part of speech. The same statement is true also of the interrogative *hwæðer*, 'which of two,' which was originally inflected like the indefinite adjective. The dual sense of this word was beginning to fail even in the Anglo-Saxon period, and in consequence it was sometimes strengthened by the numeral, as in Matthew, chapter xxi. verse 31, where, in the Anglo-Saxon version, we read, —

Hwæðer þara twegra dyde þæs fæder willan?

which, in the sixteenth-century translation, now used by us, has the same construction: "Whether of them twain did the will of his father?" The use of *whether* as an interrogative pronoun steadily gave way, and died out in the seventeenth century entirely. Its place was taken by *which*.

99. An interrogative pronoun, signifying "who of many," existed in the primitive Teutonic, and was transmitted to the Gothic and the Old Norse, but was not preserved in any dialect of the High Germanic or the Low Germanic groups. Compound forms of the interrogatives have been in use during every period of English; but the inflection of the simple forms has not been in the least modified by this fact. In conclusion, it is to be remarked that the instrumental case of *hwæt* (96) has given to the tongue the two interrogative adverbs *how* and *why*.

The Relative Pronouns.

100. The Teutonic did not possess a relative in the strict sense of the word; and, for the representation of it, the English, during every period of its history, has been obliged to have recourse to other pronouns. In Anglo-Saxon the duty of the relative was performed by the following words or phrases: —

1. By the correlative form of the demonstrative *se*, the indeclinable *þe*. As this was indeclinable, it could be employed for an antecedent in any gender, number, or person.

2. By the demonstrative pronoun *se*, *seó*, *þæt*.

3. By the joining of the indeclinable *þe* to the form of the demonstrative, giving, for example, in the nominative singular, *se þe*, *seó þe*, *þæt þe*, or *þætte*.

4. Sometimes, though far less commonly, by the joining of *þe* to the personal pronouns.

101. After the Conquest the use of *þe* was the first to be given up, — a result which was unavoidably hastened by the disposition to employ that form exclusively for the definite article: still it was used occasionally as late as the beginning of the thirteenth century. All the forms of the demonstrative *se*, *seó*, *þæt*, were maintained as relatives down to the end of the twelfth century with a fair degree of vitality; but the only one that was much in use was the neuter nominative and accusative singular, which speedily took the place of the old indeclinable *þe* as the representative of all persons, genders, numbers, and cases.

By the middle of the thirteenth century the use of *that* as a general relative, referring both to persons and things, was universally established, and such it has remained through every subsequent period of English. Other words have taken their place alongside of it; but there has never been a time since the twelfth century when it has not been in constant employment as a relative.

102. With this form alone, however, the language was not content, and at an early period it began to resort to the interrogative pronouns for additional relatives. The first that came into general use was *which*. The employment of this interrogative as a relative goes back to the beginning of the thirteenth century, and by the end of the fourteenth it was thoroughly established. It was sometimes preceded by the definite article, giving us the expression *the which;* it was sometimes followed by *that;* but it was more frequently used alone.[1] From the fourteenth to the seventeenth century it was as regularly employed in reference to persons as to things, an idiom which had been made familiar to all by the phrase "Our Father *which* art in heaven," occurring in the Lord's

[1] The use of *which* as a relative without *that* was common in the fourteenth century; but, as the assertion is frequently made that such is not the case, it has been thought best to add the following references, which might be multiplied indefinitely, — in Chaucer's Parlament of Foules, lines 29, 34, 84, 111, 126, 136, 142, 170, 248, 287, 333, 395; in Purvey's Recension of the Wycliffite Version of the Bible, Mark ii. 4; iii. 28; iv. 16, 20, 31; v. 3; vi. 2; viii. 5, 28; ix. 2; x. 5, 30, 38–40; xi. 2; xii. 14, 40; xiii. 2, 19, 20; xiv. 24; xv. 40, 42; xvi. 10; Dan. i. 4, 18, 20; ii. 11, 23, 28, 38, 41; iii. 2–5, 7, 12–15, 18, 27, 28, 31, 36, 52, 88, 91, &c.

Prayer. In the seventeenth century the tendency manifested itself, with the increasing use of *who* as a relative, to confine the reference of *which* to things; and this has now become the general practice in the language, though exceptions are still to be met with, especially in poetry. It shows how thoroughly the sense of the ancient usage had been lost, and how complete the distinction between the two pronouns had become in the beginning of the eighteenth century, that this particular expression quoted above was attacked by Steele in No. 78 of "The Spectator," which appeared in May, 1711. He appended to this paper "the humble petition of *who* and *which*," wherein a protest was uttered both against the constant employment of *that* instead of them as a relative, and against their being confounded with each other. "In the first and best prayer children are taught," says the petition, "they learn to misuse us. 'Our Father *which* art in heaven' should be 'our Father *who* art in heaven;' and even a convocation, after long debates, refused to consent to an alteration of it."

103. About as early as *which*, *whose*, and *whom*, the oblique cases of the interrogative *who* were also used as relatives. This practice may be said to have begun early in the thirteenth century, and to have steadily increased in use from that time. But it was not till the beginning of the sixteenth century that the use of the nominative *who* as a relative was established, though occasional instances of such an employment of it occur earlier. Nor was *who*, even during the

sixteenth century, common as a relative, though constantly becoming more so; but in the seventeenth century it came into general use. From the beginning it had not been limited to persons, but also referred to things. From the latter, however, it was gradually shut out by the distinction that gradually developed itself between it and *which*, in accordance wherewith the former was confined to personal and the latter to impersonal antecedents. In this matter the objective *whom* has the same history as the nominative *who;* but the genitive *whose* has, during all the periods of Modern English, been applied equally to persons and to things. In the latter usage it is etymologically the genitive, not of *who*, but of *what* (96); but in sense it corresponds to 'of which.'

104. The confusion between the nominative and objective of the interrogative *who* naturally extended itself to the word when used as a relative. In one instance the confusion has perpetuated itself to our own time, and has become established in usage. This is in the phrase *than whom*, which has been both common and classical from the latter half of the sixteenth century. Modern grammarians, in this case, are often disposed in consequence to treat *than*, not as a conjunction, but as a preposition.

105. The indefinite pronouns, as has been stated, had either the inflection of the noun or of the adjective, usually the latter. Those which existed in Anglo-Saxon, excluding the compound forms, have been transmitted to Modern English, with two exceptions:

these are *fela*, 'many,' and *man*, 'one.' The former, in Early English, passed into the form *fele;* the latter, into *men*, or, with the *n* dropped, into *me;* and both died out in the fifteenth century. *Hwa*, 'some one,' was in Anglo-Saxon also used as an indefinite pronoun, and lasted down to the seventeenth century in certain phrases, such as, "as *who* should say," which, indeed, in poetry, are not yet entirely obsolete. Another indefinite pronoun, *án*, 'a certain,' was also the numeral 'one,' and, even during the Anglo-Saxon period, had sometimes the force merely of the indefinite article. Its confinement to this usage became more thoroughly established after the Norman conquest; and in Early English the custom arose of dropping the final *n* before vowels, or a silent *h*, which, with slight exceptions, has been followed to the present day.

CHAPTER V.

THE VERB.

THE TEUTONIC VERB. GENERAL STATEMENTS.

106. To all the Teutonic languages the following parts of the verb were common from the earliest period of their history: —

1. Two leading conjugations.
2. One voice, — the active.
3. Three finite moods. These are the indicative, the subjunctive, — sometimes called the conjunctive, and corresponding to the Greek optative, — and the imperative.
4. An infinitive, and an active and a passive participle.
5. Two simple tenses, — the present and the preterite.
6. Two numbers, — the singular and the plural.
7. Three persons, — the first, second, and third.

107. Besides these forms common to all, the Gothic retained a middle voice (used generally in a passive sense) and a dual number (confined to the first and second persons). The primitive method of forming the preterite by reduplication, exemplified also in Latin by such forms as *mordeo, mo-mordi, tundo, tu-tudi,* it likewise preserved in some forty verbs; but of this traces only can be found in the other Teutonic languages.

108. Excluding the Gothic, the Teutonic has accordingly lost, of the parts belonging to the primitive Indo-European verb, the middle voice (also used as a passive), the mood corresponding to the Greek subjunctive, the imperfect, aorist, and future tenses, and the dual number.

109. According to its method of forming the preterite, the Teutonic verb is divided into two great conjugations. One is variously called the Old, the Primary, or the Strong conjugation; the other, the New, the Secondary, or the Weak conjugation. The distinguishing characteristic is, that verbs of the latter conjugation add an additional syllable to the root to form the preterite. This additional syllable, in some modern Teutonic tongues, noticeably in English, has been, in many cases, cut down to a single letter. Examples of this conjugation are words like *kill, kill-ed, love, love-d.* On the other hand, verbs of the former conjugation add nothing to form the preterite. Thus, in Anglo-Saxon, *singan* meant 'to sing:' the present tense, first person singular, was *sing-e;* the preterite of the same person was *sang.* No syllable was added, as in the case of *kill* and *love.* But to this

conjugation belongs a variation of the radical vowel, which, in the instance just cited, is exemplified by the change of *i* to *a*. This is, indeed, one of its most marked features, and one which has been preserved in its whole subsequent history. But as variation of the vowel, though not due to the same cause, is found in a few verbs of the conjugation which adds a syllable to form the preterite, this variation cannot be regarded as a distinctive peculiarity. Thus, the Anglo-Saxon present *sell-e* has for its preterite *seal-de*, the *e* of the one tense having become *ea* in the other; and Modern English still retains this peculiarity in the present *sell* and the preterite *sol-d*. Accordingly, it is the adding, or not adding, of a syllable, which is the original fundamental distinction between the two conjugations, and not the variation of vowel.

110. The terms Old and Primary are employed because the verbs belonging to the conjugation so-called are the primitive verbs of the Teutonic. It is from them, or from nouns, that the verbs of the New or Secondary conjugation have been derived, and their name corresponds to their origin. The terms Strong and Weak were first applied by Grimm, on the theory that verbs of the one conjugation expressed the idea of past time by a mere modification of their own resources, that is, by changing the radical vowel; while those of the other had to call in the help of an additional syllable to achieve the same result. Though this terminology is somewhat fanciful, it is convenient, and has come into general use, and in this treatise

will be ordinarily employed. The terms Regular and Irregular, found generally in English grammars, are scientifically incorrect, because they blend in one class the strong verbs and the anomalous verbs of the weak conjugation.

111. The syllable which is added to form the preterite of verbs of the weak conjugation is supposed, according to the generally received theory, to be the reduplicated perfect of a verb corresponding to the English verb *do*. In Anglo-Saxon the infinitive of this was *dôn*, and its preterite, *dide*, the present *did*: in Old High German the corresponding forms were *tuon* and *teta*. The reduplicated form of this verb is not preserved in its complete state in the preterites of any of the weak verbs in the Teutonic languages, except in Gothic; and there it is not found in the singular, but is found in the dual and plural. For illustration, the first person plural of the preterite of the Gothic verb *haban*, 'to have,' is *habai-dêdum*, which is strictly *have-did-we*, equivalent to *we did have*.

112. One further distinction also exists between the strong and the weak conjugation. This is in the passive participle. In the former, the suffix was *-an*, usually weakened into *-en*, as seen still in the English *driv-en*: for the latter it was *-d* or *-t*, as seen in English *love-d*, *taugh-t*.

113. These are characteristics which English shares with all the other Teutonic languages. In the Anglo-Saxon these two conjugations above described, with

all their distinctive peculiarities, were flourishing, and they have lasted down to the present time. But in the course of their history great changes have taken place in their relative size and importance. The most obvious fact is, that verbs of the strong conjugation have in Modern English become so few, and verbs of the weak conjugation so numerous, that the former, when compared with the latter, are apt to seem like exceptions to the general rule. Many strong verbs have disappeared altogether; many have passed over to the weak conjugation; a few have complete forms of both conjugations; in others, again, the conjugations have been confounded, the preterite being formed according to the one, and the past participle according to the other; while, on the other hand, a still smaller number have passed over from the weak to the strong. The details of all these changes will be given in the history of the losses and gains of the two conjugations.

CONFLICT OF THE STRONG AND WEAK CONJUGATIONS.

114. In the English of the Anglo-Saxon period the strong conjugation was divided into a number of subordinate conjugations, the distinctions between which will be given later. The diminution in the number of verbs belonging to the strong conjugation — either by the loss to the language of the verbs themselves, or by their transition to the weak conjugation — is the matter of most essential importance, bringing to light, as it does, the origin of the anomalies that are to be found in the existing inflection of the verb in our tongue.

115. In the Anglo-Saxon there were more than three hundred simple verbs of the strong conjugation: in Modern English there are less than one hundred, showing a diminution of more than two-thirds. But even this gives no adequate conception of the loss. As the number of formative prefixes was far larger in Anglo-Saxon than in Modern English, the number of compound verbs created by the addition of these prefixes to the simple verb was necessarily much larger. Thus, in Anglo-Saxon, some ten new verbs were formed by the addition of ten different prefixes to *standan*: of these ten, Modern English has retained only *with* and *under*; so that, from this same verb, we now form two verbs only, *withstand* and *understand*, instead of the original ten. The disproportion between the earlier and the later form of the language, in respect to the number of strong verbs, is consequently much greater than would be implied by a loss of two-thirds.

116. The causes of this loss are not hard to find. Even during the Anglo-Saxon period all verbs derived from nouns or other verbs were inflected according to the weak conjugation. Such was the case also with the few foreign verbs that were from time to time introduced. On the other hand, the strong conjugation received no accessions. Under any circumstances, therefore, the number of weak verbs would be constantly increasing; while the strong, by simply remaining the same, would become a proportionally smaller fraction of the whole. It was an inevitable result of this, that the tendency would manifest itself at some

time to inflect all verbs in the way that the majority of them were inflected; and there is evidence that this was beginning to exert some influence in the language as it is found written before the Norman conquest. Many of the strong verbs have weak derivative verbs with precisely the same meaning alongside of them. In some cases a weak derivative verb exists as the representative of a strong verb that had gone out of use in Anglo-Saxon, but has been preserved in other early Teutonic languages. But a special cause operated to hasten the change in the relative numbers of the two conjugations, and to widen vastly the disproportion already beginning to exist. The Norman conquest made French the language of the cultivated classes, and left the native tongue to be used exclusively by the more uneducated portion of the community. Confusion speedily sprang up between the two conjugations in the speech of ignorant men, and, in process of time, became established by custom in the speech of all. The tendency to bring about uniformity at any cost now began to make itself powerfully felt in causing the inflection of verbs belonging to the smaller class to conform to that of the larger; just as, in modern times, under the influence of this same tendency, children and uneducated men say *drinked* for *drank*, *drawed* for *drew*, *seed* for *saw*, and *knowed* for *knew*. This was inevitably the source of much loss; but, great as it was, it was not to be compared with the effects produced by the influx of foreign words from the French, which, beginning toward the end of the thirteenth century, culminated in revolutionizing the vocabulary in the century following. All the new verbs taken from the French were inflected according to the weak conjugation; and with their introduction dropped out of use a large number of Anglo-Saxon verbs. Many of these belonged to the strong conjugation, and their loss to it could never be replaced. The consequence was, that, at the beginning of the Middle English period, the whole number of strong verbs in the language had become comparatively small. Not only was this true, but it seemed as if, under the influence of the tendency to uniformity, they were about to disappear altogether.

117. The transition of verbs of the strong conjugation to that of the weak was arrested, however, as soon as the influence of literary models — the great conservative agency in speech — began to make itself widely felt. The movement in this direction, which had been going on steadily since the Norman conquest, received its first check in the latter half of the fourteenth century with the rise of a native literature of a high order. The usage of Chaucer, so far as it is exemplified in "The Canterbury Tales," has been already pointed out, and contrasted with that of the present time.[1] From his age the tendency of the strong verbs to become weak became less and less conspicuous, and at the end of the Middle English period had ceased entirely. Modern English has lost

[1] See pp. 119, ff.

not a single one since the reign of Queen Elizabeth. What the language then had it has ever since retained, nor does it manifest the least disposition to abandon any it now has. True, there have been periods in which weak preterites and past participles, like *choosed*, *blowed*, *chided*, *comed*, *weaved*, and numerous others, have been, to a greater or less extent, in use, and in most periods have been persistently urged by some grammarians. But their use has never broadened and perpetuated itself. In fact, the present disposition of the language is not only to hold firmly to the strong verbs it already possesses, but to strengthen their hold, and even to extend their number whenever possible. Forms once common, and in the best usage, such as *shaked*, *shined*, *strived*, and *thrived*, are now much rarer than *shook*, *shone*, *strove*, and *throve*, or else are not met with at all. *Woke*, though not found in Shakspeare, Milton, and the English Bible, has become, during the last century, full as common as *waked* as the preterite of *wake*; while *dug* may be said to have supplanted *digged*, the regular preterite, not only of the sixteenth and seventeenth centuries, but of all preceding periods.

118. The history of the English verb is, therefore, from one point of view, the history of a conflict between the weak and the strong conjugations, in which the former steadily tended for three centuries to become the one exclusively in use. The arrest of the development in this direction, which overtook the verb in the fourteenth century, was the main cause that all our

verbs are not now inflected according to the weak conjugation. Still it was inevitable that the stoppage of the transition that had been going on from the strong to the weak inflection should cause many apparently anomalous and irregular forms to appear in the language; and a satisfactory account of the later history of the strong conjugation has been made a task of no slight difficulty, in consequence of the irregularities that appear in many verbs, and the seemingly capricious changes that have taken place in their inflections at various periods.

119. The first point of importance to be mentioned in the history of the strong conjugation is, that more than a hundred simple verbs originally belonging to it have disappeared from the language entirely. Some of these had clearly become obsolete in later Anglo-Saxon; but of those that were in common use during that period, and have since been dropped, the places have, in the majority of instances, been taken by verbs derived from the Norman French.

120. The next point is, that a hundred and eight verbs, which, in Anglo-Saxon, belonged to the strong conjugation, have passed over wholly or partially to the weak. The list embraces many of the most common words of the language, and, in enumerating them, they will be arranged according to the classes of strong verbs as laid down in sections 142 to 148 inclusive. In some of them there has been only a partial transfer. They have retained strong forms in equal authority with the weak, or even in greater. They have

retained strong forms in poetry, while dropping them in prose; or they have retained simply either a strong participial form, or a strong preterite form. These variations will be discussed later. In the following lists the verbs that still exhibit any of the original inflections will be denoted by Italics.

121. Of the verbs originally belonging to Class I. of strong verbs (142) the following have become weak:—

1. ban.
2. blend.
3. blow ('to bloom').
4. *crow.*
5. dread.
6. flow.
7. fold.
8. *hang.*
9. *hew.*
10. hight.
11. leap.
12. let.
13. low.
14. *mow.*
15. row.
16. sleep.
17. *sow.*
18. span.
19. sweep.
20. walk.
21. weep.
22. well.
23. whoop.
24. wield

122. Of the verbs which originally belonged to Class II. of the strong conjugation (143), the following are now inflected, wholly or partially, according to the weak:—

1. bark.
2. bellow.
3. braid.
4. burn.
5. burst.
6. carve.
7. delve.
8. ding.
9. *help.*
10. melt.
11. milk.
12. mourn.
13. quench.
14. spurn.
15. starve.
16. stint.
17. swallow.
18. *swell.*
19. thresh.
20. warp.
21. *wind.*
22. yell.
23. yelp.
24. yield.

To these might be added *swink*, 'to toil,' which is still found at times in poetry, though obsolete in prose.

123. Of Class III. (144) about half of the original number survived, and, of these, a small proportion

only went over to the weak conjugation. They are the following: —

1. fret (compound of *eat*).
2. knead.
3. mete.
4. (be-) queathe.
5. *shear.*
6. sneak.
7. *weave.*
8. wreak.

124. Most of the Anglo-Saxon verbs belonging to Class IV. (146) have been preserved in Modern English, though the large majority of them have gone over entirely or partially to the weak conjugation. The following is the list of these: —

1. ache.
2. bake.
3. drag.
4. fare.
5. flay.
6. gnaw.
7. *grave.*
8. *heave.*
9. *lade,* } *load.* }
10. laugh.
11. scathe.
12. *shape.*
13. *shave.*
14. step.
15. wade.
16. wash.
17. wax.

Of these verbs *lade* and *load* come directly from the same primitive, as also the strong verb *draw* is derived from the same word as the weak verb *drag*.

125. Of the verbs belonging to Class V. (147) the following have become weak wholly or partially: —

1. *cleave* ('to adhere').
2. glide.
3. gripe.
4. reap.
5. *shrive.*
6. sigh.
7. slip.
8. slit.
9. spew.
10. streak ('to go').
11. twit.
12. writhe, } wreathe. }
13. wipe.
14. yawn.

Here, again, *writhe* and *wreathe* come from the same original, and *twit* is a compound, and not a simple verb: it comes from the Anglo-Saxon *ætwîtan;* and the simple verb *wîtan* lasted to the Middle English period as *wite,* 'to blame,' 'to find fault with.'

126. But few verbs of Class VI. (148) preserved the strong inflection. Nearly half of the original number went over to the weak conjugation. They are the following: —

1. bow.
2. brew.
3. brook.
4. chew.
5. *cleave* ('to split').
6. creep.
7. dive.
8. flee.
9. float.
10. lie ('to deceive').
11. lock.
12. lose.
13. reek.
14. *rive*.
15. rue.
16. *seethe*.
17. shove.
18. slip.
19. smoke.
20. sprout.
21. suck.
22. sup.

127. Of the above-mentioned verbs of all the classes, many have, even in Anglo-Saxon, weak derivative forms along with the strong ones; so that, in some instances, it would be more proper to say that the strong verb has been dropped entirely, and the weak verb, possessing the same signification, has been retained, rather than that the existing verb has passed over from the strong to the weak conjugation. Thus, besides the Anglo-Saxon strong verb *smeócan*, 'to smoke,' there is also a weak derivative verb, *smocian*, 'to smoke;' and it is from the latter of these, rather than the former, that the Modern English verb may, perhaps, more justly be said to come. The same is the case with the strong verb *blandan*, and the weak verb *blendan*, derived from it. Both mean 'blend;' and our modern word is as much derived from the weak verb as from the strong, if the former is not to be regarded as the real original. There are about twenty instances in which verbs in the above lists can be

referred to two Anglo-Saxon verbs, one weak and one strong, of which two of the most conspicuous are *hang* and *yawn*.

128. Many of the verbs mentioned in these lists, and not Italicized, can be found, especially in Early and Middle English, and even in the first century of Modern English, exhibiting strong forms. This is particularly true of the passive participle, of which the adjective use caused it sometimes to be retained in the speech when the rest of the verb had disappeared from the tongue entirely, or exhibited only the weak inflection. This past participle of the strong conjugation invariably ended in *en* in the earliest period of the language. When a verb of this conjugation became weak, it occasionally left behind its original participle, though very rarely used save as an adjective. *Bursten* and *carven* and *molten* and *writhen* or *wreathen* are examples of strong past participles, which remain as adjectives after the verbs to which they belong have passed over to the weak conjugation. Even more marked are *lorn* and its compound *forlorn*, originally the participles of *lose* and *forlose*. To this list may perhaps be added the adjective *rotten*, though the strong Anglo-Saxon verb from which the form comes has a different meaning. The earlier literature furnishes frequent instances of such survivals, as *baken*, *kneaden*, *yolden*, *washen*, and others, which lasted down to the sixteenth century, and occasionally even later.

129. Certain verbs originally strong have under-

gone a partial transfer to the weak conjugation; that is to say, while taking the weak inflection, they have also retained the strong. They have, in consequence, a double set of forms. In some cases, it may be said that the strong inflections are confined to the language of poetry, or to the colloquial speech; in others, they are used only in certain styles, especially in the archaic; while in others, again, they are far more common than the weak forms. On all these points, usage is so various, it differs so much at different times, that all special statements are liable to occasional exceptions. The following is the list of verbs, originally strong, that are now inflected throughout according to both conjugations: —

Infinitives.	Preterites.	Past Participles.
1. cleave ('to split'),	clove, cleft *or* cleaved,	cloven, cleft *or* cleaved.
2. hang,	hung, hanged,	hung, hanged.
3. help,	helped, holp,	helped, holp *or* holpen.
4. heave,	heaved, hove,	heaved, hove.
5. seethe,	seethed, sod,	seethed, sodden.
6. shear,	sheared, shore,	sheared, shorn.
7. shine,	shined, shone,	shined, shone.
8. shrive,	shrived, shrove,	shrived, shriven.

Infinitives.	Preterites.	Past Participles.
9. thrive,	thrived, throve,	thrived. thriven.
10. weave,	weaved, wove,	weaved. woven.
11. wind,	winded, wound,	winded. wound.

For *stave* and *strive*, see sects. 135, 137.

In reference to the verbs included in this list, it is to be added that *hang* derives its weak inflection from the Anglo-Saxon weak verb *hangian, hangode;* and that *wīnd* as an original strong verb means strictly 'to turn about something fixed;' and that, in the sense of 'to sound by blowing,' it is derived from the noun *wĭnd*, and etymologically should have a weak preterite *winded.* But the two inflections have become inextricably involved, and are used of the word in both its significations, with a decided preference in each for the strong.

130. But, in addition to these, there are certain verbs originally strong which have adopted in the passive participle the weak form, but have preterites belonging to both conjugations. Of these there are the following four: —

Infinitives.	Preterites.	Past Participles.
1. cleave ('to adhere'),	cleaved, clave,	cleaved.
2. climb,	climbed, clomb,	climbed.
3. crow,	crowed, crew,	crowed.
4. wake,	waked, woke,	waked.

In regard to these it is to be remarked that *clomb* and *clave* belong to the language of poetry rather than that of prose; and also that the forms of *cleave*, meaning 'adhere,' and *cleave*, meaning 'split,' have been and still are frequently confounded. The preterite *woke*, after almost disappearing for several centuries from the language of literature, — so much so that it is not even recognized in our dictionaries, — has, during the present century, become full as common as the weak form *waked*, and, indeed, has occasionally made its way into the passive participle; and it might perhaps be more proper to add both *wake* and *climb* to the list of those verbs that have strong and weak forms throughout.

131. It is the preterite that strictly decides whether a particular word belongs to the strong or the weak conjugation; but it is a striking fact that the strong passive participle has been retained in many cases where the strong preterite has been abandoned. There are some nine verbs originally inflected strong, but now weak, that still cling also to their ancient participial form. The following is the list: —

1. grave,	graved,	graved, graven.
2. hew,	hewed,	hewed, hewn.
3. lade,	laded,	laded, laden.
4. mow,	mowed,	mowed, mown.
5. rive,	rived,	rived, riven.

6. shape,	shaped,	shaped, shapen.
7. shave,	shaved,	shaved, shaven.
8. sow,	sowed,	sowed, sown.
9. swell,	swelled,	swelled, swollen.

To these may perhaps be properly added *gnaw* and *wax*, which occasionally exhibit the strong participial forms *gnawn* and *waxen*. For the forms *hidden*, *loaden*, *sawn*, *shown*, *strown*, and *proven*, see sects. 134, 138, 139.

132. These complete the list of existing verbs in the language that were, in Anglo-Saxon, inflected according to the strong conjugation, but are now inflected wholly or partly according to the weak. It is to be added, however, that the forms here given are the ones found more or less in present usage. If we go back to that of the seventeenth and eighteenth centuries, we shall find a number of strong verbs, which in the language of certain writers, if not of all, have weak inflections that are not mentioned here. Forms, indeed, such as *shaked*, *chided*, *wringed*, *freezed*, *comed*, and several others, are to be met in some or in all periods of Modern English, just as, in the fourteenth century, *growed* was constantly used along with *grew*, by the best writers, and, indeed, seemed to be preferred.

133. It is evident from the above that the English strong conjugation has steadily lost, from the Norman

conquest up to the sixteenth century, in the number of verbs belonging to it. Still there have been some compensating gains. The general rule has been given, that all verbs derived from nouns or from other verbs, and all verbs taken from foreign tongues, are inflected according to the weak conjugation. But to this certain words are exceptions, and each of them has a separate history of its own.

134. The following are the verbs which were originally inflected weak, but have, at a later period, passed over to the strong conjugation: —

1. *Dig* is a word of somewhat uncertain origin, though the derivation from A. S. *dīcian*, *dīcode*, 'to make a dike, mound, or ditch,' seems much the most reasonable. In the form in which it now appears it does not seem to have been used before the fourteenth century. It had then, and for several centuries following, the weak preterite and past participle *digged*. The strong form, *dug*, apparently did not become common, if, indeed, it was known at all, until the eighteenth century.

2. The verb *spit*, as early certainly as the Middle English period, developed a strong inflection — *spit*, *spat*, *spitten* — alongside of the weak one; but the former never seems to have been as common at any time as the latter, though it is found occasionally at all times since its origin. The verb comes directly from the Anglo-Saxon weak verb *spittan*, *spitte*; and the strong forms are unknown till much later. It is not impossible that the analogy of verbs like *sit*, as origi-

nally inflected, *sit*, *sat*, *sitten*, may have had some influence in causing a transition, unless, in all such cases, we assume that a strong verb was in use in the original colloquial speech, but did not find its way into literature.

3 *Stick* is derived directly from the weak Anglo-Saxon verb *stician*, *sticode*, having precisely the same meaning. The forms *stiked* for the preterite and past participle are common in the literary language of the fourteenth century; but, in the sixteenth, *stuck* had taken its place as the regular form. There was an Early English strong verb, *stiken*, *stek*, or *stak*; but to this the transition does not seem to have been due.

4. *Wear* is derived directly from the Anglo-Saxon weak verb *werian*, *werede*. In the literary language of the fourteenth century *werede* and *wered* are the forms of the preterite and passive participle; but, by the end of the Middle English period, the preterite *ware* or *wore* came in, and the participle *worn*. There is not much doubt that the transition to the strong conjugation was brought about by the influence of the strong inflection, as seen in such words as *bear*, *tear*, and *swear*, closely related in sound.

5. To this list the word *hide* may be added, though it is still generally reckoned among the verbs of the weak conjugation which have suffered contraction in the preterite and passive participle. In the Middle English period, however, *en*, the characteristic termination of the strong past participle, was added to the weak past participle *hid*; and from that time *hidden*

and *hid* have both been in established use. It seems better, therefore, to regard this inflection *hide*, *hid*, *hidden* or *hid*, as now one of the strong conjugation, like *chide*, *chid*, *chidden* or *chid*, and *slide*, *slid*, *slidden* or *slid*, than as an irregular verb of the weak conjugation.

135. These are the only verbs, originally weak, that have passed over entirely to the strong conjugation. Besides these there are the two following, which are derived from nouns that have, in the later periods of the language, received the strong inflection:—

1. *String* is a verb that has apparently been formed from the Anglo-Saxon noun *string* or *strenge*, 'string. It is certainly not common before the sixteenth century, though it would be venturesome to assert that it had not a much earlier existence. Though the participial adjective *stringed* has been much in use, it is most likely that the verb, from the beginning of its formation, was inflected *string*, *strung*, *strung*, according to the strong conjugation, after the analogy of *swing*, *swung*; *sing*, *sung*; and numerous others.

2. The verb *stave* seems to be, like *string*, a modern formation, and is formed directly from the substantive *stave* or *staff*. It has both a weak and a strong preterite, *staved* and *stove*, and corresponding passive participles. The weak forms are far more common, however, before the present century.

136. The two following, of somewhat uncertain derivation, are also inflected strong. Neither of them is known to the earliest period of the language.

1. The first is *fling*, which, perhaps, came to our tongue from the Norse. It is first found in the Early English period, and has never been inflected otherwise than according to the strong conjugation.

2. The second is the technical naval verb *reeve, rove, rove*. Its derivation is uncertain, and it probably belongs exclusively to Modern English.

137. One Romance word has also passed over partially to the strong conjugation: this is the verb *strive*, taken directly from the old French *estriver*, which is itself, however, derived from a Teutonic noun. From its very entrance into the language it was inflected according to both conjugations, the strong inflection having, doubtless, been assumed by it after the analogy of *drive, drove, driven; thrive, throve, thriven:* and from the fourteenth century to the present time the strong and weak preterites *strove* and *strived* can be found side by side, as likewise the passive participles *striven* and *strived*. The language at present prefers the strong forms.

138. Three weak verbs showed a tendency to pass over to the strong conjugation, and, in the case of each, a strong passive participle has been added to their inflection. They are the following: —

1. **show,**	**showed,**	**showed, shown.**
2. **strew,**	**strewed,**	**strewed, strewn.**
3. **saw,**	**sawed,**	**sawed, sawn.**

The first of these is derived from the Anglo-Saxon weak verb *sceawian, sceawode:* the second, which is often written and oftener pronounced as *strow*, is from the Anglo-Saxon weak verb *strewian, strewode.* It was in the Middle English period that the strong participial forms of these two words came into use alongside of the weak ones; and, as in like instances, the analogy of verbs like *know*, *blow*, *grow*, and others, had the most powerful influence in their production and wide employment. But the strong forms never extended beyond the past participle, though the strong preterite *shew* for *showed* early established itself in the provincial dialects, and has never died out. *Saw*, as a verb, does not apparently go back to an early period. It was doubtless derived from the noun spelled in the same way, and its strong past participle seems to have been developed first in Modern English. To this list might justly also be added the verb *load*, which still has at times a passive participle *loaden*, though this is far from being as common as *laden*. But *lade* and *load* are both derived from the same Anglo-Saxon strong verb.

139. The addition of the strong participial ending *en* to verbs originally weak has met with success in the case of *hidden*, *shown*, *strown*, and *sawn*. It is probable, though it has never been proved, that some, if not all, of these forms came originally into the literary language from the Northern dialect. When, two or three centuries after the Norman conquest, that dialect re-appears once more in literature, one of its

special characteristics is its inclination to retain the full form *en* of the strong passive participle; while, on the other hand, the dialect of the South was early disposed to drop the *n*. The modern participle *sung*, in consequence, would be in the thirteenth century in the one speech *sungen*, in the other *sunge*, or *y-sunge*. But not only did the Northern dialect so prefer the termination *en* as to retain it in the cases where it strictly belonged, it also manifested the disposition to add it to words to which it did not properly belong. Certain weak verbs, such as *cast*, *cut*, *put*, *thrust*, mainly of Scandinavian origin, added to the weak passive participle, which by contraction had become the same as the infinitive, as in Modern English, the ending *en*, giving us such forms as *casten*, *cutten*, *putten*, *thrusten* or *throssen*; and precisely of a similar formation is the verbal adjective *boughten*, not infrequent in America. It cannot be said that such forms as these have ever made their way to any extent beyond the dialects in which they originated; but scattered through the whole of Modern English literature are occasional instances of the substitution of a strong participial termination for that of a weak one; as, for instance, *paven* as used by Milton (Comus, line 886). One marked form is, however, here to be noticed: this is the past participle *proven* for *proved*. The word is derived from the French, and in literary use has been inflected, until the present century, like all other foreign verbs, according to the weak conjugation throughout. But the strong participial form *proven* has made its way from the Scottish sub-dialect of the Northern dialect into the language of literature, and not only has grown common, but promises to become universal; for it is widely employed by many of the best modern writers, and, in particular, occurs frequently in the later poems of Tennyson.

The English Strong Conjugation.

140. The variations and modifications that took place within the strong conjugation naturally involve the discussion of its preterites and past participles, not as distinguished from those of the weak conjugation, but as distinguished from each other. It therefore becomes necessary to introduce at this point much in regard to those parts of the verbs which strictly would find place elsewhere; for, in the history of the strong conjugation, numerous anomalies have arisen in consequence of the confusing of preterite and participial forms.

141. The Anglo-Saxon strong verbs may be divided into six classes,[1] the origin of the distinctions between

[1] For convenience of reference, and of comparison with other works, the following statement is made in reference to the classes as here given: Class I. corresponds to the first five strong conjugations in Grimm's system of the Teutonic strong conjugation; Class II., to Grimm's twelfth conjugation; Class III., to his tenth and eleventh conjugations; Class IV., to his seventh conjugation; Class V., to his eighth conjugation; and Class VI., to his ninth. Further, Class I., as here given, includes all the verbs that in Anglo-Saxon showed traces of primitive reduplication; the other classes, those that exhibit vowel-change proper. To Class II. belong all verbs that have the radical vowel *a* before a double consonant; to Class III., all that have the radical vowel *e* before a single consonant; to Class IV., all that have the radical vowel *a* usually before a single consonant, lengthened into *ō* in the preterite; to Class V., all that have *ī* as the radical vowel; and to Class VI., all that have *ū* as the radical vowel.

which it is not necessary to enter into here. Under each of these classes will be given those verbs originally belonging to it, which have been preserved with their strong inflections in Modern English. The principal parts given are, 1, the infinitive; 2 and 3 the preterite singular (excluding the second person) and the preterite plural; 4, the passive participle. Modern English forms are placed under the corresponding Anglo-Saxon; and, when one of the former has not been directly derived from the one under which it falls, the fact is marked by enclosing the modern word in parentheses.

142. CLASS I.—To this in Anglo-Saxon belonged about fifty verbs. The vowel of both numbers of the preterite was either *ê* or *eô*. Of these verbs nine remain to Modern English, and the preterite has *e* as its vowel, in one case *ea*.

	1	2	3	4
1. beat,	beâtan;	beôt,	beôton;	beâten.
	beat	*beat*		*beaten*
2. blow,	blâwan;	bleôw,	bleôwon;	blâwen.
	blow	*blew*		*blown*
3. crow,	crâwan;	creôw,	creôwon;	crâwen.
	crow	*crew*		(*crowed*)
4. fall,	feallan;	feôll,	feôllon;	feallen.
	fall	*fell*		*fallen*
5. grow,	grôwan;	greôw,	greôwon;	grôwen.
	grow	*grew*		*grown*
6. *hang* (II.),	hangan; } hôn; *hang*	hêng, (*hung*)	hêngon;	hangen. (*hung*)
7. hold,	healdan;	heôld,	heôldon;	healden.
	hold	*held*		(*held*) *holden*
8. know,	cnâwan;	cneôw,	cneôwon;	cnâwen.
	know	*knew*		*known*
9. throw,	þrâwan;	þreôw,	þreôwon;	þrâwen.
	threw	*threw*		*thrown*

Of this class it will be noticed, that, in Modern English, *hang* has passed from it to Class II. and it, in turn, has gained *draw* and *slay* from Class IV., and *fly* from Class VI.

143. Class II.—Of this class there were some eighty verbs in Anglo-Saxon. The vowel of the preterite singular was *a* or *ea*, in a few cases *æ;* that of the plural, invariably *u*. The Modern English preterite, when derived from the singular, has invariably *a;* when from the plural, *u* or *ou;* in two cases it has *o*. Twenty-three of the original verbs survive:—

1. bind,	bindan;	band,	bundon;	bunden.
	bind		*bound*	*bound*
2. climb,	climban;	clamb,	clumbon;	clumben.
	climb	*clomb*		*clomb?*
3. cling,	clingan;	clang,	clungon;	clungen.
	cling		*clung*	*clung*
4. drink,	drincan;	dranc,	druncon;	druncen.
	drink	*drank*	*drunk*	*drunk*
5. fight,	feohtan;	feaht,	fuhton;	fohten.
	fight		*fought*	*fought*
6. find,	findan;	fand,	fundon;	funden.
	find		*found*	*found*
7. -gin,	-ginnan;	-gan,	-gunnon;	-gunnen.
	-gin	*-gan,*	*-gun*	*-gun*
8. grind,	grindan;	grand,	grundon;	grunden.
	grind		*ground*	*ground*
9. ring,	ringan;	rang,	rungon;	rungen.
	ring	*rang*	*rung*	*rung*
10. run,	rinnan;	ran,	runnon;	runnen.
	(*run*)	*ran*		*run*
11. shrink,	scrincan;	scranc,	scruncon;	scruncen
	shrink	*shrank*	*shrunk*	*shrunk*
12. sing,	singan:	sang,	sungon;	sungen.
	sing	*sang*	*sung*	*sung*

13. slingan,	slingan; *sling*	slang,	slungon; *slung*	slungen. *slung*
14. slink,	slincan; *slink*	slanc,	sluncon; *slunk*	sluncen. *slunk*
15. spin,	spinnan; *spin*	span,	spunnon; *spun*	spunnen. *spun.*
16. spring,	springan; *spring*	sprang, *sprang*	sprungon; *sprung*	sprungen. *sprung*
17. sting,	stingan; *sting*	stang,	stungon; *stung*	stungen. *stung*
18. stink,	stincan; *stink*	stanc, *stank*	stuncon; *stunk*	stuncen. *stunk*
19. swim,	swimman; *swim*	swam, *swam*	swummon; *swum*	swummen. *swum*
20. swing,	swingan; *swing*	swang,	swungon; *swung*	swungen. *swung*
21. win,	winnan; *win*	wan,	wunnon; *won*	wunnen. *won*
22. wind,	windan; *wind*	wand,	wundon; *wound*	wunden. *wound*
23. wring,	wringan; *wring*	wrang,	wrungon; *wrung*	wrungen. *wrung*

Of these verbs, *clingan*, in Anglo-Saxon, does not have its modern meaning, but signifies 'to wither.' To this class have been added *hang*, from Class I., and *strike*, from Class V. In literary English, *hang* had for its preterite *heng*, the representative of the original form, until the fifteenth century, and perhaps later; but in the sixteenth this had usually given way to *hung*.

144. Class III.—To this belonged, in Anglo-Saxon, about forty verbs. These had, as the vowel of the preterite singular *æ*, *ea*, or *a*, and, correspondingly in the plural, *ǽ*, *eá*, or *á*. Sixteen of these verbs are still found in Modern English:—

1. bear,	beran; *bear*	bær, bæ̂ron; *(bore)*	boren. *born(e)*
2. bid,	biddan; *bid*	bæd, bæ̂don; *bade (bid)*	beden. *(bidden)*
3. break,	brecan; *break*	bræc, bræ̂con; *(broke)*	brecen, } brocen. } *broken*
4. come,	cuman; *come*	cam, câmon; *came*	cumen. *come*
5. eat,	etan; *eat*	æt, æ̂ton; *ate*	eten. *eaten, eat*
6. get,	getan; *get*	geat, geâton; *(got)*	geten. *(gotten, got)*
7. give,	gifan; *give*	geaf, geâfon; *gave*	gifen. *given*
8. lie,	licgan; *lie*	læg, læ̂gon; *lay*	legen. *lain*
9. see,	seohan; } seôn; } *see*	seah, sâwon; *saw*	segen, } sên. } *seen*
10. shear,	sceran; *shear*	scær, scæ̂ron; *(shore)*	scoren. *shorn*
11. sit,	sittan; *sit*	sæt, sæ̂ton; *sat*	seten. *(sat)*
12. speak,	specan; *speak*	spæc, spæ̂con; *(spoke)*	specen, } spocen. } *spoken*
13. steal,	stelan; *steal*	stæl, stæ̂lon; *(stole)*	stolen. *stolen*
14. tear,	teran; *tear*	tær, tæ̂ron; *(tore)*	toren. *torn*
15. tread,	tredan; *tread*	træd, træ̂don; *(trod)*	treden. *(trodden)*
16. weave,	wefan; *weave*	wæf, wæ̂fon; *(wove)*	wefen. *(woven)*

145. To this class belongs the defective verb ***quoth***, found only in the preterite in Modern English. In Anglo-Saxon the principal parts were as follows: —

cweðan, cwæð, cwæ̂don, cweden.

By the fourteenth century it was rare that any other part of this verb beside the preterite was used; but the preterite itself was then very common. It appeared indifferently with the consonant of the singular or of the plural, as *quoth* or *quod;* but the former became the prevalent form before the end of the Middle English period. The compound *be-queathe* (123) has retained the full verbal inflection, but has passed entirely over to the weak conjugation.

146. Class IV. — In this class there were in Anglo-Saxon nearly thirty verbs. The vowel for both numbers of the preterite was *ô;* in Modern English it is *oo* or *o*. Nine of these verbs still remain in our language with the strong inflection: —

1. *draw* (I.),	dragan; *draw*	drôg, drôgon; (*drew*)	dragen. *drawn*
2. heave,	hebban; *heave*	hôf, hôfon; *hove*	hafen. (*hove*)
3. (for)sake,	sacan; *-sake*	sôc, sôcon; *-sook*	sacen. *-saken*
4. shake,	scacan; *shake*	scôc, scôcon; *shook*	scacen. *shaken*
5. *slay* (I.),	slahan; sleân; *slay*	slôh, slôgon; (*slew*)	slagen. *slain*
6. stand,	standan; *stand*	stôd, stôdon; *stood*	standen. (*stood*)
7. swear,	swerian; *swear*	swôr, swôron; *swore*	sworen. *sworn*
8. take,	tacan; *take*	tôc, tôcon; *took*	tacen. *taken*
9. wake,	wācan; *wake*	wôc, wôcon; *woke*	wacen. (*woke?*)

Of these verbs *draw* and *slay* have, in Modern English, passed over to Class I., in the preterite.

147. CLASS V. — This class numbered over fifty verbs in Anglo-Saxon. The preterite singular had for its vowel *â;* the plural had *i*. In Modern English the vowels of the preterite are *a*, *o*, and *i*. Fifteen of these verbs survive: —

1. (a)bide,	bîdan; *-bide*	bâd, *bode*	bidon;	biden. (*-bided*)
2. bite,	bîtan; *bite*	bât,	biton; *bit*	biten. *bitten*
3. chide,	cîdan; *chide*	câd,	cidon; *chid*	ciden. *chidden*
4. cleave ('to adhere'),	clîfan; *cleave*	clâf, *clave*	clifon;	clifen. (*cleaved*)
5. drive,	drîfan; *drive*	drâf, *drove*	drifon;	drifen. *driven*
6. ride,	rîdan; *ride*	râd, *rode*	ridon; *rid*	riden. *ridden*
7. rise,	rîsan; *rise*	râs, *rose*	rison;	risen. *risen*
8. shine,	scînan; *shine*	scân, *shone*	scinon;	scinen. (*shone*)
9. shrive,	scrîfan; *shrive*	scrâf, *shrove*	scrifon;	scrifen. *shriven*
10. slide,	slîdan; *slide*	slâd,	slidon; *slid*	sliden. *slidden*
11. smite,	smîtan; *smite*	smât, *smote*	smiton;	smiten. *smitten*
12. stride,	strîdan; *stride*	strâd, *strode*	stridon;	striden. *stridden*
13. *strike* (II.),	strîcan; *strike*	strâc, (*struck*)	stricon;	stricen. *stricken*
14. thrive,	þrîfan; *thrive*	þrâf, *throve*	þrifon;	þrifen. *thriven*
15. write,	wrîtan; *write*	wrât, *wrote*	writon; *writ*	writen. *written*

Of these verbs, *strîcan*, in Anglo-Saxon, meant 'to go rapidly;' and the modern meaning of the verb did not belong to it. It has also passed over to Class II., in Modern English, in the preterite, though it retains sometimes its regular past participle, *stricken.*

148. Class VI. — To this class belonged, in Anglo-Saxon, about fifty verbs. The preterite in the singular had for its vowel *eá;* for the plural, *u.* In Modern English the vowel of the preterite is *o* or *oo.*

1. choose,	ceósan ;	ceás,	curon ;	coren.
	choose	*chose*		*cho(s)en*
2. cleave ('to split'),	cleófan ;	cleáf,	clufon ;	clofen.
	cleave	*clove*		*cloven*
3. *fly*,	fleógan ;	fleáh,	flugon ;	flogen.
	fly	(*flew*)		*flown*
4. freeze,	freósan ;	freás,	fruron ;	froren.
	freeze	*froze*		*fro(z)en*
5. seethe,	seóðan ;	seáð,	sudon ;	soden.
	seethe		*sod*	*sodden*
6. shoot,	sceótan ;	sceát,	scuton ;	scoten.
	shoot		*shot*	*shot*

Of these words, *fly*, *flew*, has gone over to the first class in Modern English, its forms apparently having been confounded with the preterite and past participle of *flówan*, 'to flow.' *Shoot* may also be regarded as a contract verb of the weak conjugation, the old strong participle *shotten*, having gone out of use.

149. The above lists embrace seventy-seven verbs. They are all which are now in use that can trace their origin to a known Anglo-Saxon strong verb; and some of them, as has already been shown, have developed weak forms along with the strong ones. But, in addition to these, ten other verbs have been pointed out as now having the strong inflection, which were either

not known to the Anglo-Saxon at all, or were known only as weak verbs. It is no easy matter to state definitely the time of their introduction into the language, or of their transition from the weak to the strong conjugation; and all assertions are liable to be proved mistaken as the earlier literature is more closely studied. But, apparently, it may be said with a fair degree of certainty, that *fling*, *stick*, and *strive* belong to the Early English period; *hide*, *spit*, and *wear*, to the Middle English; and *dig*, *stave*, *string*, and the technical sea-term *reeve*, belong to Modern English. Within the strong conjugation, they may be assigned to the following classes:—

II.	III.	V.
dig.	wear.	hide.
fling.	spit.	reeve.
stick.		stave.
string.		strive.

150. The strong verbs now existing in the language consequently number eighty-seven. Necessarily, this assertion is made of the simple verbs only, and does not refer to their compounds, which follow the conjugation of the simple verb. These compounds, however, are few in number; as compared with the earliest period of the speech, the loss in them has been enormous. The word *fret*, it is to be added, is inflected weak; though the simple verb *eat*, of which it is a compound, belongs to the strong conjugation: and *forsake* is a single instance also of the preservation of a compound while the simple verb *sake* has perished.

There are, besides, a few verbs, such as *bide* and *gin*, that are rarely to be met with, except as compounded.

151. An examination of the inflection of verbs of the strong conjugation, as given above, brings to light two facts which it is important to comprehend clearly; for they serve to explain much that may seem peculiar in the later history of the verbs. These facts may be stated as follows:—

1. That, with the exception of the verbs belonging to Classes I. and IV., there is in Anglo-Saxon a difference of vowel, or of vowel-sound, between the preterite singular and the preterite plural. The verbs in which this vowel variation appeared constitute more than three-fourths of the strong verbs now existing in our tongue.

2. That, in the second and fifth classes,—embracing about one-half of the Anglo-Saxon strong verbs that have been transmitted to Modern English,—the vowel of the preterite plural and of the past participle is precisely the same. *We wrote*, for illustration, would be, in Anglo-Saxon, *we writon; written* would be *writen;* and the only essential difference between the two forms would be the vowels *o* and *e* of the endings. In one instance in the second class, and in all the verbs of the sixth class, the vowel of the preterite plural was *u*, and that of the participle *o;* but as, in Early and Middle English, *o*, in such cases, was used for *u*, even here a distinction ceased to exist.

152. From these two facts have resulted in Modern English varying forms for the preterite and passive

participle, the origin of which can now easily be traced Let us take, for illustration, the history of the preterite of the Anglo-Saxon verb *singan*, 'to sing;' for the comprehension of the development of one verb involves that of all.

153. In the earliest period of English, when one wished to say, *I sang*, or *sung*, he used the form *ic sang:* when he wished to say, *we sang*, or *sung*, he used the expression *we sungon*. The plural preterite differed from the singular by having a termination *on*, and by change of vowel. After the break-up of Anglo-Saxon, the first thing to be affected was this ending *on*. In accordance with the principle already so often stated, the vowel *o* was weakened into *e*, and *sungon* became *sungen*. But, along with this weakening of the vowel, there was also a tendency to drop the final *n;* and *sungen* became *sunge*. The next steps were to drop the final *e* in pronunciation, and then in writing; and we have, in consequence, for the preterite plural, the form *sung*. Hence, there remained as a result two forms for the preterite,—one for the singular and one for the plural,—differing from each other only by a single letter, and that letter a vowel. This statement requires a slight modification. The second person singular of the preterite had the same vowel as the plural. *Sangest*, for illustration, would, in Anglo-Saxon, be *sunge*. The use of this person, much more common than at present, helped to increase the confusion that soon arose in the usage of an uneducated people. It was inevitable that a distinction seem-

ingly arbitrary, and serving no useful purpose, should break down; and this was what happened. For a while, doubtless, the distinction was kept up by individuals long after it had disappeared from the language of the great mass of men. To say *I sang* and *we sung* was, probably, vaguely felt by many, and loudly maintained by some, to be the only correct usage; even after, in the ordinary speech, men had become accustomed to say indifferently, *I sang* or *we sang*, or *I sung* or *we sung*. In particular verbs, also, the distinction lasted much later than it did in others. An examination of the best manuscripts of Chaucer's poetry leaves little doubt, that, with him, *gan* was regularly the singular of the preterite, *gunnen*, *gunne*, or *gun*, the plural; and the same statement may be made as to his use of *schal*, 'shall,' and *schullen* or *schulle*. But even in his time the distinction between the preterite singular and plural of most verbs had broken down generally, and the forms originally belonging to one number were used for both; and, not unfrequently, both forms were used indifferently and interchangeably. Hence arose a double set of preterite forms, such as *drank* and *drunk*, *began* and *begun*, *rang* and *rung*, *sprang* and *sprung*, *rode* and *rid*, *wrote* and *writ*, which have been transmitted to Modern English.

154. These double preterites were far more numerous in the Middle English period than now. The tendency of the language has been to steadily reduce their number; and many forms, which, even in the

early period of Modern English, were in good use, have now disappeared altogether, or are heard only in the language of low life. Ben Jonson, in his grammar, gives a long list of verbs that had two different forms for the preterite in his time; and, in a large proportion of them, one form is now obsolete or antiquated. Especially is this true of Class V., in which, according to him, *bide* has for preterite *bode* or *bĭd*, *chide* has *chode* or *chĭd*, *drive* has *drove* or *drĭve*, *rise* has *rose* or *rĭs*, *slide* has *slode* or *slĭd*, *smite* has *smote* or *smĭt*, *stride* has *strode* or *strĭd*, and *write* has *wrote* or *wrĭt;* and in Class II. he gives to *climb* the two preterites *clomb* and *clĭmb;* to *fling*, the preterites *flang* and *flung;* to *swing*, the preterites *swang* and *swung;* to *wring*, the preterites *wrang* and *wrung*, and, in like manner, double forms to many others.

155. In all these instances it is observed that one form comes from the singular of the preterite, the other from the plural. In the majority of instances only one form continues now in use; but there are still a number of verbs which retain the two, — one derived from the original singular of the preterite, the other from the original plural. They all belong to the second or fifth classes of the strong verbs; and, in the following list, the Anglo-Saxon original forms are added in parentheses.

156. The verbs now possessing double forms for the preterite are the following: —

	Original Singular.	Original Plural.
drink,	drank (*dranc*),	drunk (*drunc-on*).
(be)gin,	-gan (*gan*),	-gun (*gunn-on*).
ring,	rang (*rang*),	rung (*rung-on*).
shrink,	shrank (*scranc*),	shrunk (*scrunc-on*).
sing,	sang (*sang*),	sung (*sung-on*).
spring,	sprang (*sprang*),	sprung (*sprung-on*).
stink,	stank (*stanc*),	stunk (*stunc-on*).
swim,	swam (*swam*),	swum (*swumm-on*).
ride,	rode (*rád*),	rid (*rid-on*).
write,	wrote (*wrát*),	writ (*writ-on*).

To these must be added the word *bid*, from *biddan* of Class III., whose forms have been confounded in later English with those of *bídan*, 'to abide,' of Class V.; thus giving the following preterites: —

	Original Singular.	Original Plural.
bid,	bad(e) (*bæd*, III.), (*bád*, V.),	bid (*bid-on*, V.).

This list includes only those forms in present use, and even some of these may be said to belong to the language of poetry rather than of prose.

157. But most of the strong verbs have now but one form of the preterite. The following lists show the forms that have been derived from the singular, and those from the plural, in the classes already mentioned.

1. Forms derived from the singular of the preterite: —

V.

(a)bide,	-bode (*bád*).	smite,	smote (*smát*).
cleave,	clave (*cláf*).	shrive,	shrove (*scráf*)

drive,	drove (*drāf*).	stride,	strode (*strād*).
rise,	rose (*rās*).	II.	
shine,	shone (*scān*).	run,	ran (*ran*).
thrive,	throve (*þrāf*).		

In earlier English it is also to be added, in regard to these verbs of Class V., that the vowel *a* was more common than *o*, the latter gradually supplanting it in these verbs in the Middle English, and in many cases even earlier. But *drave* lasted down to the sixteenth century, and is still used in poetry; while other forms with the vowel *a* survive in the dialects.

2. Forms derived from the plural of the preterite: —

II.		V.	
1. bind,	bound (*bund-on*).	1. bite,	bit (*bit-on*).
2. cling,	clung (*clung-on*).	2. chide,	chid (*cid-on*).
3. fight,	fought (*fuht-on*).	3. slide,	slid (*slid-on*).
4. grind,	ground (*grund-on*).		
5. sling,	slung (*slung-on*).		
6. slink,	slunk (*slunc-on*).		
7. spin,	spun (*spunn-on*).		
8. sting,	stung (*stung-on*).		
9. swing,	swung (*swung-on*).		
10. win,	won (*wunn-on*).		
11. wind,	wound (*wund-on*).		
12. wring,	wrung (*wrung-on*).		

Clomb, the preterite of *climb*, may have come either from the Anglo-Saxon preterite singular or plural.

It is hardly necessary to add that other forms derived from the singular are also occasionally to be met with, especially in Middle English and in the earlier period of Modern English. *Span* and *swang*, and *slank* and *chode*, and others, are by no means infrequent in our past literature, and may be revived in the future.

158. It is evident, that in the verbs of the second class, wherever only one form has been selected, the Modern English has preferred the plural. The only exception, indeed, is in the case of *run;* and this was doubtless due to the fact that the vowel *u* had made its way into the present, where it had no right: and so, instead of *rin*, that form became *run;* and, to distinguish the preterite from the present, the vowel of the singular was chosen. On the other hand, the verbs of the fifth class have, in most cases, chosen the singular forms. This may seem the result purely of accident; but, while partly so, it was far from being so entirely. The choice of the plural in verbs of Class II. was largely owing to the influence of the vowel of the passive participle, which, with them, was either the same as the plural of the preterite, or came to be the same. When *u* was the vowel of the preterite plural, either *u* or *o* was the vowel of the participle, as can easily be seen by reference to the examples. In Early and Middle English, *o* became the representative, frequently, of the original *u* and *o*. *Songen* and *wonnen*, for illustration, might be either the plural of the preterite or the passive participle; and, as in both forms, the dropping of the termination took place at about the same time, *song*(*e*) and *won*(*ne*) became the shortened form of both these parts of the verb; and when, at a still later period, the *u* took the place in pronunciation, and also in writing (with the excep-

tion of *won*), of the *o*, it entered alike into both these parts of the verb. But in the weak conjugation the preterite and past participles had now assumed precisely the same form; and the influence of this inflection was insensibly brought to bear upon these verbs, so as to make them conform in this respect to the practice of the vast majority of verbs in the language. The plural was, therefore, naturally chosen, when the selection was limited to one form. This similarity of form of the preterite and past participle has led some grammarians to assert that the forms now exhibited by the preterite in these verbs are intrusions of the passive participle; but this is a mistake. They are simply in their origin preterite plurals, which the similarity of the participle aided to establish over the preterite singular as the exclusive form in Modern English.

159. Why, then, did not this become the practice in the verbs of Class V.? Why was it that here the singular form has been preferred in Modern English? This is due to the fact, that, in verbs of this class, the original participle either dropped out of the language entirely, or retained its termination *en*. *Shinen* and *cliven*, the participles of *shine* and *cleave*, early disappeared. *Abidden*, from *abide*, lasted to a later period; but it never could be called common. On the other hand, most of these verbs retained their full participial forms, such as *risen*, *driven*, *smitten*, and the like; and, in consequence, there was not a constant resemblance between them and the shortened

form of the preterite, such as *drive* and *ris* and *smit*. The latter, in consequence, gave way generally to the singular form. In the three cases of *bite*, *chide*, and *slide*, in which the plural form has been the one adopted in Modern English, the influence of the participle must be regarded as having decided the matter; for in each of them *bit*, *chid*, and *slid* have been common shortened forms of that part of the verb.

160. But there are, nevertheless, a number of verbs in which there has been an intrusion of the vowel of the participle into the preterite: these belong to Class III. (144). In Anglo-Saxon, verbs of this class whose stem ended in a liquid belonged to a group which had *o* or *u* as the vowel of the participle; as *cuman*, 'to come,' had for the passive participle *cumen*, and *beran*, 'to bear,' had *boren*. Of the two, the vowel *o* was much the more common. But there was another group of verbs belonging to this class, whose stem ended in a consonant not a liquid, and with these the vowel of the passive participle was almost always *e*; thus *etan*, 'to eat,' and *tredan*, 'to tread,' had for participles *eten* and *treden*. But, even in the Anglo-Saxon period, the *o* of the participles of the first group sometimes supplanted the *e* of the participles of the second group; and *spocen* and *brocen* are more common than *specen* and *brecen*, the strictly regular forms. This tendency to use *o* as the vowel of the past participle increased after the break-up of the Anglo-Saxon inflection; and from the parti-

ciple it made its way into the preterite, supplanting the older forms in *a* of verbs belonging to this class. There are, consequently, two forms of the preterite of these verbs, — one derived from the vowel of the original preterite, and the other from the vowel of the passive participle. The first of these are the older; but in most cases they have now gone out of use. The verbs of this class which have exhibited, or do exhibit, these double forms of the preterite, are the following: —

Infinitive.	New Preterite.	Old Preterite.
bear,	bore,	bare.
break,	broke,	brake.
get,	got,	gat.
shear,	shore,	share.
speak,	spoke,	spake.
steal,	stole,	stale.
tear,	tore,	tare.
tread,	trod(e),	trad.
weave,	wove,	wave.

By a false analogy with these verbs, *swear*, which belongs to Class IV. (146), and whose preterite is, in consequence, strictly *swore* (A.S. *swór*, *swór-on*), took to itself another form with *a*, *sware*, which is now rarely used outside of poetry. The weak verb *wear*, which, on becoming strong, entered this class, developed likewise two preterites, *ware* and *wore*.

161. The other verbs of this class generally follow the ancient inflection. *Bid*, as already mentioned, has mixed its forms with those of *bide* (Class V.). The verb *eat* may be said to have a peculiar history of its

own, a long vowel-sound having not only taken the place of the original short vowel-sound of the stem *ĕt* in the infinitive and passive participle; but the vowel of the preterite in Modern English is sometimes long as in *āte*, sometimes short as in *ĕat:* in the latter, the barbarous spelling, as not unusual, gives no clew to the pronunciation.

162. The verbs of the first and fourth classes, having the same vowel-sound in the singular and the plural of the preterite, have never developed double strong forms, with the single exception of *swear*, which, as already mentioned, had given to it the preterite *sware*, through what was, strictly speaking, a blunder. In verbs of the sixth class, the *o* of the preterite can have come either from the vowel of the plural or from that of the participle; for in Early and Middle English the *u* of the plural had become *o*, and this was sufficient to establish the exclusive use of that vowel in the preterites of the few verbs now in use that belonged to that class.

163. A few verbs of this sixth class underwent, in the Anglo-Saxon period, rhotacism in the preterite plural and the passive participle; that is, changed their *s* into *r*. Thus the Anglo-Saxon *leósan*, 'to lose,' had for the preterite plural *luron* instead of *luson*, and the participle *loren* instead of *losen;* and when this verb, at a later period, passed over to the weak conjugation, it left behind it its participle *loren* in the adjective *lorn*, seen more frequently in the compound *forlorn*. There was another verb of this kind which is still in

flected strong, — the word *freeze;* but it has given up its rhotacism, though a poetic adjective, *froren* or *frore,* still recalls the form of the original past participle.

164. The account given of the preterite of the strong conjugation has, to a large extent, involved an account of the past participle. Still the latter has, in some respects, a special history of its own; but, on account of its close alliance in form with the preterite, it will be considered next.

The Past Participle of the Strong Conjugation.

165. The passive participle of strong verbs was originally formed in all the Teutonic languages by adding to the stem the suffix *-na* with the connective *a,* thus making the termination, exclusive of the case-signs, *ana.* In the Anglo-Saxon the final *a* of this ending had dropped, and the initial *a* had been weakened into *e.* The termination, therefore, in the earliest period of English, was regularly *-en,* except in a few instances when the *e* was syncopated.

166. After the Norman conquest the *n* was frequently dropped, especially in the South of England. Usage on this point was, however, very variable during the whole of the Early and Middle English periods; and as a result the form of the passive participle came into Modern English with a good deal of variation. These diversities can be arranged under the following heads, though in a few cases the differences are rather orthographical than real.

167. (1.) Some verbs have lost the termination entirely. This includes nearly all of Class II. (143), but none outside of it. Forms like *begunnen*, *rungen*, *sungen*, *sprungen*, and others of this class, in very few cases were in existence at the beginning of Modern English. Chaucer occasionally exhibits the full form as *songen* (C. T. 1531); but with him the *n* is usually dropped, and *begonne*, *songe*, and *spronge*, and similar forms, are those almost invariably met with. Even *bounden*, *drunken*, *foughten*, *shrunken*, which are the only full forms of this class that have been retained in Modern English, are almost always used, when used at all, as adjectives. *Come*, of Class III. might, perhaps, be properly added to this group; for in pronunciation, though not in writing, it has dropped the termination entirely. *Comen* is not uncommon in Elizabethan English, being frequently met with in Bacon's works; but it is not often used after the beginning of the seventeenth century.

168. (2.) Some verbs have retained the termination, though in some of them the *e* is syncopated; but this is the only contraction they undergo, as they never drop the *n*. They come from all classes except the second (143) and sixth (148), and are about the same in number as those belonging to the preceding group. The participles *fallen*, *known* (I.), *given*, *torn* (III.), *shaken*, *taken* (IV.), and *driven*, *risen* (V.), may be instanced as representatives of this group, in which the final *n* never disappears.

169. (3.) Between these groups stands a third

which has double forms for the past participle, — one with the ending *n*, the other without it. A still further distinction might be made in the fact that some words drop *en* entirely, others drop only *n;* but this is a distinction existing merely on paper, as this final *e* is never sounded. The following is the list of verbs which exhibit double forms of the past participle, with the classes to which they belong: —

I.	beat,	beaten, beat.
II.	bind,	bounden, bound.
II.	drink,	drunken, drunk.
II.	fight,	foughten, fought.
II.	shrink,	shrunken, shrunk.
III.	bid,	bidden, bid.
III.	break,	broken, broke.
III.	eat,	eaten, eat.
III.	get,	gotten, got.
III.	speak,	spoken, spoke.
III.	steal,	stolen, stole.
III.	weave,	woven, wove.
III.	tread,	trodden, trod.
V.	bite,	bitten, bit.
V.	chid,	chidden, chid.
V.	ride,	ridden, rid.
V.	slide,	slidden, slid.
V.	write,	written, writ.
VI.	choose,	chosen, chose.
VI.	cleave,	cloven, clove.
VI.	freeze,	frozen, froze.
VI.	shot,	shotten, shot.
VI.	seethe,	sodden, sod.

To these may be added the originally weak verb *hide* (Class V.), which has the two forms *hidden* and *hid* for the participle.

In regard to most of these verbs it is sufficient to say that the full forms are now generally preferred, outside of those belonging to the second class, which, indeed, can now hardly be reckoned as participles. But there is no established rule in regard to these forms, and the widest diversity of usage has existed, and still continues to exist, in respect to many of them.

170. (4.) A certain number of verbs have been mentioned in which the participial forms made their way into the preterite. On the other hand, the reverse operation has happened in a number of instances: the preterite has made its way into the past participle. In some cases it has entirely superseded the regular form; in others, it has taken its place alongside of it. The following is the list of verbs in which this transition of the preterite into the participle has occurred, and is still in use: the older forms, when entirely obsolete, are printed in Italic: —

Infinitive.	New Passive Participle.	Old Passive Participle.
I. hold,	held,	holden.
II. drink,	drank,	drunk.
III. sit,	sat,	*sitten*, *sit*.
IV. stand,	stood,	*stonden*.
IV. wake,	woke,	*waken*.
V. (a)bide,	(a)bode,	(*a*)*bidden*.
V. shine,	shone,	*shinen*.

The participles *waken* and *shinen* disappeared early; but the weak form of *waked* was and is so generally used, that the use of *woke* as a participle may even now be regarded as uncommon. It was in the sixteenth century that most of these transitions were effected; in particular, it was then that *held*, *sat*, *stood*, and *abode* were established as passive participles. *Drank* and *drunk* are both in use at the present time, and the choice varies with the writer.

171. These words, however, are only the relics of what was once a general movement, which has been completely arrested. In the sixteenth and seventeenth centuries the use of the preterite for the past participle was common in a large number of verbs in which it is no longer seen. The literature of the Elizabethan period, and even later, abounds in instances of the use of *drove* for *driven*, *fell* for *fallen*, *rode* for *ridden*, *rose* for *risen*, *forsook* for *forsaken*, *shook* for *shaken*, *smote* for *smitten*, *strove* for *striven*, *took* for *taken*, *wrote* for *written*, and doubtless numerous other like forms. In some cases these preterites used for the regular past participle lasted down to a late period. *Wrote*, for illustration, is very common for *written* in the literature of the eighteenth century; and at the present day these forms occasionally appear. But the language at the present time is averse to their use, and, with the exception of those mentioned in the preceding section, is disposed to exclude the employment of them wholly.

172. Two other participial forms are worthy of attention. The verb *bear* has two forms, *born* and *borne*, and in ordinary usage limits the former to the sense of 'brought forth.' The difference is, in its origin, a

difference of spelling; and the distinction is unknown to the periods before Modern English. The verb *strike*, also, which has passed from the fifth class (147) to the second (143), has usually *struck* for both the preterite and the past participle; but it sometimes makes use of the original participial form *stricken*, and along with this it developed a form *strucken*, by adding the participial ending *en* to the preterite.

173. The origin of *y*, as prefixed to the past participle, will be given in the account of the past participle of the weak conjugation (201).

174. This concludes the discussion of the principal parts of the strong conjugation. It will be seen from this, that, since the beginning of the Modern English period, that conjugation has lost none of the verbs belonging to it; though there have been times when it seemed as if weak forms of all would become universal. The tendency of the language at present is unquestionably to prefer the strong form wherever there is any choice; and it is not impossible that many verbs now inflected weak will, in the future, receive back their old inflection. The use of *clomb* in poetry is becoming more and more common; and *dive* (originally of Class VI.) frequently assumes, in the language of common life, its ancient preterite *dove*, and this, in consequence, occasionally makes its way into the written speech. Cases of this kind may be always expected to occur. The English dialects also have retained the strong form in some cases where the literary language has assumed the weak,

and at any moment the original inflection may be taken up by the latter from the former. These dialects, indeed, have often developed strong forms in verbs that are strictly weak, as has already been seen in the case of *show, shew,* which is found both in England and this country. So, also, *squeeze* has a strong preterite *squoze* in the dialects of some parts of England; and this can be heard, likewise, in various parts of the United States in the speech of the uneducated. Sporadic forms like these crop up here and there constantly in our literature; and their occurrence renders it unsafe to assert that particular forms are never employed. It can only be said that they are not the ones usually employed.

The Weak Conjugation.

175. It has already been pointed out that the distinguishing characteristic of the weak conjugation was, that it added a syllable to form the preterite; that this syllable was nothing more than a verbal form corresponding to the reduplicated perfect of the English verb *do,* so that to illustrate an ancient usage by a modern hypothetical formation, instead of employing an expression equivalent to *I did love,* the preterite was denoted by an expression equivalent to *love-did-I;* that this appended verb was so cut down, and so closely united with the leading verb, that it was only in the dual and plural numbers of the Gothic preterite that its full form was seen. In Anglo-Saxon it was represented in the first person of the preterite singular

by *de*, as *bernan*, 'to burn,' had for its past tense *bernde*, 'burned;' and in general terms it may be that the said Anglo-Saxon weak verb formed its preterite by adding *de*.

176. Its passive participle was also distinguished from that of the strong conjugation by the fact that the latter ended in *en;* while in the former the termination was *d*, or occasionally *t*.

177. But the Teutonic weak verb had originally a connective which entered between the stem and the termination. This connective in its full form was *aja;* but this was never actually seen, for, from an early period, it was modified in three ways. Either the initial *a* was dropped, and the connective, in consequence, became *ja*, vocalized into *ia;* or the *j* was dropped, and the two vowels *aa*, coming together, were contracted usually into *ó;* or the final *a* was dropped, leaving the connective *aj* vocalized into *ai*. According to the use of these three connectives arose in the Teutonic three conjugations of weak verbs, all of which are preserved in Gothic and Old High German. But in the other early Teutonic tongues the third conjugation above mentioned, the one with the connective *ai*, had disappeared. In the Anglo-Saxon the two first-named conjugations were still found; though that with the connective *ó* was showing, in some respects, signs of decay, the forms belonging to the conjugation with the connective *ia* having taken its place in certain parts of the verb. But, even in this latter conjugation, the *ia* was generally weakened to *e*.

More than this, the connective *e* was dropped in the preterite in the case of all verbs with long stems. The verb *hŷr-an*, 'to hear,' with its long stem *hŷr*, formed, for example, the preterite *hŷrde*, 'heard,' not *hŷr-e-de*. And, as most of the verbs of this conjugation had the vowel of the stem long by nature or by position, there were comparatively few that formed their preterites by adding *ede*.

178. In the English of the Anglo-Saxon period, consequently, there may be said to be two conjugations of the weak verb, — one forming the preterite by adding *de*, and occasionally *ede*, to the stem, the other by adding *ode*. The following examples will illustrate the differences between them: —

dêm-an, *deem*,	dêm-de.	I.
der-ia-n, *harm*,	der-e-de.	
luf-ia-n, *love*,	luf-o-de.	II.

179. These represent the two early weak conjugations as distinguished from each other in the preterite; for already in the present tense the connective *ia* of the first conjugation had made its way into the second. But within certainly a century and a half after the Norman conquest the distinction had disappeared. The connective *o* of the second conjugation was generally weakened to *e*, although it is occasionally found even as late as the end of the thirteenth century, and perhaps still later. A necessary result of this was, that verbs of the original Anglo-Saxon second conjugation formed their preterites precisely like short-stemmed

verbs of the first conjugation, both having the connective *e*. To this conformed, in the latter part of the Early English period, and still more in the Middle English period, many, and perhaps most, of the long-stemmed verbs of the first conjugation. Instead of *dēmde*, for instance, the preterite became *demede*. The connective *e*, consequently, became, by the beginning of the Middle English period, the general connective of the weak preterite, which it has always since remained. There were, and still are, exceptions to this statement; but, as a general statement, it is sufficiently accurate.

180. It may therefore be said that *ede* in the Early English period was added to the stem of weak verbs to form the preterite; thus the past tense of *thank* was written and pronounced *thankèdè*. But in the fourteenth century certainly, and perhaps earlier, the *e* final of *ede* began to disappear from pronunciation, and in the fifteenth century the rule became general not to sound it. At the beginning of Modern English it had disappeared entirely. Its disuse in pronunciation led, likewise, to its disuse in writing or printing, and *thankèdè*, to continue the same illustration, became *thankèd*. This left *ed* as the addition with which to form the preterite in Modern English. It was also attended by another consequence. As the past participle usually ended in *ed*, the dropping of the final *e* of the preterite was followed necessarily by the result that the forms for the preterite and past participle became the same.

181. But the modification of the preterite did not stop here. At the beginning of the Modern English period the connective *e* of the preterite — and the statement is likewise true of the past participle — began to be dropped in pronunciation. During the latter part of the sixteenth, and the earlier part of the seventeenth century, usage seems to have varied. In some words, or by some persons, the *ed* was pronounced as a distinct syllable; and in other words, or by other persons, the *e* was not sounded, and the *d* was joined directly in pronunciation to the preceding syllable, where it necessarily had often the sound of *t*. *Thankèd* of Middle English came, in consequence, in Modern English, to have the sound of *thankt*. The tendency to drop the *e* of *ed* in pronunciation went on steadily increasing, and became general; though, in writing, the full orthographic form was, in the large majority of instances, retained. At the present time the *ed* is rarely heard as a distinct syllable, save in verbs ending in *d* or *t*, as *dread, dreadèd, wet, wettèd;* and in certain participles used as adjectives, such as *agèd* and *learnèd*, to distinguish them from the same words when used strictly as participles. The dropping of this *e* in many cases caused a change of pronunciation, which, in return, re-acted upon the form of the preterite; but this will be considered later.

182. *De, ede, ode,* and, finally, *ed,* have, accordingly, been the terminations usually added to form the weak preterite during the various periods of the history of the language But, even in Anglo-Saxon, the

ending *de* was subjected to an important modification, the influence of which has been widely extended in Modern English; and from it have sprung a number of peculiar forms for the preterite, different from those regularly formed. As the connective *ia* weakened to *e* was dropped in the vast majority of verbs of the first weak conjugation, the result was, that *de* was added directly to the stem, as in the preterite *dêmde*, given above as an example of the first weak conjugation. The effect of this was often to change the pronunciation; and, the spelling conforming to the sound, *d*, after certain consonants, became *t*; and *te* was the syllable added, and not *de*. In Anglo-Saxon, this was regularly the case when the stem of the verb ended in *c*, *p*, *t*, *x*, and sometimes in *s*, as will be seen by the following examples, in which the past participles are given, as well as the preterites. It will be noticed that *c* final of the root passes, in the preterite, into *k*.

Infinitives.	Preterites.	Past Participles.
sêcan, *seek*,	sôhte,	sôht.
cêpan, *keep*,	cêpte,	cêped.
cyssan, *kiss*,	cyste,	cyssed.
grêtan, *greet*,	grêtte,	grêted.
lixan, *shine*,	lixte,	lixed.

183. In the Early English, some of these verbs resumed the original connective *e* before the ending, in which case the common termination *de* was again employed, as, *kepede*, *kissede*, for *kepte*, *kiste*; and this, to a certain extent, diminished the number of verbs which had in Anglo-Saxon formed their preter-

ites by adding *te*. But, on the other hand, during the Middle English period their numbers were largely swelled by other agencies which were in operation. The dropping of the final *e* of *ede*, both in pronunciation and in writing, it has already been shown, was followed by the dropping of the connective *e* of *ed* in pronunciation, and sometimes in writing; so that *d* was added directly to the stem. After certain consonants, it assumed the sound of *t*. In some cases, this sound was denoted in the orthography, as it should have been in all; but in many other cases it was not. One result of this is, that a large number of verbs exist in Modern English which have their preterites ending in *ed* in writing, but which, in speaking, are almost invariably sounded as if they ended in *t*. It is hardly necessary to observe that it is the spoken language only that has any vitality; and a spelling of the written tongue that does not represent the sounds of the spoken tongue is essentially unscientific, not to say barbarous. Another result of this is, that, in Modern English, a number of double forms for the preterites and past participles have been developed, differing from each other, in some cases, only in spelling, and not at all in pronunciation; and, when differing in pronunciation, they differ only in the sound of final *d* or *t*. They usually occur in words ending in *l*, *ll*, *n*, *p*, *sh*, and words ending in the sound of *s*. The following list will furnish some of the more common illustrations: —

spell,	spelled, spelt.	spoil,	spoiled, spoilt.
pen,	penned, pent.	bless,	blessed, blest.
learn,	learned, learnt.	curse,	cursed, curst.
dip,	dipped, dipt.		
fix,	fixed, fixt.		

There are many double forms, like these, to be found at various periods in our literature; but, in general, it is true that the ending in *t*, when the word is so pronounced, is found much oftener in the early printed literature of Modern English than in that which appears at the present time.

184. The dropping of the final *e* of the termination *de* or *te*, had, likewise, necessarily the effect of producing a contracted form for the preterite, in the case of verbs whose stems ended in *d* or *t*, and, as a consequence, a number of verbs exist in Modern English which undergo no change of form in their principal parts. The precise history of these verbs can be clearly understood by a comparison of the changes which the Anglo-Saxon conjugation underwent in these particulars in the case of two, — ***sprǣdan***, 'to spread,' and ***settan***, 'to set.'

Infinitives.	Preterites.	Past Participles.
sprǣdan,	sprǣdde,	sprǣded.
settan,	sette,	setted, set.

When the *e* final disappeared in the fifteenth century from the preterite of such verbs, the second *d* or *t*, being now entirely unnecessary, was also dropped; and as, by that time, the infinitive had dropped its termination *an* weakened into *en*, and the present most of its personal endings, the forms of the infinitive, of the present, and of the preterite came, in consequence, to be precisely alike. To this, the past participle also early conformed, showing, even in the Anglo-Saxon period, a decided leaning toward contraction, as witnessed above in the case of *set*, found alongside of *setted*. The verb, as a result of these various changes, and droppings of the terminations, exhibited the same form throughout. But the tendency to bring about this result was not limited to the verbs of the kind which has just been mentioned. Words were brought also into this class which did not belong to the Anglo-Saxon, but came from the Norse or the Norman-French; and words which in Anglo-Saxon added *ode* to form the preterite, and not simply *de*, were in like manner made to conform to this inflection. But after many verbs had thus been stripped of their original endings, and been reduced to one unvarying form in their principal parts, a reaction set in. In the Middle English period began the practice of adding the regular termination *ed* to these contract forms, and this gathered strength as time went on. In some instances this has been wholly successful. The verb *start*, for illustration, which during much of the Middle English period had the preterite and past participle *start*, adopted the fuller form *started*, which has now become the only one. In other cases, contract and full forms of the preterite came into use, and have since been retained side by side. In a few instances only have the contract forms become the exclusive ones. The general present practice of the language in regard to these verbs will now be exhibited.

185. (*a.*) The following are those which have only contract forms in the preterite and the past participle, and therefore have all the principal parts the same: —

1. rid.	8. cost.	15. put.
2. shed.	9. cut.	16. set.
3. shred.	10. dight (poetic)	17. shut.
4. spread.	11. hit.	18. spit.
5. (be)stead.	12. hurt.	19. thrust.
6. burst.	13. hight (poetic).	
7. cast.	14. let.	

186. (*b.*) The following are those which have double forms for the preterite and past participles: —

1. bet,	betted, bet.	6. sweat,	sweated, sweat.
2. knit,	knitted, knit.	7. wet,	wetted, wet.
3. quit,	quitted, quit.	8. whet,	whetted, whet.
4. slit,	slitted, slit.	9. wont,	wonted, wont.
5. split,	splitted, split.		

187. Whether the full or the contract form shall be

employed is merely a question of usage, and of usage that has varied at different periods. In the above list it is largely a matter of individual preference which shall be adopted. The number, indeed, might be largely extended, if the various forms that have appeared at various times in the writings of good authors were to be included. The contracted form *wed* for *wedded* is not infrequent. In the early period of Modern English, *lift* for *lifted* is sometimes met with, and other unusual forms, either full or contract, are occasionally to be found in our literature. On the other hand, it is not at all uncommon to find, especially in the earlier authors of the Modern English period, forms like *casted*, and *hurted*, and *bursted;* and they are liable, in the very nature of things, to appear at any time, in obedience to that desire to bring about uniformity of inflection, which plays so important a part in the development of language.

188. Somewhat resembling these in their history is another series of contract forms for the preterite, which arose in certain verbs whose stems ended in *nd*. The conjugation of the Anglo-Saxon verb *sendan*, 'to send,' will show the original forms: —

sendan, sende, sended.

In such verbs as these, the dropping of the *e* of the preterite had the effect of changing the final *d* into *t*: *sende*, in consequence, became *sent*. It is not impossible, indeed, that this termination came into the preterite from the past participle, as contract forms for that part, such as *sent* for *sended*, appeared not infrequently in the Anglo-Saxon period. Here, again, the same course of proceeding took place as in the verbs whose history has just been given. After the contracted forms for the preterite and past participle had become established, new and strictly regular forms were developed in some cases by the adding of *ed*. The following list includes the verbs that have this contract form: —

1. bend,	bent.	5. send,	sent.
2. blend,	blent.	6. spend,	spent.
3. lend,	lent.	7. (wend,	went).
4. rend,	rent.		

Of these, *bend* and *blend* have often the fuller forms *bended* and *blended;* while *went* has become the preterite of the verb *go*, and *wend* has developed, to take its place, the regular form *wended* (265).

189. After this same method, several verbs not having the termination of the stem in *nd*, but in *ld* and *rd*, have likewise developed a contracted preterite and past participle, and, along with it, a full form. The following is the list: —

1. build,	builded, built.	3. gild,	gilded, gilt.
2. geld,	gelded, gelt.	4. gird,	girded, girt.

These are to be distinguished from such preterites as *learned* and *learnt*, *dwelled* and *dwelt*, *mixed* and *mixt*, *passed* and *past* (183); for in these latter, while there is an actual difference in the spelling, there is usually no additional syllable heard in the pronunciation.

190. All of the irregular weak verbs that have so far been mentioned, not only retain the same vowel through all their principal parts; they retain also the same length of that vowel. We now come to the discussion of certain verbs of which the vowel of the stem was either shortened in the preterite and the past participle, or was changed entirely.

191. This first class, which shortened the stem-vowel, is a development of the Early and Middle English periods; for no such shortening was known to the Anglo-Saxon. It seems to have been largely due to the influence of the short vowel of the preterite plural in certain strong verbs, which plural had become, with them, the usual form for both numbers; as, *chide*, *chĭd*, *shoot*, *shŏt*. This class may be conveniently subdivided into two. The first will embrace the verbs whose stems ended in *d* or *t*, especially the former. These dropped the *de* or *te* of the termination, like the class to which *spread* and *set* belonged (184); but they differed from them in having the vowel of the preterite shorter than that of the infinitive or present. The list embraces the following verbs, to which the Anglo-Saxon primitives are subjoined:—

1.	bleed, *blēdan*	blĕd. *blēdde*	5.	meet, *mētan*	mĕt. *mētte*
2.	breed, *brēdan*	brĕd. *brēdde*	6.	read, *rēdan*	rĕad. *rēdde*
3.	feed, *fēdan*	fĕd. *fēdde*	7.	speed, *spēdan*	spĕd. *spēdde*
4.	lead, *lēdan*	lĕd. *lēdde*	8.	(be)tide, *tīdian*	-tĭd. *tīdde.*

It will be noticed that *read*, in Modern English, actually shortens the vowel of the preterite and past participle, although no change takes place in the spelling. To the list may also be added *heat* (A.-S., *hǽtan, hǽtte*), which in Elizabethan English had a preterite and participle *hĕt*, along with the full form, *heated;* and this is still heard in the language of low life. To it may also be added the two following verbs, with their double forms for the preterite and participle: —

plead,	pleaded, } plĕad. }	light,	lighted, } lĭt. }

Hide, hĭd, etymologically should also be reckoned here; but, as explained in sect. 134, it seems best to regard it as a strong verb. *Betide* sometimes exhibits the full regular form *betided*, as also *speed* in certain senses has *speeded.*

Plead is of Romance origin; while *light* represents two Anglo-Saxon verbs, *lýhtan*, 'to shine,' and *lihtan*, 'to make lighter,' and 'to alight.'

192. The second subdivision embraces those verbs whose stem ends in a vowel, in the liquids, *l, m, n*, and *r*, and in *p, f*, and *s*. The list embraces the following words, of which *flee, creep, leap, sleep, sweep, weep*, and *lose*, belonged, in Anglo-Saxon, to the strong conjugation; while *kneel* is not a form known to the original tongue. To the others the Anglo-Saxon forms are added.

1. flee,	flĕd.	3. deal,	dĕalt.
2. shoe,	shŏd.	*dǽlan*	*dǽlde*
sceóan	*sceóde*	4. feel,	fĕlt.
		félan	*félde*

5. kneel,	knĕlt.	11. keep,	kĕpt.
		cēpan	*cēpte*
6. dream,	drĕamt.	12. leap,	lĕpt.
drēman	*drēmde*	13. sleep.	slĕpt.
7. lean,	lĕant.	14. sweep,	swĕpt.
hlinian	*hlinode*	15. weep,	wĕpt.
8. mean,	mĕant.	16. lose,	lŏst.
mǣnan	*mǣnde*		
9. hear,	hĕard.		
hȳran	*hȳrde*		
10. creep,	crĕpt,		

To these may be added three verbs which now change a *v* of the infinitive into *f* in the preterite and participle: of these, *cleave* was originally strong:—

cleave,	clĕft.	leave,	lĕft.	(be)reave,	-rĕft.
		lǣfan,	*lǣfde.*	*reáfian,*	*reáfode.*

In a large number of these words, Middle and Modern English have developed full forms alongside of the contracted ones, and some of the former are even more common than the latter. The verbs which have had, or still have, these double forms, are *deal, kneel, dream, lean, leap, cleave*, and (*be*)*reave*, which exhibit, either generally or occasionally, the regular forms *dealed, kneeled, dreamed, leaned, leaped, cleaved,* and (*be*)*reaved.* Full, regular forms of some of the others likewise occur, but not often.

193. The vowel-variation that took place in the above verbs was, as has been said, unknown to the earliest period of the language. At that time, nearly every one of the above-mentioned verbs that existed in it and was inflected weak had a long vowel in all the principal parts, as the primitive forms show dis-

tinctly. In Anglo-Saxon there were, however, a number of verbs of the weak conjugation, in which there was a real variation of vowel in the preterite. A few of these have disappeared from the tongue altogether, others have become perfectly regular; but, of those that have continued to show this vowel-variation, the following list gives the principal parts as found both in Anglo-Saxon and Modern English. It is to be noticed, that in the former, a *c* or *g* final of the stem became, in the preterite, *h*.

194.

Infinitives.	Preterites.	Past Part.	Infinitives.	Preterites.	Past Part.
bringan,	brohte,	broht.	bring,	brought,	brought.
bycgan,	bohte,	boht.	buy,	bought,	bought.
sêcan,	sôhte,	sôht.	seek,	sought,	sought.
sellan,	sealde,	seald.	sell,	sold,	sold.
tellan,	tealde,	teald.	tell,	told,	told.
þencan, *think*,	þohte,	þoht.	think,	thought,	thought.
þyncan, *seem*,	þuhte,	þuht.	(me)thinks,	(me)thought.	
wyrcan,	worhte,	worht.	work,	wrought,	wrought.

Of these verbs, *work* has developed also a regular form, *worked;* and, although this did not come into common use before the eighteenth century, it is now much more widely employed than the earlier *wrought*. On the other hand, *tǣcan*, 'to teach,' which had no variation of the vowel-sound in Anglo-Saxon, its preterite being *tǣhte*, has developed a variation in later periods in the forms *teach, taught;* while *catch*, a word that did not make its appearance in the language until after the Norman conquest, has, in like manner, formed a preterite, *caught*. *Reach* (A.-S., *rǣcan, rǣhte*) and *stretch* (A.-S., *streccan*, *streahte*) are also verbs, which, in Old and Middle English, had their preterites *raught* and *straught;* but during the Modern English period they have been almost invariably inflected *reached* and *stretched*, though the earlier forms sometimes occur. At various periods, also, some other of these verbs have been inflected regularly. Especially is this true of *catch*, *teach*, and *tell*, and the compound *beseech*, all of which occasionally exhibit the forms *catched*, *teached*, *telled*, and *beseeched;* but the earlier preterites have always been preferred.

195. The form *fraught* is also to be reckoned with the foregoing. When employed at all, it is almost invariably used as the past participle of *freight;* but it belongs, in its origin, to a verb spelled in precisely the same way, which was an allied form of the verb *freight*, and probably the older of the two, but which has now gone out of use. *Fraught* may therefore be described as the obsolescent participle of an obsolete verb.

196. Three verbs have undergone contractions peculiar to themselves. These are *have*, in which the existing preterite has been cut down from the Old English *havede;* *make*, in which *made* has been similarly cut down from the Old English *makede;* and *clothe*. The Anglo-Saxon inflection of the last-named was *clāðian*, *clāðode*, *clāðod;* but in Early and Middle English the contracted forms for the preterite and past participle, *cladde* and *clad*, were used along with the fuller forms, and the two have lasted down to our time.

197. With the statement that certain verbs ending in *y* change this *y* to *i* in the preterite, as *say, said, pay, paid,*—which is nothing more than an orthographic variation,—the history of all the anomalous forms of the weak verbs now existing has been given. Anomalous forms not mentioned here can, indeed, occasionally be found; but they are all explainable according to the analogy of the contracted forms that have been described. In general, also, the history of the past participle of the weak verb is, since the fifteenth century, the same as the history of the preterite, when the dropping of the final *e* by the latter brought about in them both identity of form. The few additional explanations in its history, not involved in the history of the preterite just given, will now be stated.

PAST PARTICIPLE OF THE WEAK CONJUGATION.

198. The past participle of weak verbs was formed in the primitive Indo-European by adding to the stem the suffix *ta*. Of this the consonant appeared in the early Teutonic tongues as *th*, *t*, or *d*. In Anglo-Saxon it was *d;* and, as the vowel of the suffix had disappeared, it was *d* only that was added. This was joined on directly to the connective *o* of the second weak conjugation, as *luf-o-d*, 'loved;' or to the connective *e* of the first weak conjugation, as *dēm-e-d*, 'deemed' (178). But sometimes this connective *e* was dropped, in which case *d* often became *t*.

199. When the distinction between the two weak

conjugations disappeared in the Early English period, *e* became, in general, the connective for all verbs, and *d* or *t* was usually added to it, though sometimes they were added directly to the stem. The dropping of the final *e* of the ending *ede* of the preterite, in the Middle English period, had, necessarily, the direct effect of bringing about a perfect similarity of form between the preterite and past participle; and, as has already been shown, the latter was subjected to precisely the same changes which befell the former. To this there is one slight exception.

200. Either after the analogy of verbs whose past participle is precisely the same in form as the present, as *hit, hurt*, or because they were made to resemble their Latin primitives, a number of verbs in the Middle English period did not always add *d* to form the past participle; as *consummate* (Lat. *consummat-us*) for *consummated, create* (Lat. *creat-us*) for *created pollute* (Lat. *pollut-us*) for *polluted.* These forms without final *d* usually belong to words that are derived from Latin verbs of the first conjugation; but they are not limited to them. The usage extended down to the Modern English period, and can hardly be said to have been abandoned before the end of the seventeenth century. Certain writers are remarkable for their fondness for such forms. As a general use, they are employed in an adjectival sense; but even then their participial character is plainly apparent. The participle *situate* for *situated*, common in legal phraseology, is a survival of this usage.

201. The Anglo-Saxon prefix *ge* has had also a special history of its own in connection with the past participle both of the weak and of the strong conjugation. In the earliest period of the language it was affixed indifferently to nouns, adjectives, pronouns, adverbs, and verbs. There was not, in the case of the verb, any disposition originally to restrict it to the past participle; but this became, in Early and Middle English, the prevailing, though not absolutely exclusive, practice. But the prefix sometimes suffered a change of form before the Conquest, which change, after the Conquest, became habitual. For *ge*, either *y* or *i* is found from the twelfth century on; and in the manuscripts these two letters frequently appear as capitals, *Y* or *I*. During the thirteenth, fourteenth, and even the fifteenth centuries, this *y* or *i* was widely used, but more particularly in the speech of the South. Participial forms like *ilent*, *ymaked*, *isworn*, *ygo*, 'gone,' *ybe*, 'been,' are exceedingly common in the literature of the fourteenth century. And not only was this *y* or *i* applied indifferently to verbs of the weak or of the strong conjugation, it was applied with equal indifference to foreign or native words. The Northern dialect, however, never made use of this prefix to any extent, hardly even at all, except in the writers who directly imitated the language of Chaucer; and it seems as if the influence of that dialect of the language had in this respect prevailed over the usage of the South and the Midland. In the fifteenth century the employment of *y* or *i* with the participle began to be given

up, and in the sixteenth century it practically disappeared. It occasionally made its appearance much later, and is even seen at times in poetry to this day, especially in burlesque, or in imitation of the archaic style.

Number and Person.

202. As regards the three primitive numbers, the Gothic was the only one of the Teutonic languages that retained the dual of the verb; but, even in that, it was confined to the first and second persons. At the time that language was committed to writing, the third had disappeared; and, in order to say that "they two" had done any thing, the plural form had to be used. The English verb, through all the stages of its history, knows only of the singular and plural numbers: no trace of a dual appears in its earliest monuments.

203. The commonly received theory as to the origin of the personal endings is, that the personal pronoun, as the subject of a verb, was originally placed after it, and not before it as now; just as if we, instead of saying *I hate*, *ye hate*, should say, *hate I*, *hate ye*, and so on for the other persons. These pronouns, appended to the stem of the verb, gradually united with it so as to form one word; as even in Early English, for illustration, *thinkest thou* or *sayest thou* often appears as one word, *thinkestow*, *seistow*. Thus joined to the verb, they came at last to be regarded as an inseparable part of it, as really belonging to it, and were then used to form the inflection of the tense; and, as the per sonal pronoun originally appended to each person to denote the subject was different, the endings were necessarily in all cases different at first. When these pronouns, however, had become so thoroughly united with the verb as to form one word, the recollection of their original pronominal character passed away: they were simply looked upon as an integral part of the inflection of the verb, and not as separate words or syllables denoting the subject. After this result had been reached, a personal pronoun was frequently put before the verb as its subject; and this naturally became more and more common as the sense of the original pronominal nature of the personal ending became fainter and fainter. When it had become a common practice to employ the personal pronoun as the subject of the verb, and usually preceding it, the necessity of an ending to denote the person was gone: that was denoted by the personal pronoun which was the subject. The value of distinct terminations for the persons was accordingly destroyed. Under such circumstances, it was inevitable that in some cases the terminations should be confounded, and, if much confounded, that many of them in course of time should disappear. This has been fully exemplified in the history of the Teutonic languages, and of our own in particular. In Gothic there is a distinct termination for each of the three persons of the plural of the present indicative,—*m* for the first person, *th* for the second, and *nd* for the third; but in Anglo-Saxon this diversity of endings had been given up: the endings of the first and third persons had been entirely abandoned, and the ending of the second person, *th*, had become the common ending of the three. In the Anglo-Saxon subjunctive there was a distinction of form between the singular an l the plural; but the three persons of the singular had all the same termination, as had likewise the three persons of the plural the same; in this respect differing again from the older tongue, the Gothic, which in this mood still preserved the distinction of persons by the endings. In the preterite plural the Anglo-Saxon had only one termination for the three persons, which termination was originally that of the third person, and had been extended to the other two. But barren of these endings as is our earliest speech when compared with the Gothic, it is rich when compared with what we have to-day. The history of the tenses will show the steady loss in this respect that has overtaken the inflection.

TENSES OF THE VERB.

204. The English, like all the Teutonic tongues, has but two simple tenses, — the present and the preterite. About them as centres have been developed verbal phrases which express the ideas and relations conveyed by the fuller forms to be found in other languages. The use of these two tenses is far more limited in Modern English than it was in the ancient speech; for the present then generally expressed also the ideas for which we now use, not merely the future

but the future-perfect; while the preterite denoted what is now conveyed by the imperfect, the perfect, and the pluperfect. These forms have, moreover, undergone changes so various, that it will be necessary to consider each one of the two simple tenses by itself.

THE PRESENT TENSE, INDICATIVE AND SUBJUNCTIVE.

205. The following paradigms of the strong verb *singan*, 'to sing,' and the weak verb *lufian*, 'to love,' will show the inflection of the present indicative and subjunctive in the Anglo-Saxon period. To them is also appended the indicative singular of the verb *rîdan*, 'to ride,' both in the full and also the contract forms, which are often found in verbs whose stems end in *d* and *t*, and even *s*.

206.

Sing.		Indicative.	Subjunctive.	Indicative.	Subjunctive.
1.	*ic*	sing-e,	sing-e,	luf-ie (ige),	luf-ie,
2.	*þu*	sing-e-st,	sing-e,	luf-a-st,	luf-ie,
3.	*he*	sing-e-ð.	sing-e.	luf-a-ð,	luf-ie.
Pl.					
1. 2. 3.	*we*, *ge*, *hi*	sing-a-ð.	sing-en.	luf-ia-ð.	luf-ie-n.

Sing.			
1.	*ic*	rîd-e,	rîd-e
2.	*þu*	rîd-e-st,	rîst,
3.	*he*	rîd-e-ð.	rît.

In these paradigms it will be seen that the stem of *singan* is *sing*; the connective is *a* weakened to *e* in the singular of the indicative and in both numbers of the subjunctive; and the personal endings, so far as they have been preserved, are *st* of the second, and ð of the third person singular, ð of the plural indicative, and *n* of the plural subjunctive. Most verbs of the first weak conjugation do not differ here from the strong verb in their inflection. In the second weak conjugation it will be noticed that the connective *o* has been abandoned in this tense, and its place taken by the connective *ia* of the first conjugation (177), which, however, is only seen pure in the plural indicative.

207. This is the common inflection in the Anglo-Saxon, as it is exhibited in the classical dialect, the West-Saxon. But, after the Norman conquest, the present tense of the verb presented marked differences of form in the three great dialects of the English speech that arose and developed literatures of their own during the thirteenth and fourteenth centuries. According to each of these, the verb *singe(n)* would exhibit the following forms in this tense; and what is true of it is true also of verbs of the weak conjugation.

Sing.	Southern.	Midland (East).	Northern. 1st Form.	Northern. 2d Form.
1.	sing-e,	sing-e,	sing,	sing-e(s),
2.	sing-est,	sing-est,	sing-es,	sing-es,
3.	sing-eth.	sing-eth.	sing-es.	sing-es.
Pl.				
1. 2. 3.	sing-eth.	sing-en.	sing.	sing-es.

208. It is evident at a glance that the Southern

forms are much nearer the classic Anglo Saxon than either of the others; and that the Midland are nearer the Southern than they are to the Northern. On the other hand, it is to be remarked that the Northern forms in *s* go back to a period before the Conquest, although the dearth of the Northumbrian literature, and the uncertainty attending the date of composition of the little that has been preserved, make positive statements hazardous as to the time of the transition of the final ð into *s*, or the extent of usage of the latter. It will be observed, however, that there are two sets of Northern forms, one of which, though going back to the thirteenth century, is far nearer Modern English than either of those found in the Midland or the South. In general, it may be said of these two, that, when the verb has for its subject a personal pronoun directly preceding it, it uses the first form; but in other cases the forms in *s* are usually though not invariably found. In consequence, in the Northern English of the thirteenth and fourteenth centuries, *they think* and *men think* would ordinarily be represented by *thai thynk* and *men thynkes;* and this is still a peculiarity of the Scotch dialect.

209. It is the Midland form, however, though largely influenced by the Northern, that has been the ruling one in Modern English. The connective *a* or *ia* of the Anglo-Saxon had in Early English become, in all cases, *e;* and this had reduced the inflection of all verbs, whether weak or strong, to one form so far as that was concerned. As regards the first person, which in the earliest period had dropped the personal ending, the connective *e*, which in consequence had become the termination, disappeared also from the verb in the Middle English. In this, the Northern dialect preceded the Midland, and, doubtless, largely influenced it. This ending *e* really disappeared from all verbs: but it was retained in the spelling of many, though never sounded in pronunciation, as in *I love;* and this has continued the practice down to the present time. The Northern dialect also added *s* at times to the first person, probably from a false analogy with the other persons, which all had this ending. This occasionally appears in English literature as late as the sixteenth century, though in many cases it is hard to tell whether the termination was due to design or to typographical errors. The colloquial expressions, *I says, thinks I to myself*, and others, are modern representatives of this peculiarity of the Northern dialect: though it is noticeable, that, in nearly all such cases, the present tense is the historic present, and is used to recount a fact or feeling which is already past; and the historic present is not known to the Anglo-Saxon.

210. The second person, through all the periods of English, outside of the distinctively Northern dialect, has invariably ended in *st*, and there has never been a time when the supremacy of this termination has been seriously shaken. During the Elizabethan period the Northern form in *s* is occasionally found alongside of it, as can be seen in the following instances: —

Thou art not thyself;
For thou *exists* on many a thousand grains
That issue out of dust.
SHAKSPEARE, *Measure for Measure*, act iii. scene 1

My sharpness thou no less *disjoints*.
JONSON, *Epigram* 58.

But in such cases the final *t* was almost always dropped, in order to prevent the crowding together of numerous consonants, caused by the previous dropping of the connective *e*. In the examples above given, the full forms would be *exist-e-st, disjoint-e-st*.

211. The suffix ð of the third person singular was in the Anglo-Saxon period frequently changed into *s* in the North of England; and, in the works still extant in the Northumbrian dialect, forms in ð and *s* stand side by side. By the thirteenth century, however, the latter had completely supplanted the former in this division of English speech. Outside of it, the ending *th* was regularly employed, not only during the Early English, but during the Middle English period. Chaucer almost invariably has the third person singular terminating in *th*, except when he designedly represents the dialect of the North. The very few instances in which he otherwise has the ending *s* (as in "The Boke of the Duchesse," line 257) are due to the necessity of rhyme.[1] But in the sixteenth century

[1] Instances occur, however, in which the forms in *s* are found where the necessity of rhyme cannot be alleged, as in the following extracts from Langlande's Vision of Piers Plowman Text B.

And as his loresman *leres* hym, bileueth and troweth.
Passus, xii. 183.

Thus the poete *preues* that the pecok for his fetheres is reuerenced.
Passus, xii. 260

the termination in *s* gradually made its way from the Northern dialect into the language of literature, and, after the middle of that century, became with each succeeding year more common. For about a hundred years, the forms in *s* and *th* lasted side by side with apparently little general difference in their usage. Books and writers naturally varied. The authorized version of the English Bible does not employ the third person singular in *s;* and in Bacon's works it is comparatively infrequent. Ben Jonson does not even mention it in his grammar, although it is of constant occurrence in his writing. But, by the middle of the seventeenth century, the form in *s* had become the prevailing one, and has since that time become nearly the exclusive one. It is the English Bible that has kept alive the form in *th;* but it is rarely employed now, save in poetry and in the solemn style.

212. The Midland plural *en* is of uncertain origin, though by some it is regarded as being nothing more than an intrusion of the subjunctive ending *en* into the indicative. To whatever due, it was a distinctive characteristic of the Midland dialect, and showed itself as early as the end of the twelfth century. The Southern speech, as has been seen, varied little from the classic Anglo-Saxon, and formed its plural in *eth;* while the Northern, having often changed the *að* into *as* before the Norman conquest, adopted after that event the form *es* or *s* exclusively, or dropped the termination altogether. These three terminations of the plural lasted side by side for centuries; and, though

strictly denoting different dialects, they were to some extent interchanged, and there are but few Early English and even Middle English manuscripts in which at least two forms are not represented, though one is naturally much more common than the other. It is from the form in *en*, however, that the modern English has been derived; though it is scarcely possible not to believe that the Northern forms, existing as early as the thirteenth century, without any terminations at all, should not have had some influence in bringing about the result we now see. The *n* began to be widely dropped, even early in the Middle English period; and this was followed by *e*. This vowel naturally disappeared first in pronunciation, in this as in so many other cases; and its disuse in pronunciation was generally, though not invariably, followed by disuse in orthography. The dropping of the *n*, and the dropping or retention in the spelling of the *e*, caused all the persons of the plurals to assume the same sound and form as the infinitive and the first person of the singular. It has already been stated[1] that, according to Ben Jonson, this *en* was employed until the time of Henry VIII. "But now," he adds, "whatever is the cause, it hath quite grown out of use, and that other so generally prevailed, that I dare not presume to set this afoot again; albeit, to tell you my opinion, I am persuaded that the lack hereof, well-considered, will be found a great blemish to our tongue." The termination *en* is occasionally found through the whole of the

[1] Page 117.

sixteenth century; but it is entirely confined to poetry. In the latter part of it, it was made somewhat more current in a certain class of writings by Spenser, who introduced it largely, and in this was followed by a number of his admirers and imitators. In the seventeenth century it disappeared even from literature of this kind, though it was and is occasionally revived as an archaism; as, for instance, it is employed frequently in Thomson's "Castle of Indolence."

213. The plural forms in *s* and *th* in reality lasted to a much later period than the full forms in *en*. In the prose literature of the sixteenth century they are far from uncommon, and they can be found even later, in the seventeenth. These statements are especially true of the third person: the first and second with these endings are far from being frequent, though occasionally found. But there are more than two hundred plurals in *s* to be found in Shakspeare's plays, though these are changed wherever possible in the modern editions; but *doth* and *hath* are the only plurals in *th* which he regularly employs. In general, it may be said that the plurals in *s* are common during the whole Elizabethan period; but, by the middle of the seventeenth century, they had pretty generally gone out of use. The language of low life, however, retains to some extent this form to the present day.

214. The contracted forms of the present singular, exemplified by the paradigm of the Anglo-Saxon verb *rídan* (206), were very common in the earliest period of our speech, much more common, indeed, than the

fuller forms. They were, however, confined to verbs whose stem ended in *d*, *t*, or *s*. Through the whole of the Early and of the Middle English period they are constantly to be met with in the third person; as *rit* from *rideth*, *sit* from *sitteth*, *rist* from *riseth*, *glit* from *glideth*, *stant* from *standeth*. By the beginning of the Modern English period, the full forms had generally taken their place; or perhaps it would be better to say they were displaced by the form in *s*. The verb *list*, meaning 'please,' still continues to show in the modern language the contracted form *list*, along with the full form *listeth*.

215. It is hardly necessary to say, that, in all the early periods of the language, there are many variations from the forms here given. The connective *e* is often syncopated; it is replaced often by *y* or *i*; the *th* of the endings frequently appears as *t* or *d*; and numerous other variations could be mentioned which need here no more than a general reference, as they have had no influence upon the forms existing in the modern speech.

216. The adoption of the ending *en* by the indicative necessarily caused its plural to assume the same form as that of the subjunctive. The history of the one is therefore the history of the other. The disappearance of the *n* from both took place at the same time, as did also the disappearance of the *e* when it occurred at all. It is only in the second and third persons of the singular that the subjunctive forms differ at all from those of the indicative; and it is mainly

owing to these two moods assuming the same forms, that the distinct shades of thought once expressed by the subjunctive, as contrasted with the indicative, have practically disappeared. To denote these the language is now obliged to resort to other methods, the discus sion of which belongs to syntax exclusively.

THE PRETERITE INDICATIVE AND SUBJUNCTIVE.

217. It is the form of the preterite which distinguishes a verb of the weak conjugation from one of the strong: it is therefore desirable to give full forms of both. Of the Anglo-Saxon strong verbs, the inflection of the preterite of *singan*, 'to sing,' and *tacan*, 'to take,' will be given; of the weak, the preterites of *dêman*, 'to judge,' and *lufian*, 'to love.'

Sing.	Indicative.	Subjunctive.	Indicative.	Subjunctive.
1. *ic*	sang,	sung-e,	tôc,	tôc-e,
2. *þu*	sung-e,	sung-e,	tôc-e,	tôc-e,
3. *he*	sang.	sung-e.	tôc.	tôc-e.
Pl.				
1. *we* } 2. *ge* } 3. *hi* }	sung-on.	sung-en.	tôc-on.	tôc-en.

218. The history of the modern forms of the preterite has been largely given in the account of the weak and strong conjugations. But, in addition to what has already been said, there are three things to be especially noted in the Anglo-Saxon inflection: —

1. The personal endings have entirely disappeared from the first and third persons of the singular.

2. The termination of the second person singular of the indicative is not the usual *st*, but *e*.

3. In the preterite of *singan*, the vowel of the second person singular of the indicative is different from that of the first and third persons of the same number; but it is precisely the same as the vowel of the plural indicative, and both numbers of the subjunctive.

The first two statements were true of all strong verbs: the first part of the third was true of about four-fifths of them.

219. These paradigms should be compared with those of the weak verbs, which follow:—

Sing.	Indicative.	Subjunctive.	Indicative.	Subjunctive.
1. *ic*	dêm-de,	dêm-de,	luf-o-de,	luf-o-de,
2. *þu*	dêm-dest,	dêm-de,	luf-o-dest,	luf-o-de,
3. *he*	dêm-de.	dêm-de.	luf-o-de.	luf-o-de.
Pl.				
1. *we* 2. *ge* 3. *hi*	dêm-don.	dêm-den.	luf-o-don.	luf-o-den.

220. As the history of the subjunctive is here, as in the present tense, involved in that of the indicative, it may be disregarded; and the preterite indicative of the four verbs may be placed side by side, as they appeared in Early English, with the changes, whatever they are, that have already been described in the account of the conjugations:—

Sing.				
1.	sang,	took,	demede,	lovede,
2.	sung(e),	took(e),	demedest,	lovedest,
3.	sang.	took.	demede.	lovede.
Pl.				
1, 2. 3.	sunge(n).	tooke(n).	demede(n).	lovede(n)

221. For the strong verbs these are a theoretically correct inflection, rather than the ones invariably employed; for, even in the Early English period, the vowels of the singular and plural were confounded (153). By the fourteenth century, the main distinction between the singular and the plural in the case of strong verbs was, that the latter added *e* or *en* to the singular: the vowel difference was frequently disregarded. In the second person singular, the tendency toward uniformity began to make itself felt in the latter part of the fourteenth century; and the *est* or *st* of the weak conjugation was, in consequence, substituted for the *e* of the strong, so that *sunge*, for illustration, became *sang*(*e*)*st* or *sung*(*e*)*st*. In the fifteenth century this became the established practice. The dropping of the final *en* of the plural resulted, as has already been shown (153), in causing the two numbers to have precisely the same form as soon as there ceased to be any variation of vowel.

222. In the case of the weak verbs, the final *n* was frequently dropped, even as early as the twelfth century; and this practice became more and more common in the centuries which followed. By the beginning of the Middle English period it was the usual, though not invariable, practice in the Midland dialect. At that time, also, the final *e* which remained after the dropping of the *n* was more often neglected than retained in the pronunciation; and in the fifteenth century this *e* disappeared entirely, leaving the forms as they are now seen. In this stripping from the preterite plural the

ermination *en*, the Northern dialect had, as usual, taken the lead. As early as the thirteenth century, it not merely showed occasional instances of such forms as *loved* and *demed*, instead of *lovede(n)* and *demede(n)*: they were even then the regular rule.

223. Besides these two original tenses, English has had from the beginning, or has developed, certain verb-phrases which correspond in power and use to the tenses found in other languages of the Indo-European family. The primitive Indo-European had itself five tenses; and of these, the imperfect, the future, and the aorist, were not found in any of the earliest Teutonic tongues. Their places, however, have all been supplied by compound forms, which it will be best to consider under the titles usually given them in English grammars.

THE FUTURE TENSE.

224. As the Anglo-Saxon had no future tense, the present was usually employed to express the relation denoted by it. This was a peculiarity shared by our speech with all the Teutonic languages; and in all of them it continues to exist to the present day. Phrases like 'To-morrow is Sunday,' 'I am going to the city next week,' and numerous others, are common in every period of our language and in every great writer of our literature. But Modern English does not use the present for the future by any means as commonly as do several of the other Teutonic languages, in particular the Modern High German.

225. But, even in the Anglo-Saxon period, the necessity for more precise and definite expression was beginning to be felt. The verbs *sceal*, 'I am obliged,' 'I ought,' and *wyle*, 'I wish,' 'I have a mind to,' are, even at that early time, occasionally found joined to the infinitive of another verb to express its future; though, generally, and perhaps it is right to say invariably, there was, in the employment of these, more or less reference to the original idea of obligation involved in the one, and of inclination or intention in the other. Still, in the Northumbrian dialect, the idea of simple futurity may be said at times to be distinctly conveyed, and this certainly became the common usage in the Early English period. In the sixteenth century a delicate distinction in the use of the auxiliaries *shall* and *will* began to be prevalent, and in the seventeenth century was firmly established; though this statement is strictly true only of England, and not of the English spoken in Scotland or Ireland. Immigration has largely broken down this distinction in the United States: the Irish do not know it, and the Germans do not acquire it.

FUTURE-PERFECT TENSE.

226. The future-perfect was the last of the verb-phrases denoting the relation of time to be formed. As its name denotes, it is a compound of the future and of the perfect. It was, consequently, unknown to the Anglo-Saxon; but it likewise, rarely, if ever, appeared in Early English, and it is certainly not com-

men before Modern English. Its use, indeed, is easily avoided, as its place can be, and often still is, taken by the compound-perfect, and even sometimes by the present. It was the former of these that was usually employed during the Middle English period. In fact, the same sentence, involving the conception expressed by this tense, has been and can be represented in a variety of ways, as may be seen in the following illustrations —

1. Before the cock crow twice, thou deniest me thrice.
2. Before the cock crow twice, thou shalt deny me thrice.
3. Before the cock has crowed twice, thou shalt deny me thrice.
4. Before the cock shall crow twice, thou shalt deny me thrice.
5. Before the cock has crowed twice, thou shalt have denied me thrice.
6. Before the cock shall have crowed twice, thou shalt have denied me thrice.

The first of these expressions is the one employed in Anglo-Saxon: the last is found only in Modern English, which, however, employs all the rest. The second and third belong to the Early English period: the fourth and fifth, to the Middle English.

THE PERFECT AND PLUPERFECT.

227. The perfect and pluperfect are compound tenses, formed of the past participle, with the present and preterite respectively of either the verb *be* or *have*. The use of these forms goes back to the earliest period of English; but the simple preterite was then also frequently employed to represent the idea expressed by both. Originally, the auxiliary *have* seems to have

been joined only with transitive verbs, and *be* with intransitive; but the employment of the former has as steadily increased as that of the latter has diminished during the whole history of our speech. Even in Anglo-Saxon, though *be* was the strictly correct auxiliary with verbs of motion, *have* can be found joined with them also, as, *siððan hie tôgædere gôegân hæfdon*[1] (BEOWULF, *line* 2631); and this has now become far the more common usage. The verb *be* was, from the beginning, added as an auxiliary to certain intransitive verbs denoting motion, rest, or change, as, *is gone*, *is set*, *is grown*, and others; and this has maintained itself down to the present time. But so steady has been the encroachment of *have*, that this auxiliary may now be regarded as the regular one to form the perfect and pluperfect in Modern English.

228. Besides these forms, there are two other methods of inflection that need to be considered,—the one commonly called the progressive form, and the other the emphatic.

229. The former of these is compounded of the tenses of the verb *be* and of the present participle of another verb, as, *I am coming*, *I was coming*. The forms as used with the present and the preterite go back to the very earliest period of the language, and throughout the whole history of our speech there has been but little variation in the extent or character of their usage. They need, therefore, no remark, save that, as compound tenses have been added to the sub-

[1] After they had gone together.

stantive verb, a full set of corresponding forms with the present participle have been successively added, as, *I shall* or *will be coming*, *I have been coming*, *I had been coming*, and have gone into general use. Even the form for the future-perfect, *I shall* or *will have been coming*, is recognized in grammars, though it is certainly rare in usage.

230. The history of the so-called emphatic forms is far more varied. These are compounded of the present and preterite of the verb *do* with the infinitive of another verb. These forms cannot be said to have come into general use until the early part of the fifteenth century; and they were, as a matter of fact, preceded by the infinitive used with the present, but more particularly with the preterite of the verb *gin*, which in the Anglo-Saxon period was rarely seen outside of its compounds, especially *on-ginnan*, and in later English is rarely seen save in the compound *be-gin*. The use of the preterite of *on-ginnan*, with an infinitive to express the relation denoted by the preterite, can be traced back to the Anglo-Saxon;[1] but, in the thirteenth and fourteenth centuries, the infinitive with the preterite of the simple verb *gin* had become exceedingly common. *Gan* was strictly used as the singular, and *gunne(n)* or *gonne(n)* as the plural, as can be seen in the following lines from "The Canterbury Tales:" —

It was ten of the clokke he *gan* (i.e., did) conclude. *l.* 4434.
For in a bath thay *gonne* (i.e., did) hir faste schetten. *l.* 12455

[1] For illustration see the Anglo-Saxon poem of Elene, ll. 303, 306, 311.

The use of the present of *gin* in this manner was far from being as common as that of the preterite *gan*; and this statement is in the beginning true also of *do*.

231. *Do* itself, at this period, when employed with the infinitive, ordinarily meant 'to cause;' in which usage *make* has taken its place in Modern English. It is from this causative sense that many suppose that *do* and *did* came at last to be looked upon as having, with the infinitive, the force of a present and a preterite. 'He did arrest the man' would, in the fourteenth century, strictly have meant, 'he caused the man to be arrested;' and the transition from the earlier usage to the modern does not seem difficult. But it is far more reasonable to attribute the rise of the idiom to another method of expression which has been common in English during all the periods of its history. This is the wide employment of the present and preterite of *do* to supply, in a following clause, the place of the principal verb of the preceding one. In such a sentence, for instance, as, 'He thinks upon this subject as I do,' the transition by which the principal verb would be supplied in many cases after *do* is a natural and an easy one. There is, indeed, but little doubt that this is the true origin of the modern form. As already stated, this usage of *do* has been common during all periods of English, and is as frequently met with in the Anglo-Saxon as in any other.

232. But, whatever may be the fact as to its origin, this so-called emphatic form did not come into general use till the fifteenth century. Scattered instances

of its employment can be found much earlier, extending up even into Anglo-Saxon. In the thirteenth century it was occasionally used; but neither during that nor the following century can it be said to be at all common: the form for the preterite made by compounding *gan* with the infinitive is in altogether wider employment. The great writers who flourished at the beginning of the Middle English period — Chaucer, Langlande, Gower, and Wycliffe — rarely made use of the forms of *do* to express this relation.[1] But, with their immediate successors at the beginning of the fifteenth century, the verb, in this usage, seems to have become a favorite; and from that time the employment of it steadily increased. It was in the Elizabethan era that the use of *do* and *did* with the infinitive, in declarative sentences, was most wide-spread. In this respect, a great change took place during the seventeenth century, so that, in such cases, the auxiliary seemed out of place, unless used for the specific purpose of making the expression emphatic. Pope's line, published in 1711, —

> While expletives their feeble aid *do* join,

[1] *Do* and *did*, especially the latter, are common in Lydgate's writings. In the King's Quhair, by James I., they occur in cantos iii. 11, 15; iv. 18, 27; vi. 7. On the other hand, the following is the only instance I have observed in Langlande, though there may be others: —

> Is in drede to drenche that neuere *dede* swymme.
>
> *Passus*, xii, 169.

The form is certainly more common in Robert of Gloucester than in either Chaucer or Langlande, though these two were nearly a century later in time than he.

would have had no special point had it been composed a century earlier. The language still continues ordinarily to reject the *do*, and to a less extent the *did*, in declarative sentences; but in negative and interrogative sentences the use of these auxiliaries has become almost universal. Men no longer say, under ordinary circumstances, *You go not*, but, *You do not go;* nor, again, do they say, *Go you?* but, *Do you go?*

THE IMPERATIVE.

233. The imperative is found in Anglo-Saxon only in the second person; but it has distinct forms for the singular and the plural: that for the latter is precisely the same as the plural of the present indicative, as will be seen in the following examples of the imperative in the verbs already given:—

Sing.	sing.	lufa.
Pl.	singað.	lufiað.

The distinction between the two numbers was very generally kept up until the fourteenth century. By that time, however, not only was the plural termination *ath*, weakened to *eth*, sometimes dropped, but the two numbers were frequently used interchangeably for each other. This, no doubt, was largely due to the employment of the pronoun *ye* for addressing individuals (94). As difference of form for the two numbers lost, in consequence, its usefulness, the ending of the plural went out of use in the fifteenth century.

234. For the first and third persons of the impera-

tive, the subjunctive, followed generally by the personal pronouns, was widely employed in Anglo-Saxon; and this usage has lasted down to modern times, and is found to this day, at least in poetry. *Return we to our subject,* meaning 'Let us return to our subject,' is a method of expression which has been employed from the earliest period of our speech. The place of the first person plural of the imperative was also supplied in Anglo-Saxon by an infinitive preceded by *utan*, which meant strictly of itself 'let us go.' This went wholly out of use within the second century after the Norman conquest, and the place of both these methods of expression was wholly or mainly supplied by the verb *let.* Though this made its appearance in the thirteenth century, it can hardly be called very common even in the fourteenth; but it has now become, with an infinitive complement, an ordinary method of representing the imperative.

THE INFINITIVE AND PARTICIPLES.

235. The infinitive was formed in the primitive Indo-European by adding to the verbal stem the suffix *ana*, which in all the early Teutonic languages had dropped the final *a*, and, becoming *an*, had been appended directly to the verb without any connective. Or perhaps it may more properly be said that it had dropped the initial *a* also, and that *n* alone was the sign of the infinitive; thus 'to bind' is, in the Anglo-Saxon period, represented simply by the form *bind-a-n*, made up of the root *bind*, the connective *a*, and *n* the

infinitive sign. In the Old Frisian and the Old Norse this final *n* had also disappeared, and the infinitive regularly terminated in *a;* and, though the West-Saxon dialect clung firmly to *an*, the Northumbrian showed a constant and increasing tendency to follow the Frisian and the Norse in giving up *n;* thus the infinitive *come* is in West-Saxon *cuman;* in Northumbrian it is both *cuman* and *cuma*.

236. The weakening of the *an* to *en* speedily became universal after the Conquest; but, as to the retention or abandonment of the *n*, usage was exceedingly variable. In fact, it remained for several centuries; and the Romance verbs that were brought into the language assumed it as naturally as they did the inflections of the tenses. It is not to be understood that it was anywhere in exclusive use; for infinitives without *n* were always just as common as the fuller form, if not more so. In the fourteenth century the disposition to drop this letter became more pronounced; in the fifteenth, it had become general; in the sixteenth, the *n* was used only for poetic effect, or as a designed imitation of the archaic style. In all cases the final *e* which was left ceased to be sounded: in some cases it was dropped also, in other it was retained. The latter was more apt to take place when the connective was *ia* rather than *a;* as, for instance, our word *hate* comes from *hat-ia-n*, whereas from *bind-a-n* we have *bind*, and not *binde*. But the retention of a final *e* is very arbitrary.

237. The infinitive is in its nature a verbal noun,

and in Anglo-Saxon it had a dative case, ending in *anne*, invariably preceded by the preposition *tó;* as, *tó bindanne*. This is frequently called the gerundial infinitive. The termination in *anne* speedily passed, after the Conquest, into *enne* or *ene*, and at last, dropping the final *e* entirely, its form became the same as that of the root infinitive, originally terminating in *an*. One effect of this unification of form was, that the infinitive in Early English assumed the preposition *to* before it, except when preceded by certain verbs. The use of *tó* with the root infinitive (as *tó sécan*, PHŒNIX, *line* 275) is exceedingly rare in Anglo-Saxon; but this has now become so general, that, with the disappearance of the ending, the preposition itself has almost come to be regarded as a part of the infinitive. The gerundial infinitive occasionally preserved a distinct form down to the end of the fourteenth century, and it was frequently confused with the present participle in *ende;* but, before the beginning of the Modern English period, it had disappeared from the language, though relics of its original use continue to be common to this day in such phrases as, "the house to let."

238. The infinitive of the past *to have told*, for example, is not known to the Anglo-Saxon. It originated in the Early English period, apparently toward its conclusion, and was frequently employed during the Middle English and first part of the Modern English periods. Certain of its ancient uses there seems to be at present a disposition to confine within narrower limits, if not to reject altogether.

239. The history of the past participle has already been given in the discussion of the two conjugations. In both of these the present participle was formed the same way; that is, by the adding of the suffix *ende* to the radical syllable, as, *sing-ende*, 'singing.' During the Early English period this suffix appeared frequently in the dialect of the South as *ind*(*e*), in that of the North as *and*(*e*). In the former it was, as early as the twelfth century, often confounded with the gerundial infinitive in *enne*, and also with the verbal substantive, which in Anglo-Saxon ended usually in *ung*, but sometimes in *ing*. Of this last termination, which after the Norman conquest became the exclusive one for the verbal substantive, it finally assumed the form in the Southern dialect, and from that it was adopted into the Midland. From the fourteenth century *ing* has, in consequence, been almost the exclusive form of the present participle, though Northern forms, such as *glitterand*, *followand*, *comand*, have occasionally been employed.

240. The compound participial forms have all been of comparatively later formation; and, indeed, the use of any of them is one that can easily be avoided. The composition of *being* with the present participle, though perfectly legitimate in theory, has never been common in practice. Expressions like *being going*, found in Shakspeare's "Cymbeline" (act iii. scene 6), are very rare. On the other hand, the composition of *being* with the past participle, as *being loved*, is now very frequent. These forms did not become generally

current, however, till the earlier part of the sixteenth century; nor even then are they often met with, though in this respect there is great difference in writers of that time. It was not until the latter half of that century that the compounds of *having* with the past participle came much into use. Necessarily the compounds with *having been* were still later. Of these, the joining of this compound to the past participle seems to have long preceded its joining to the present; that is to say, such participial phrases as *having been gone* were earlier, as even now they are much more common, than those represented by *having been going*. The former were certainly in use in the latter half of the sixteenth century.

PASSIVE FORMATIONS.

241. The primitive Indo-European tongue had two voices, — the active, and the middle or reflexive, which, from the very beginning, seems to have assumed the functions of the voice we call the passive. The use of the reflexive to do the office of the passive is common enough in many modern tongues where the reflexive pronoun is not united with the verb, nor changed at all in form; and how easy the transition is in sense can be shown in our own speech by many familiar examples. *I persuade myself*, for illustration, differs very slightly, and in some cases not at all, from *I am persuaded*. It is from the reflexive that the passive has been developed in the history of the languages of the Indo-European family.

242. But in the Teutonic branch only one of these voices can be said to exist. The Gothic, indeed, had a middle form, which, with some few exceptions, was used in a passive sense; but it was only found in the present tense, and in that the persons were much confounded; and these and other signs show, that, at the time of the translation of the Bible by Ulfilas, the form was going out of use. In the other Teutonic tongues, occasional traces of a passive, which must once have existed, can be found; but they are few in number, and slight in importance. In all of the earlier tongues of this class, the loss of the form was supplied by compounding the passive participle with the present and preterite of verbs corresponding in meaning to our verbs *be* and *become*.

243. In the Anglo-Saxon, the participle was compounded with the above-named tenses of the verbs *beón* and *wesan*, both meaning 'to be,' and of *weorþan*, 'to become;' with these the passive was formed. The last verb has now gone out of use in our tongue; but it existed as an independent verb down to the beginning of the Modern English period, though almost always in the phrase *woe worth*, meaning 'woe be.'[1] In German, the corresponding form *werden* was chosen as the auxiliary to form the passive; but in English it was never common after the Anglo-Saxon

[1] "Thou cursed pen," quoth he, "woe *worth* the bird thee bare!"
SURREY.

What will *worth*, what will be the end of this man?
LATIMER, *Lent Sermons* (Arber's reprint, p. 180).

period, though it is sometimes met with. The formation of the passive with the present and preterite of *wesan* and *beón* became early predominant, and *worthe(n)* gradually went out of use. It, however, lasted down to the end of the fourteenth century; but, when used, it had generally, and perhaps always, the signification of a future; and accordingly it is the present, and not the preterite, that is employed, as in this extract: —

Chastite withoute charite *worth* (i.e. shall be) cheyned in helle.[1]

244. The forms of *worthe(n)*, 'to become,' having been driven out, those of the substantive verb *be* were the only ones left to express the passive. It was, from the nature of things, an office for which it was ill calculated; for, with a verb which expresses a simple action, and not a continuous state, the compounding of its past participle with the present tense of *be* did not denote something actually taking place, but something which had taken place. *The field is reaped* corresponds in form to *the man is hated;* but it does not correspond in the sense given to the verbal phrase. With the latter expression there is continuous action implied; in the former, only a completed result. This was a difficulty inherent in the employment of this form. To avoid it, the language resorted to expedients of all kinds: it changed the construction of the sentence, it adopted various circumlocutions, and at last, in the latter part of the eighteenth century, it

[1] Langlande's Piers Plowman (text B). — *Passus*, i 168.

began the formation of verb-phrases made up of the present and preterite of *be* and the compound passive participle. The more detailed history of the passive formations in such expressions as *the field is being reaped* has already been given on pp. 132, ff, and need not be repeated here. As stated there, the use of these forms, like that of the emphatic forms with *do* and *did*, is confined to the present and the preterite tense.

245. The discussion of the use of the passive belongs strictly to syntax, and finds properly no place here; and it is only necessary to repeat what has been previously said, that in the freedom in which, and in the extent to which, the passive is employed, English has gone far beyond other cultivated tongues. The use of such expressions as *he was given a book, he was told the truth*, and the like, runs back to the Middle English period, and occurs in all the great writers of our tongue.

PRETERITE-PRESENT VERBS.

246. In all the early Teutonic tongues there were a number of strong verbs whose preterite tense had assumed the signification of a present; and along with this, and perhaps in consequence of it, the original present tense had gone entirely out of use. A familiar illustration of this assumption by a past tense of a present meaning can be seen in the colloquial use in Modern English of *I have got* in the sense of 'I have,' 'I possess.' The process, however, had not stopped at the

point indicated by this common expression. When the original present had disappeared, and the original preterite had assumed entirely the signification of a new present, it went on to develop a new past tense. This latter was always of the weak conjugation. So, in the inflection of the new present tense, the peculiarities of the preterite of the strong conjugation are found; while in the new preterite the inflection is the one which regularly characterizes the weak verbs.

247. In Anglo-Saxon there were twelve of these verbs, of which seven continue to exist in some form, or to some extent, in Modern English. As each has had a history of its own, each will necessarily be treated of by itself, so far as the changes which it has undergone have not already been treated of in the account given of the inflection of the verb in the previous pages. Only the forms of the present and the preterite indicative are here laid down; for the subjunctive has nothing about its history different from that of other verbs, and the other parts are developed in some of these verbs, and absent in others.

Cunnan.

248. The verb which has developed this new infinitive originally belonged to the second class of strong verbs (143). The following is the Anglo-Saxon inflection; —

Sing. Present.		Preterite.
1.	can, *can,*	cûðe, *could.*
2.	cunne, canst,	cûðest,
3.	can.	cûðe.
Pl.		
1, 2, 3.	cunnon.	cûðon.

249. It will be seen, that, even in the Anglo-Saxon, the weak termination of the second person, *canst*, was taking the place of the regular strong form, *cunne*, which is, indeed, looked upon by many as never being used save in the subjunctive. Early and Middle English showed for the preterite *couthe* and *coude*, the latter of which became the prevailing form in Modern English. In the sixteenth century an *l* was inserted, by a false analogy with *would* and *should;* but it has never been pronounced. The verb never had a present participle, and its past, *cûð*, has gone out of use though, as an adjective, it survives in the last syllable of *un-couth*. The infinitive has also disappeared, save as it still survives in the independent verb *con:* it was common, however, in the fourteenth and fifteenth centuries, in the sense of 'to be able.'

Durran.

250. This belonged to the same strong class as the preceding.

Sing. Present.		Preterite.
1.	dear, *dare,*	dorste, *durst,*
2.	dearst,	dorsted,
3.	dear.	dorste.
Pl.		
1, 2 3.	durron.	dorston.

251. In this verb the original form *durre*, of the second person, seems to have been entirely supplanted by *dearst*, even in the Anglo-Saxon period. As the existing present is in its origin a preterite, the third person of the singular is precisely the same as the first; but the tendency to make it conform to the regular inflection, and form its third person in *s*, has been powerful since the beginning of Modern English. Both forms, *he dare* and *he dares*, have flourished side by side during the last three centuries. The verb, however, shows a disposition to go over entirely to the regular form of the weak conjugation, and even to discard the preterite *durst*, which is now far less common than formerly. Throughout all its forms it is now, indeed, frequently inflected regularly, and has developed all the parts of the verbs.

Sculan.

252. This belonged to Class III. of the strong verbs (144).

Sing.	Present.	Preterite.
1.	sceal, *shall*,	sceolde, *should*,
2.	scealt,	sceoldest,
3.	sceal.	sceolde.
Pl.		
1. 2. 3.	sculon	sceoldon.

253. In Anglo-Saxon, *ic sceal* meant ordinarily 'I am under obligation,' 'I ought,' 'I must.' Its transition to express the future has already been pointed out in the account of that tense. It has remained

throughout its history, comparatively speaking, faithful to the Anglo-Saxon form; and the distinction between the vowel of the singular and of the plural was kept up, at least by some writers, as late as the fifteenth century. In fact, this verb preserved this distinction after most of the other strong preterites had abandoned it; *shal* and *shul(en)* being, in the fourteenth century, the respective methods usually found of denoting the singular and the plural.

Mágan.

254. This also belonged to Class III. of the strong verbs (144).

Sing.	Present.	Preterite.	
1.	mæg, *may*,	meahte, mihte,	*might*
2.	meaht, miht,	meahtest, mihtest,	
3.	mæg.	meahte, mihte.	
1. 2. 3.	mágon.	meahton, mihton.	

The second person singular of the present *thou might* lasted down even to the Middle English period, and was not entirely supplanted by *mayst* until the fifteenth century.

Mótan.

255. This verb belonged to Class IV. of the strong verbs (146).

Sing. Present.	Preterite.
1. môt, *mote*,	môste, *must*,
2. môst,	môstest,
3. môt.	môste.
Pl.	
1, 2, 3. môton.	môston.

256. This verb has had a history different from most of the others, in that its strong preterite-present has practically disappeared from Modern English, and its new weak preterite has come to assume the force of a present; and, to supply the place of a new preterite to *must*, the language has had recourse to *was obliged*. The original *mote* is occasionally heard; but it is limited to a few phrases, or to imitation of the archaic style.

Âgan.

257. This has given rise to both a defective and a regular weak verb in Modern English. The defective verb *ought* is in its origin the new weak preterite of a preterite-present verb; and its relations can only be comprehended clearly by examining the original forms. The verb from which it came belonged to Class V. of the strong conjugation (147).

Sing. Present.	Preterite.
1. âh, *I own, possess*,	âhte, *ought*,
2. âht, âhst,	âhtest,
3. âh.	âhte.
Pl.	
1. 2. 3. âgon.	âhton.

258. By comparing the Anglo-Saxon forms with those of its class, it will be seen, that, even in the

earliest period, this verb had deviated from the regular inflection; for the vowel of the plural had become the same as the singular, and we have *âgon* instead of *igon*. The present forms were in use in the Early English period, but were gradually supplanted by the preterite; while from the infinitive the word *owe* came into use, and, after having for a while *ought* as its preterite, developed the regular form *owed*. This left *ought* to be used exclusively in the sense of duty, obligation, fitness, and it is now confined to this one signification and tense.

Witan.

259. This verb, whose forms have been much misunderstood, belonged, also, to Class V. of the strong conjugation (147). All difficulties connected with it disappear at once on an examination of the original form:—

	Present.	Preterite.
Sing. 1.	wât, *wot*,	wiste, *wist*,
2.	wâst,	wistest,
3.	wât.	wiste.
Pl. 1. 2. 3.	witon.	wiston.

260. The infinitive of this verb *to wit* still exists in Modern English, especially in legal phraseology, used in the adverbial sense of 'namely.' Another form of this, *to weet*, is occasionally found in our earlier poetry The present and preterite are still retained, mainly through their occurrence in the Bible. The singular form *wot* of the present, and the plural present *witen*

or *wite*, lasted down to the fifteenth century; but, after that, *wot* was generally used of both numbers. Very curiously a singular blunder produced a new verb as the supposed present of *wiste*. It has already been stated that the Anglo-Saxon prefix *ge* was turned, in Early and Middle English, into *y* or *i* (201). The Anglo-Saxon adjective *gewis*(*s*), 'certain,' became in Early and Middle English the adverb *iwis*, or *ywis*, 'certainly.' In the sixteenth century this was frequently printed *Iwis*, and, in consequence, the capital *I* was supposed to be the personal pronoun, instead of the modern representative of the prefix *ge;* and *wis* was accordingly assumed to be a verb, and regarded as the present of *wiste*. *Wis* has rarely, if ever, been used outside of the phrase *I wis*, which is, however, by no means uncommon in poetry, even in our own day. A verb *wis*, or *wiss*—from Anglo-Saxon *wissian*, 'to show,' 'to instruct'—died out in the Middle English period, and has no connection with the present word. There are numerous anomalous forms of the verb wit to be met with in Modern English, such as, *he woteth* for *he wot*, the participle *wotting* for *witting* (seen in *unwitting*), and others; but they are all explainable as formed on false analogies with other verbs, or misunderstanding of the character of this one.

261. To this list of preterite-present verbs of the early language that still survive, in some form, to our day, may be added one, which, even in its original form, presents great irregularities. This is *willan*, one of the auxiliaries now used by us to express the future

Willan.

This belonged to Class V. of the strong verbs (147) It was originally a subjunctive of the preterite, but had discarded some of the forms belonging to the subjunctive, and taken those of the indicative in their place: —

Sing.	Present.	Preterite.
	1. wille, *will*,	wolde, *would*,
	2. wilt,	woldest,
	3. wille.	wolde.
Pl.		
	1. 2. 3. willað.	woldon.

262. In Early English, forms of the present with *o* instead of *i* were common, and *wol* and *wil* stood side by side until the fifteenth century. Indeed, a relic of the former is still preserved in the colloquial form *won't*, which is a contraction of *wol not*, which itself was sometimes written as *wonot*.

263. Apparently, by analogy with the preterite-present verbs, the verb *need* frequently drops the *s* of the third person singular of the present tense when followed by the infinitive of another verb; and 'he *need* not do it,' for instance, would, perhaps, be regarded as more common than 'he *needs* not do it.' This usage certainly goes back to the beginning of the sixteenth century, and is perhaps earlier.

IRREGULAR VERBS.

264. Beside the preterite-present verbs, there are three which deserve special mention. One of these is

the verb *do*, which still exhibits the peculiarity of that primitive reduplication by which the preterite was originally denoted. The modern forms exhibit little variation from the Anglo-Saxon *dôn*, *dide*, *dôn*, except that, in the present singular, they have abandoned the vowel-variation of the second and third persons. The original forms for that number were *dô*, *dêst*, *dêð*, and the plural *dôð*.

265. The verb *go*, both in the earliest and latest periods, has supplied its preterite by one taken from another stem. In Anglo-Saxon, while it had the form *geông* for the preterite, it more commonly made use of *eode*, and this appeared as the usual preterite in Early and Middle English, with the spelling *yode*. There was also another Anglo-Saxon verb, *wendan*, 'to go,' which in Early English was inflected *wenden*, *wende*, *went;* and to this the compound tenses *I have went*, *I had went*, frequently met with in the fifteenth century, belong. When, in the fifteenth century, *yode* was given up, the preterite *wende*, contracted into *went*, came to take its place as the preterite of *go;* the participle *went* disappeared; and the verb *wenden*, which had now become *wend* by the dropping of the final *en*, developed the regular form *wended*.

266. Finally, there remains the substantive verb, in which the roots of several verbs have been and still are represented. The following are the forms of the present tense, in both the indicative and subjunctive, in the West-Saxon dialect of the Anglo-Saxon :—

Sing.	Indic.	Subj.	Indic.	Subj.
1.	eom,	sî,	beô(m),	beô,
2.	eart,	sî,	bist,	beô,
3.	is.	sî.	bið.	beô.
Pl.				
1, 2. 3.	sind, sindon.	sîn,	beôð.	beôn.

267. The subjunctive form *sî* did not last beyond the Anglo-Saxon period, nor did the plural *sind*, or *sindon;* but the singular indicative forms, *eom*, *eart*, *is*, have been preserved, with little change, through all the periods of the language. In the Northumbrian dialect of Anglo-Saxon appeared also, as the plural of the present indicative, the form *aron*, the ancestor of the present form *are*. It has also been pointed out, in two instances, in early West-Saxon poetry; but it was from the Northern dialect, aided by its exclusive use in the language of the Scandinavian invaders of England, that we owe its general adoption into our tongue. Even in the beginning of the Middle English period, *are* was far from common in the Midland and Southern dialects. Chaucer almost invariably uses *be* or *ben* as the plural of the present; and the same remark is true of Langlande, though *are* is more common with him than with Chaucer. The Northern writers, however, use *are* regularly, and from them the practice extended, in the fifteenth century, to all. *Be*, however, was constantly used as an indicative form, down to the seventeenth century, and even later, and is still occasionally employed in poetry, especially in the phrase, *there be*. The tendency showed itself, in

the sixteenth century, to limit the verb *be* to the subjunctive, and this has now become the established geneıal rule.

268. The preterite is from an obsolete strong verb, *wesan*, of Class III. (144), meaning 'to dwell,' 'to exist,' and was thus inflected: —

Sing. Indicative	Subjunctive.
1. wæs,	wǽre,
2. wǽre,	wǽre,
3. wæs.	wǽre.
Pl.	
1, 2, 3. wǽron.	wǽren.

269. This is the only verb existing in Modern English in which the original rhotacism has been preserved. In addition to the retention of the change of *s* into *r*, this preterite also shows vowel variation between the singular and the plural.

270. These forms have remained substantially unchanged during all the periods of English language, subject only to the droppings of endings that have taken place in the case of the other verbs. An exception is to be made in the case of the second person singular, which is strictly *were;* and, in fact, *thou were* has been always in use in poetry. But the abandonment of vowel-change in the second person of the preterite of strong verbs naturally led to the disuse of this form. In the Early English period the modern inflection *wast* showed itself; and *wast* and

were asted side by side for several centuries, the former coming steadily more and more into use, and gradually displacing the latter from the language of prose. But along with these a new form, *wert*, was developed, somewhat after the analogy of *shal-t* and *wilt-t*, the final *t*, in fact, being an older suffix for the second person than the usual *st*. *Wert* does not seem to have been common before the sixteenth century, if it even be known at all; and it was often falsely spoken of as belonging to the subjunctive. Like *were*, it is now mainly confined to poetry; but this may be due to the fact that the second person itself of the verb is little used in prose.

271. The infinitive *wesan*, with the imperative and participle, early disappeared, and, as they have had no influence on the later language, need not be mentioned here. Our present infinitive, imperative, and participles are all derived from the Anglo-Saxon *beón*.

272. It is to be added, that, in some of the Northern dialects, *is* was early used for all persons of the present singular and plural, and *was* for the same numbers and persons of the preterite. From the North, *is* has sometimes made its way into the literary language; but its use has been comparatively rare. The employment of *was* as a plural has been on a much more extensive scale; and in the eighteenth century, even, the preterite is sometimes inflected with *was* as the regular plural, instead of *were*. This is more especially true of the second person, which is often *you was*. Cases

of its employment in the first and third persons are much more infrequent.

With the verb ends the foregoing brief consideration of the changes that have taken place in the inflection of English. As a result of this consideration, a few general inferences can be safely drawn. One of them is, that the history of language, when looked at from the purely grammatical point of view, is little else than the history of corruptions. The account contained in the preceding pages is largely a record of endings that have been dropped, or perverted from their proper use; of declensions that have been intermixed; of conjugations that have been confounded; of inflections in every part of speech that have either passed away altogether, or have been confused with one another, and consequently misapplied. There are but few forms in use, which, judged by a standard once existing, would not be regarded as gross barbarisms. Terminations and expressions which had their origin in ignorance or misapprehension are now accepted by all; and the employment of what was at first a blunder has often become subsequently a test of propriety of speech.

Nothing of this need be denied or even questioned: all of it may be ungrudgingly admitted. But it is equally true that these grammatical changes, or corruptions if one is disposed so to call them, have had no injurious effects upon the development of the language; or if, in single instances, they have been followed by injurious effects, these have been more than counter-balanced by benefits which have been derived from other quarters; for the operation of these changes is merely on the outside. It is rare, indeed, that they impair, or even modify in the slightest, the real force of expression. It would now be looked upon as improper to say *I have shook* for *I have shaken;* yet, in the days of Shakspeare and Milton, the former was as allowable as the latter: and at this time all of us use the preterite for the past participle in a similar way in *I have stood*, or *I have understood*, and are not even conscious in so doing that we are guilty of what is, in strict grammar, a barbarism. Changes of such a character — and most changes are of this character — affect merely the garb of speech, not speech itself. To suppose that the English tongue has suffered any loss of strength, that it has entered upon a period of decline, because we now say, for instance, *stood*, where etymologically we ought to say *stonden*, is no evidence whatever of decay on its part: it is merely evidence of ignorance on our part of what constitutes the real life of language. It is, at the present time, a fashion to talk of our speech as being in some way less pure and vigorous than it was in the days of Alfred; mainly, because then it had, on the one hand, fewer foreign words, and, on the other, more inflections, more formative affixes, and therefore more capacity for self-development. But the test of the value of any tongue is not the grammatical or linguistic resources which it may be supposed to possess, it is the use which it makes of the resources it does possess. It is, on the very face, an absurdity to speak of a form of a language which has been made the vehicle of one of the great literatures of the world, which has been found fully adequate to convey all the conceptions of generations of illustrious men, as being inferior in power to a form of it, which, whatever its theoretical capacities, has embodied in its literature, as a matter of fact, little that is worth reading or remembering. As a mere instrument of expression, there is not the slightest question as to the immense superiority of the English of the nineteenth century over that of the ninth. It is equally proper to say that the former is just as pure as the latter, unless we restrict that epithet, as applied to language, to the narrow sense of being free from words that are not of native origin. Even in this respect there was no difference in the influences that operated upon the two forms of the speech; for the disposition to use foreign terms was just as potent in the Anglo-Saxon period as now, though the necessity for them was naturally far less pressing. No tongue can possibly be corrupted by alien words which convey ideas that cannot be expressed by native ones. Yet this elementary truth is far from being universally accepted; for it is a lesson which many learn with difficulty, and some never learn at all, that purism is not purity.

The third inference concerns the assurance we may feel as to the stability of our speech derived from the influence, already immense and steadily increasing, of the language of literature. This is something that places tongues now in use in a position entirely different from that occupied by those employed in any previous period in the history of the world. The cultivated speech is with us no longer confined to a small class which an irruption of barbarism, or a social and political revolution, may subject to the sway of those who speak a foreign or a corrupt idiom. It is the language of entire communities, and, through the operation of manifold agencies, is daily growing in universality and power. The whole tremendous machinery of education is constantly at work to strengthen it, to broaden it, to bring into conformity with it the speech of the humblest as well as of the highest. Day by day dialectic differences disappear; day by day the standard tongue, in which is embodied classical English literature, is widening and deepening its hold upon every class. The history here given, brief as it is, shows how violent and extensive have been the changes that have taken place in our inflection since the ninth century; and yet, of those changes, how few in number and slight in importance are such as belong to the last three hundred years. If the social and political agencies now in being continue to exist, we may confidently expect that the language of the future will never materially vary from what it is to-day. Movement there will be: differences will be developed, but they will not be important either in their nature or extent. Pronunciation will probably be most affected; but words and their meanings, grammatical inflections and constructions, will never, on any large scale, move away from usage which a great literature has made more or less familiar to all, and to the readers and students and creators of which every generation adds a constantly increasing number. English, in the form which it has had essentially for the last three hundred years, may doubtless disappear; but its destruction, if it ever takes place, will be under conditions such as have never before existed, and will be owing to agencies which differ wholly from those that have brought about the ruin of any of the great cultivated languages of the past.

INDEX OF WORDS AND PHRASES.

Abbreviations. — *Adj.*, adjective; *adv.*, adverb; *art.*, article; *compar.*, comparative degree; *comp. part.*, compound participle; *defec.*, defective; *demon.*, demonstrative; *imper.*, impersonal; *indef.*, indefinite; *indic.*, indicative mood; *infin.*, infinitive; *interj.*, interjection; *interrog.*, interrogative; *irreg.*, irregular; *n.*, noun; *num.*, numeral; *p. p.*, passive participle; *p. pres.*, present participle; *pl.*, plural number; *per.*, person; *pers.*, personal; *poss.*, possessive; *prep.*, preposition; *pres.*, present tense; *pret.*, preterite tense; *pron.*, pronoun; *v.*, verb; *v. pret.-pres.*, preterite-present verb; *v. s.*, strong verb; *v. w.*, weak verb; *v. s. (v. w.)*, strong verb originally weak; *v. w. (v. s.)*, weak verb originally strong; *v. w., v. s.*, weak verb originally strong, and still possessing some strong forms.

CPSIA information can be obtained
at www.ICGtesting.com
Printed in the USA
LVOW09s0103050617
536940LV00027BA/1003/P

9 781144 822345